kayaking
puget sound <small>and the</small>
san juan islands

kayaking
puget sound and the
san juan islands

Third Edition

60 Paddle Trips Including
the Gulf Islands

Rob Casey

THE MOUNTAINEERS BOOKS

THE MOUNTAINEERS BOOKS
is the nonprofit publishing arm of The Mountaineers,
an organization founded in 1906 and dedicated to the exploration,
preservation, and enjoyment of outdoor and wilderness areas.

1001 SW Klickitat Way, Suite 201, Seattle, WA 98134

First edition 1991. Second edition 1999. Third edition: first printing 2012, second printing 2017, third printing 2021

Manufactured in the United States of America

Copy Editor: Connie Chaplan, Icon Editing
Cover, Book Design, and Layout: Peggy Egerdahl
Cartographers: Jerry Painter and Jennifer Shontz
Photographer: All photographs by the author unless otherwise noted.

Cover photograph: *Kayakers enjoying the low tide at Crescent Beach in Salt Creek Recreational Area*
Frontispiece: *Burrows Island Light Station State Park and west view of the island*

Library of Congress Cataloging-in-Publication Data
Casey, Rob.
  Kayaking Puget Sound & the San Juan Islands : 60 paddle trips including the Gulf Islands / Rob Casey. — 3rd ed.
    p. cm.
  Includes bibliographical references and index.
  ISBN 978-1-59485-685-3 (ppb : alk. paper)
  1. Kayaking—Washington (State)—Puget Sound—Guidebooks. 2. Kayaking—Washington (State)—San Juan Islands—Guidebooks. 3. Kayaking—British Columbia—Gulf Islands—Guidebooks. 4. Puget Sound (Wash.)—Guidebooks. 5. San Juan Islands (Wash.)—Guidebooks. 6. Gulf Islands (B.C.)—Guidebooks. I. Title. II. Title: Kayaking Puget Sound and the San Juan Islands.
  GV776.W22P842 2012
  797.122'40916432—dc23
                              2012002268

ISBN (paperback): 978-1-59485-685-3
ISBN (ebook): 978-1-59485-686-0

contents

OLYMPIC PENINSULA

SAN JUAN ISLANDS AREA

GULF ISLANDS & VANCOUVER ISLAND (BRITISH COLUMBIA)

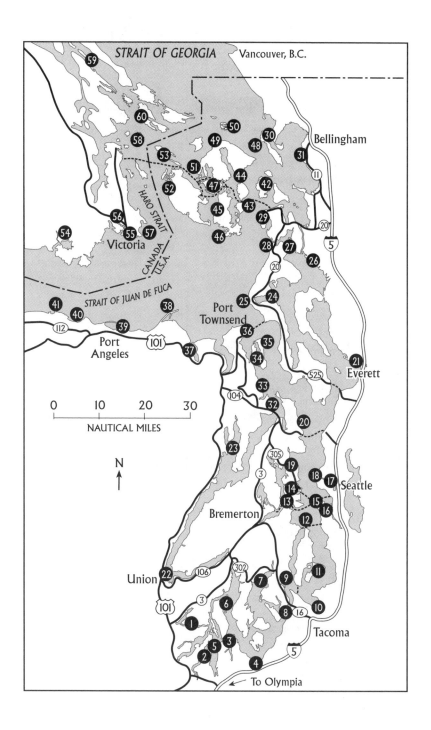

quick trip reference

(Rating: P=Protected; M=Moderate; E=Exposed)

TRIP #	TRIP NAME	RATING	DURATION
1	Hammersley Inlet	M	Full day or overnight
2	Eld Inlet	P or M	Part day to full day
3	Henderson Inlet	P or M	Part day to full day
4	Nisqually Delta	P	Part day
5	Hope Island (South)	M	Part day to overnight
6	Jarrell Cove State Park	M	Part day to overnight
7	Carr Inlet	P or M	Part day.
8	Tacoma Narrows	M or E	Part day to overnight
9	Gig Harbor	P or E	Part day to full day
10	Commencement Bay	P or M	Part day to full day
11	Maury Island	P, M, E	Part day or full day
12	Blake Island	P, M, E	Full day to overnight
13	Eagle Harbor to Bremerton	M	Full Day
14	Eagle Harbor	P	Part Day
15	Elliott Bay	M	Part Day
16	Duwamish Waterway	P	Part day to full day
17	Lake Union	P	Part day
18	West Point, Shilshole Bay, & Golden Gardens	P or M	Part day to full day
19	Port Madison & Agate Passage	M	Part day to overnight
20	Kingston to Point No Point Lighthouse	M	Part day to full day
21	Everett Harbor	P	Part day
22	Southern Hood Canal: Annas Bay	P	Part day
23	Central Hood Canal	P or M	Full day or overnight
24	Whidbey Island: Coupeville & Penn Cove	P or M	Part day to full day.
25	Whidbey Island: Keystone to Hastie Lake Boat Ramp	E	Part day to overnight
26	Skagit River Delta	P	Part day to full day
27	Hope and Skagit Islands	M	Part day to overnight
28	Deception Pass	P, M, E	Part day to full day
29	Burrows Island	M to E	Part day to overnight

CAMPING (C)
Walker County Park (CMT); Hope Island St Park (CMT)
Carlson Bay on Anderson Island (CMT)
Hope Island St Park (CMT), Joemma Beach St Park (CMT); Jarrell Cove St Park (CMT)
Joemma Beach St Park (CMT); Jarrell Cove St Park (CMT)
Kopachuck St Park (CMT)
Narrows Park (CMT)
Saltwater St Park (CMT); Pt Robinson (CMT)
Blake Island St Park: 2 St Park sites and one CMT
Manchester St Park (CMT); Fort Ward (CMT)
Fay Bainbridge Park (CMT)
Point No Point Resort
Potlatch St Park (CMT)
Mike's Beach Resort; Triton Cove (CMT); Seal Rock Campground; Herb Beck Marina: Dosewallips St Park
Windjammer City Beach Park in Oak Harbor (CMT)
Fort Ebey St Park (CMT); Joseph Whidbey St Park (CMT); Fort Casey St Park
Pioneer Park (CMT)
Skagit Island (CMT), Ala Spit (CMT)
Bowman Bay (CMT)
Alice Bight (CMT)

TRIP #	TRIP NAME	RATING	DURATION
30	Lummi Island	M or E	Overnight
31	Chuckanut Bay	P or M	Part day to full day
32	Hood Head	P or M	Part day or overnight
33	Mats Mats Bay	P	Part day
34	Indian Island	P or M	Full day to overnight
35	Marrowstone Island	P, M, E	Full day or overnight
36	Port Townsend to Point Wilson	P or M	Part day to full day
37	Sequim Bay—Protection Island— Diamond Pt Loop	P or E	Part day to full day
38	Dungenesss Spit	P or M	Part day to full day
39	Port Angeles and Ediz Hook	P to M	Part day
40	Freshwater Bay to the Elwha River	E	Part day to full day
41	Freshwater Bay to the Salt Creek Recreational Area	M, P, E	Part day to overnight
42	Cypress Island	M	Full day to overnight
43	James Island	M or E	Overnight
44	Obstruction Pass	M	Part day to overnight
45	Lopez Island: Fishermen's Bay	P	Part day
46	Lopez Island: Mackaye Harbor	P	Part day
47	Shaw Island: Circumnavigation	P or M	Full day to multiple nights
48	Clark Island	E	Full day to overnight
49	Point Doughty on Orcas Island	M	Part day to overnight
50	Patos, Sucia, and Matia Islands	E	Overnight to multiple nights
51	Jones Island	M	Full day or overnight
52	South and West San Juan Island	M or E	Part day to multiple nights
53	Stuart Island	P or E	Overnight or longer
54	Sooke Harbor	P or E	Part day to overnight.
55	Victoria Harbor, British Columbia	P	Part day to full day.
56	Victoria: The Gorge Waterway	P or M	Part day.
57	Victoria: Outer Harbor to Cadboro Bay	P, M, E	Part day, full day, or overnight
58	Portland Island	M	Full day to overnight
59	Salt Spring Island–Wallace Island	P or M	Part day to overnight
60	Pender, Saturna, & Mayne Islands	M	Part day to overnight

CAMPING (C)

Lummi Island DNR site (CMT)

Hood Head (CMT)

Kinney Pt (CMT);Portage Beach (CMT); Oak Bay (CMT); Fort Flagler St Park
Kinney Pt (CMT), Fort Flagler St Park (CMT), Portage Beach (CMT), and Oak Bay (CMT)
Fort Worden St Park (CMT)

Salt Creek Recreational Area; Crescent Beach and RV Park

Cypress Head and Pelican Beach DNR sites (CMT)
Closed Labor Day to Memorial Day
James Island St Park (CMT)
Obstruction Island Recreation Site (CMT)

Shaw Island County Park (CMT); Blind Island St Park (CMT); Jones Island St Park (CMT); Turn Island St Park
Clark Island St Park (east side only); Lummi Island Recreation Site (CMT)
Pt Doughty DNR site (CMT)
Patos camping in Active Cove; Sucia camping in Fossil, Echo, and Shallow bays and Fox Cove; Matia camping at Rolfe Cove
Jones Island St Park (CMT)
Griffin Bay (CMT), San Juan County Park (CMT);Posey Island St Park (CMT); Turn Island St Park
Reid Harbor (CMT), Prevost Harbor
East Sooke Regional Park

Discovery Island

Arbutus Point, Princess Bay; Shell Beach (BC Marine Trail sites)
Cabin Bay; Chivers Point, east of Conover Cove (BC Marine Trail sites)

Beaumont Marine Park, Port Browning, Miners Bay (BC Marine Trail sites)

acknowledgments

Many thanks to my partner Christy Cox for your assistance and for being so patient and supportive in accomplishing this revision in such a short time frame. Also thanks to my parents for their support during the project.

My sincere thanks to Jim and Nadja Zimmerman; Eric Grossman (USGS), Jory Kahn; Tammi Hinkle, Adventures Through Kayaking, Port Angeles; David Parks, geologist and wetland scientist, Department of Natural Resources; Bill Walker, Ruby Creek Boathouse; Outer Islands Expeditions; Shearwater Adventures; Northwest Outdoor Center; David Book, Talisman Books, Pender Island; Dr. Todd Switzer, oceanographer; Mark Volkart; Corey Dolan, Dolan's Board Sports; Connie Campbell, AquaTrek Marine Center; Caleb Goodwin, Ocean River, Victoria, British Columbia; Ted and Marge Mueller, authors of The Mountaineers Books' *Afoot and Afloat* series; Barb and George Gronseth, Kayak Academy; Julie Anderson, Washington Water Trails Association; Joel Rogers, photographer and author; David Burch, Starpath Publications; Reg Lake and Sterling Donaldson, Sterling's Kayaks; Werner Paddles; Ken Campbell, Azimuth Expeditions; Randel Washburne; Christopher Cunningham, *Sea Kayaker Magazine;* Greg Whittaker, Mountains to Sound; John Kuntz, Olympic Outdoor Center; Jim Marsh, *Canoe & Kayak* magazine; Don Rice, Dungeness Kayaking; Jim Emery; Urban Surf; Shawn Jennings, Stoke Harvester; Morgan Colonel, Olympic Raft and Kayak; and my editors at The Mountaineers Books: Janet Kimball, Connie Chapman, and Kate Rogers.

Nikki Gregg and her dog, Nui, teach a stand up paddling class on Seattle's Lake Union.

introduction

For thousands of years, people have used human-powered watercraft to travel through Pacific Northwest waters, also known as the *Salish Sea*. The Salish Sea includes the Strait of Juan de Fuca, Puget Sound, and Georgia Strait. Native people referred to Puget Sound as *Whulge* (or *Whulj*) an anglicization of the Lushootseed name *whulcH*, which means "saltwater."

The Coast Salish people paddled dugout canoes for fishing and transportation. Prior to the twentieth century they constructed the canoes by setting fires in the trunks of old growth cedar trees to burn out the interiors, and then later carved the canoes to precision using hand tools. The canoes varied in length depending on the region and the type of water in which they were paddled. Saltwater canoes were usually twenty to thirty feet long and designed for speed and stability in big seas.

The canoe was a vital part of Coast Salish life. Families traveled seasonally to specific locations to fish, pick berries, and for some, to harvest hops in places like the Puyallup Valley. The Makahs from Neah Bay, used canoes to hunt for gray whales, sometimes several miles offshore. Tribes used canoes to make surprise raids on other tribes, to capture slaves, or for retribution. In the mid-1800s, amateur anthropologist James Swann, who lived among several Northwest tribes, reported one incident when the Makah used their canoes to raid the S'Klallam tribe from the Port Angeles area.

The first contact the Coast Salish peoples had with Europeans was reported to be in the late 1700s, when many explorers, such as Captain George Vancouver and Spanish explorer Manuel Quimper "discovered" the region. In July of 1790, Quimper anchored in a wide bay along the Strait of Juan de Fuca near the Elwha River. Native Americans in canoes brought his crew salmonberries and fresh water from a nearby creek. The bay was later called Freshwater Bay (see chapter 40).

By the mid-1800s, the European settlers who had begun to populate the shores of Puget Sound needed a way to get around. Before steam wheelers and ferry services existed, many settlers hired Native Americans to take them in canoes to their preferred destinations. The two parties didn't necessarily agree on how or when to travel. A European couple was told by their Native American canoe guide that the day they intended to travel wasn't the best time. The couple insisted, and while they were underway, a gale began that capsized the canoe, drowning all aboard. In another incident, a settler was in a hurry to get to a destination, but tribal customs required the paddlers to take a longer, slower route around superstitious landmarks. In 1847, Canadian artist Paul Kane hitched a ride in a canoe across the Strait of Juan de Fuca and experienced a harrowing eleven-hour crossing in huge seas and gale-force winds.

In time, the new residents of the Salish Sea area learned how to get around on their own using a variety of watercraft. In 1867, Samuel Jerisch rowed a flat-bottomed skiff from British Columbia to stake the first claim in the protected inlet of what is now Gig Harbor. In 1895, Ethan Allen and his wife Sadie moved to Waldron Island. As the county superintendent of San Juan Island Schools, he rowed more than 10,000 miles over the years in his homemade rowboat to check on each school.

Northwest paddler Bill Walker once showed me a photograph of his grandfather, Forrest Goodfellow, who, in 1907, rode in a canoe down the log flume separating Lake Washington from Portage Bay in Seattle. The Montlake Cut was built in the same location in 1909. Bill commented, "My brother Dee and I followed in his paddle strokes in the 1960s and 1970s while rowing for the University of Washington Husky Crew."

Sea kayaks didn't become commonplace in the region until after the latter half of the twentieth century. Prior to this time, kayaks weren't readily available for purchase, so many people built their own. In the early 1970s, George Dyson, credited for the revival of the baidarka kayak, an Aleutian kayak originally used for hunting in the Arctic, immigrated to British Columbia to avoid the draft. Kenneth Brower's books about Dyson's exploits illustrate his superb craftsmanship and innovative kayak designs. Living in a tree house east of Vancouver, British Columbia, Dyson studied the history of the baidarka. Working with materials such as metal tubing, fabric, locally cut lumber, old metal stop signs, and nylon twine, George made several baidarkas and eventually in 1975, he completed the forty-eight-foot Mount Fairweather.

In the early 1970s, Tom Derrer relocated from Colorado to Seattle to build sea kayaks for Werner Furrer, Sr. Derrer, who was originally a whitewater paddler, was soon hooked on sea kayaking the coastal waterways of the Pacific Northwest. By the late 1980s, Werner Paddles and Derrer's company, Eddyline Kayaks, became household names in the outdoor recreation industry, as sea kayaking finally hit the mainstream. Other local companies such as Necky Kayaks, Northwest Kayaks, Easy Rider Canoe & Kayak Co., Pygmy Boats, Sterling's Kayaks, and *Sea Kayaker* magazine contributed to making the Northwest a center of the sea-kayaking industry. In the early 1990s, the Washington Water Trails Association (WWTA) founded the Cascadia Marine Trail (CMT) to provide campsites for people using human-powered watercraft from Olympia to the Canadian border. WWTA now has four other water trails throughout the region. The BC Marine Trails Network was opened in 2011 and offers access to many paddling destinations in Canada.

I grew up in Seattle with a view of Puget Sound. I finally got on the water and began sea kayaking in the late 1990s. Influenced by local writer and photographer Joel W. Rogers's books, *The Hidden Coast: Kayak Explorations from Alaska to Mexico* and *Watertrail: The Hidden Path through Puget Sound*, I wanted to explore the rocky, Madrona-lined shorelines of the San Juan Islands and the lush green estuaries of south Puget Sound.

I purchased Randel Washburne's paddling guidebook for Puget Sound—the first and original edition of the guide you now hold—which opened the door for me to learn where to go, when to go, and how to get there. I carried one copy of the guidebook in my car and left another copy by my bedside at home. I spent countless hours studying each trip. Friends would call me after finding a trip of interest in their copy of the guidebook and we'd set a date and go. Even though I am a Seattle native, Washburne's book, later updated by R. Carey Gersten, introduced me to places I had never heard of nor had visited before. It's an honor to be taking the reins of this guide from my talented predecessors.

Early trips I took included exploring Mats Mats Bay, Marrowstone Point, Point Whitney on Hood Canal, the Nisqually Delta, and running the currents of Hammersley Inlet. Intrigued by the idea of doing as little driving as possible to go kayaking, my neighbor Todd and I began to make overnight paddling trips to Blake Island from our neighborhood in Ballard, a one-way distance of 8 miles. After acquiring skills in surf and white-water kayaking, I began paddling the advanced trips in the guidebook, such as paddling the swift tidal rapids of Deception Pass, rock gardening the rugged stretch west of Freshwater Bay, and surfing the waves at Crescent Beach.

While the focus of Washburne's guidebook was on kayaking, it was always a treat to see other types of watercraft at the various campsites. On my first trip to Jarrell Cove, we camped next to a Boy Scout troop that had canoed there from Boston Harbor, and a couple who had rowed a dinghy to the island from Olympia.

Canoes have been used by native peoples in the Northwest for thousands of years. In more recent years, canoes have been used for recreation such as traveling along the Cascadia Marine Trail. Canoes are also family friendly. When local paddler Kaj Bune takes his family on canoe trips, he packs more gear than would fit in a kayak, such as a dutch oven, tables, and crab pots. His kids sat in the middle of the canoe until they were nine, and his father, now in his early eighties, can sit comfortably for long trips. Their canoe has a spray deck to reduce windage and keep them warmer. To avoid capsize, they stay out of surf, have learned how to paddle in wind and current, and paddle during calm conditions.

In an interesting blend of old and new technologies, US Geological Survey (USGS) scientist Eric Grossman from Bellingham attaches water quality testing gear to the stern of native canoes and paddles alongside using his SUP during the annual Tribal Journeys event. Tribal Journeys is held annually in the Salish Sea and marks a cultural resurgence of the canoe culture of tribes along the coasts of Washington, Oregon, and British Columbia. Canoe families travel the waterways, often in cedar replicas of their tribe's traditional canoes, to gather at a different tribal location each year.

Stand Up Paddle Boards

Nearly a decade since my first wanderings on Pacific Northwest waters, a new type of watercraft has been introduced—the stand up paddle board (SUP). Many paddlers are embracing SUPs for their simplicity and similarity to kayaking. I began paddling a SUP as another way to get on the water, and never knew that three years later I would write one of the first "how-to" guides for the sport.

Stand up paddlers are now beginning to explore the inland waters of the Salish Sea. In 2009, Tacoma resident and kayak guide Ken Campbell paddled 150 miles throughout Puget Sound in support of the Washington Water Trails Association (WWTA). Carrying thirty-five pounds of gear on the nose (front) of his board, he was able to accomplish the paddle in four and a half days.

This new edition is intended for both kayakers and paddlers of SUPs. All routes described in this edition are accessible by kayak or SUP, except where noted.

However you get on the water, I hope you will use this book to learn about new places or to rediscover old favorites. I have added several new trips and adjusted a few existing ones. A new trip, Sooke Harbor (chapter 54), is dedicated to Randel Washburne, who said this is one of his favorites. While updating this edition, I found so many great trips I could write a few more books of this kind! Enjoy, and see you on the water!

Route Legend

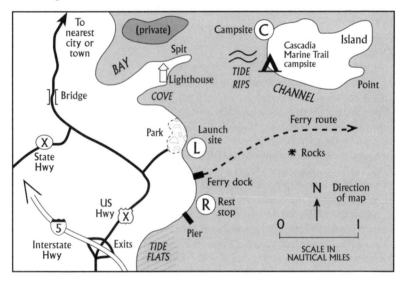

A Note About Safety

Sea kayaking, stand up paddling, and canoeing entail unavoidable risks that every paddler assumes and must be aware of and respect. The fact that an area or route is described in this book is not a representation that it will be safe for you. Trips vary greatly in difficulty and in the amount and kind of preparation needed to enjoy them safely. On the open ocean and even within the confines of Puget Sound and adjacent waters, conditions can change from day to day or even from hour to hour depending on weather, currents, tides, shipping activity, and other factors. A trip that is safe in good weather or for a highly conditioned, properly equipped kayaker may be completely unsafe for someone else or unsafe under adverse weather conditions.

When you follow any of the routes described in this book, you assume responsibility for your own safety. You can minimize your risks by being knowledgeable, prepared, and alert. Do not attempt even the easier routes described in this guidebook unless you have developed basic boat-handling and seamanship skills. The maps in this book are intended for general guidance only, not for navigation. Proper nautical charts and tide tables should always be used in conjunction with this book (see The Pacific Northwest Paddling Environment, Tides and Currents, and Going Paddling).

Always be aware of your own limitations and of existing conditions when and where you are traveling. If conditions are dangerous or if you are not prepared to deal with them safely, change your plans! It is better to waste a few hours or perhaps even abandon a long-planned-for trip entirely than to proceed in the face of dangerous conditions and pay a high price for your insistence. The publisher and author are not responsible for any adverse consequences resulting directly or indirectly from information contained in this book.

Finally, it is important to be considerate of private property. Because many of the lands in this book are subject to development and/or change of ownership, conditions may have changed since this book was written to make your use of some of these routes unwise. It is important to avoid putting in, taking out, or camping on property owned by others. Always obey posted private property signs and avoid confrontations with property owners or managers. Keeping informed on current conditions and exercising common sense are the keys to a safe, enjoyable outing.

The Mountaineers Books

A Note About Access

Due to state and local budgetary constraints, some boat launch sites may have closed. Before setting out, be sure to check with the relevant managing agency to determine the status of a particular launch site.

the pacific northwest paddling environment

The sea-kayaking environment is always characterized by certain elements: weather, water temperature, marine traffic, tides, and currents. Understanding these variables is critical for a safe and enjoyable outing.

Weather, Water, and Marine Shipping

While they are somewhat unpredictable, Northwest marine weather patterns do have some consistencies. Paying attention to both visible signs and marine forecasts can reduce uncertainties and risk about what the weather has in store for you. Sea water temperature also deserves cautionary attention. In these waters, immersion and the possibility of hypothermia are a problem serious enough to warrant special discussion. Another hazard meriting space in this chapter is the chance of being run down by a ship, especially while crossing main traffic channels. As with weather, knowledge about marine traffic can reduce the chances of having a problem.

Marine Weather

For kayakers the most important variable is wind and the resulting sea state. Unfortunately, winds are difficult for meteorologists to forecast, especially in the Pacific Northwest. Visual cues that you can use to predict what is coming are even less reliable, though there are a few that will be noted in this very brief treatment of our local marine weather. For a more thorough understanding of patterns, see Kenneth Lilly's book, *Marine Weather of Western Washington*, local TV weatherman and sea kayaker Jeff Renner's book, *Northwest Marine Weather: From the Columbia River to Cape Scott*, and Cliff Mass' book, *The Weather of the Pacific Northwest* (see Resources).

The maritime Northwest's year is almost equally divided into two seasonal weather regimes, each with characteristic patterns. The two regimes are governed by two large atmospheric pressure cells. The Pacific High is always present off the California coast but expands north in the spring to dominate the entire northeast Pacific until early fall. Then the high retreats south and is replaced by the growing Aleutian Low. This low moves south in the fall from the Bering Sea to the Gulf of Alaska to stay through the winter. In spring the low weakens and retreats to the northwest Pacific and the Bering Sea, again replaced with the high.

The summer pattern usually eases during April and gives way in September. Gales (winds stronger than 33 knots) decrease in frequency toward midsummer. This is due to the region becoming dominated by stable Pacific High pressure blocking most disturbances from entering the area. Nonetheless, lows and fronts can bring rain and strong winds, which almost always blow from a southerly direction during bad weather.

A 30-knot SSW day on Shilshole Bay in Seattle

Winds can still be quite fresh during fair weather. As the interior landmass warms, air from high-pressure areas in the Pacific Ocean is drawn in through the Strait of Juan de Fuca. It can blow 25 knots or more in the afternoon. These winds spread to the north and south at the eastern end of the strait, sending southwesterlies up into the San Juan Islands and northwesterlies down across Port Townsend and into northern Puget Sound. Other than as influenced by the Strait of Juan de Fuca, winds tend to be northwesterly during fair weather in the summer regime.

Of course, topography plays an important part in wind direction and force throughout the area. As land heats up on sunny afternoons, local onshore winds, called sea breezes, are created. Hence morning is generally the least windy time for paddling. When the sea breeze direction coincides with the prevailing northwesterly, local winds are intensified.

Mountainous seasides, such as those of Orcas Island, channel winds and deflect them as much as ninety degrees. They may also cause intensified winds where they are forced through a narrow passage or over a saddle between higher hills. For instance, Orcas Island's East Sound often has stronger-than-average winds during prevailing northerlies.

Fog is most common in late July through September, particularly during clear weather when rapid land cooling occurs during the nights. This fog usually clears by early afternoon.

As the Pacific High yields to the Aleutian Low in early fall, prevailing winds shift to southeasterly, and disturbances with gale-force winds become increasingly frequent and intense. The first gales of the season usually occur in late September. By late fall no weather pattern can be counted on for very long, as a procession of unstable fronts and depressions become the rule through the winter. Strong winds are typically southerly throughout the area, but can blow from almost any direction. One particular wintertime hazard is strong northerly winds on clear days, a result of outbreaks from arctic high-pressure fronts located in the interiors of Washington or British Columbia. On the other hand, periods of very calm weather also occur during the winter regime, particularly since the low-angle sun has less power to generate local sea breezes. Fog is also possible, especially in January and February, and may persist for several days.

In keeping an eye out for impending weather, there are a few indicators that suggest changes for the worse. Remember that strong winds can develop from very localized circumstances. Weather problems are not necessarily the result of a bad weather system.

In general, be most leery of southerly winds, as these suggest the presence of unsettled weather with potential for strong winds. Oncoming winds often can be spotted on the sea in the distance. Rapid shifts in wind direction, particularly counterclockwise changes (*backing* winds in nautical parlance) to the southeast, suggest the arrival of a front. Whatever the wind direction, weather usually arrives from the west, so note the sky in that direction. The development of high clouds or rings around either the sun or moon is a harbinger of a front.

One of the most effective predictors is the meteorologist's marine forecast via VHF radio. Continuous-broadcast forecasts and local weather reports are always available from at least one of three stations in the United States and two in Canada for the Northwest inland waters of the trips described. Most weather radios or handheld VHF transceivers get at least three of these channels (WX1, WX2, and WX4). Forecasts are reissued every six hours, with local-condition updates every three hours.

LOCATION	CHANNEL
Neah Bay	WX1
Astoria	WX2
Olympia	WX3
Seattle	WX1
Port Townsend	WX4
Victoria, BC	WX2
Vancouver, BC	21B (also WX4)

For additional information:
- National Weather Service, Seattle: www.wrh.noaa.gov/sew/
- Environment Canada, West Coast: www.weatheroffice.gc.ca/marine
        /region_e.html?mapID=03

In recent years paddlers have begun to use smart phones to access the Web to view weather, tide, and swell reports while underway, as well as satellite and chart information. Global Positioning System (GPS) units are also commonly used to assist with navigation. Whichever device you choose, get to know it prior to departure. Carry extra batteries and a solar strip to keep your batteries charged.

Cold Water

Sea temperatures near Seattle vary between 56 degrees (Fahrenheit) in August and 46 degrees in February. Being capsized results in hypothermia—body heat loss that can cause death—unless prompt action is taken to get out of the water. Survival time in 50-degree water can be as little as half an hour if you are exerting yourself by swimming, especially when your head is immersed. Or it might be as much as four hours if you have flotation and are able to hold a heat-retaining fetal position to protect the groin and side areas.

Clothing provides some in-the-water insulation, particularly tight weaves and cuffs that trap "dead-water" spaces inside, such as a paddle jacket or semi-dry suit over other garments. Full surfing wet- or dry suits can extend survival time significantly and are highly recommended. Unfortunately, many paddlers in this region forego them except in cold weather or times of higher risk.

Well-practiced recovery techniques, whether properly dressed or not, are especially important in Pacific Northwest waters. Getting out of the water quickly—either back in the boat or ashore—is critical, though hypothermia may continue due to wind chill.

Early stages of hypothermia include violent shivering, but the individual is lucid and talking clearly and sensibly. Short of a warm shower or bath, dry clothes and a chance to sit quietly and warm up (either in a warm place or wrapped up to prevent heat loss) are probably the best treatment.

If shivering is not present and/or the person's actions become clumsy or speech is slurred, more advanced hypothermia is present and an external heat source is usually needed to help the body rewarm. Avoid exercise as that may bring "after drop": cold blood from the extremities rushes into the body core with the potential to cause a heart attack. Likewise, do not rub the arms or legs to encourage circulation. Warm baths are fine, but keep the arms and legs out. Hot drinks also have been known to produce after drop, so they are best avoided unless the condition is clearly a mild one (shivering is present). Warm compresses on the torso, neck, and head; hot water bottles around these areas inside a sleeping bag; or direct body contact with another person may be required. Use artificial respiration and cardiopulmonary resuscitation (CPR) if necessary.

Marine Traffic Hazards

Some kayakers feel that other boats and ships are as much a danger to paddlers as what nature throws at us. Ships could run down a kayak or upset it in a near miss because of their inability to see it or because they spot it too late for avoidance. Pleasure boats could do the same due to inattention at the helm or even in an attempt to come in for a closer look.

Large ships suffer from two disadvantages. Visibility forward from the ship's bridge is partially obstructed by the hull: from some ships a kayaker is not visible at all when less than a half mile ahead! Also, ships cannot maneuver quickly, and emergency actions, like throwing the engines in reverse which requires some time to accomplish, are slow to have an effect and may put the ship out of control. Many ships require more than a mile to stop, even with full power astern. Tugs pulling barges are especially unable to change course or to stop quickly.

Consider how small a kayak would appear a mile ahead of a ship's bridge. To get some idea of how visible you are from that ship, imagine your kayak on top of the bridge—probably hardly noticeable—then partially obscure it with whatever waves are around you. The chances that the ship will pick you up on radar are slim. Even if you carry a reflector it would be too low to the water to produce a significant signal.

The burden is on you to stay out of a ship's path. As with all other pleasure craft you must stay at least a half mile from approaching ships and a quarter mile aside from passing ones. Fortunately, where they are going is usually quite predictable. The major shipping routes in Puget Sound, Rosario Strait, and the Strait of Juan de Fuca have defined traffic lanes which are marked in red or purple on nautical charts. Some routes are divided into one-way lanes with a separation zone between the two. Ships are supposed to stay within these lanes. If you can determine where you are in relation to the lane, you can predict where the ship will pass. Though pleasure craft can cross these lanes, they should do so as quickly as possible and otherwise stay out of them. Ships will sometimes deviate from their lane, to pass around a sailboat regatta, for example, so be sure to leave some margin for error for both you and the ship.

Suppose you see a distant ship coming down a traffic lane that you wish to cross. Should you try to cross ahead of it or wait for it to pass? Obviously, the latter is safest, but circumstances do arise when you find yourself needing to proceed ahead to get clear or when it seems apparent that you can cross ahead safely. Can you make it?

You need to know something about the ship's speed relative to yours, and your respective distances from your crossing point on the traffic lane. Most ships are much faster than they appear—16 knots is typical in our inland waters, though some freighters may move at their full 20-knot sea speed. Tugs with tows average 8 knots with up to 10 knots possible. Assuming your speed to be 4 knots, ships may be traveling at four to five times that. Make a generous estimate of their speed using the speeds given. Then compare the ship's distance from where you plan to cross with its course to how far you have to go to be clear by a quarter mile on the other side.

Another way to determine what will happen as you approach a ship on a course perpendicular to your own is by watching the ship's position off your bow as you converge. If the interior angle between your bow and the ship's bow gradually increases, that indicates that you will pass the intersection point first—how much sooner is another question. If it stays constant, you are on a collision course. A decreasing angle indicates you will pass astern.

If you find yourself in a situation where you believe you cannot get out of a ship's way, emergency signaling with flares, or orange smoke in sunny weather, may be your only remedy. However, it will probably bring the wrath of the Coast Guard down upon you, as well as the whole maritime community. The most effective solution is a marine VHF transceiver. Call the ship, let them know what and where you are, and then agree on a solution. Do this before it is too late for them to take evasive action. Though Channel 16 is the general calling and emergency frequency, ships in Washington's inland waters monitor

A Washington State Ferry threading the narrow channels of the San Juan Islands

Channel 14 (Seattle traffic) or Channel 13 (ships' bridge-to-bridge). If you cannot read the ship's name, call it by position (e.g., "the southbound black container ship off Foulweather Bluff").

Pleasure Craft

Always yield to powerboats and sailboats, particularly in busy urban areas during the summer when boating traffic is frequent. Both paddlers on SUPs and in kayaks are slower than most other boats. Many paddlers misjudge the speed of incoming powerboats and cross in front. Pay attention to boating channels where red and green buoys mark the path that boaters have to follow to avoid grounding on shallow shoals or sandbars on either side of the channel. Below the Hiram M. Chittenden Locks, nicknamed the Ballard Locks, in Seattle (see chapter 18), kayakers and paddlers on SUPs regularly cross a busy boating channel in front of fast moving boats. One to 3 knots of outgoing current released from the locks is always present. Unsuspecting paddlers who are not familiar with crossing current find themselves being pushed more quickly toward oncoming boats than they had planned. We've seen several near collisions as boaters swerve to avoid hitting the paddlers. Look both ways before crossing a boating channel and when in doubt, let the boating traffic pass.

In open water, I've seen larger boats turn directly toward me giving few options how to react. I've seen powerboats pass by me at full speed with no one at the helm, probably on auto pilot. In the case of sailboats, the captain is in the rear of the boat with limited forward visibility. Make sure you wear bright colors, have reflective tape on your PFD and paddle, and pay attention to all boating traffic around you.

Ferries

Ferries are also a hazard. Generally, the ferries have much better visibility and maneuverability than ships of comparative size, and they will do their best to go around you. When paddling in a group in narrow channels traversed by ferries, or other traffic for that matter, stay close together and avoid getting strung out across their path. If you are taking evasive action, decide on a direction and stay with it so that the ferry can react accordingly. Be especially cautious around docked ferries. Be sure that they are not about to leave as you cross ahead. As a safe practice, give them a wide berth anyhow. Also watch out for their prop wash. Paddling underneath ferry docks is both illegal and dangerous as the prop wash from a docking or departing ferry can easily wrap your boat around a piling.

Naval and Commercial Shipping Restrictions

Finally, you should be aware that there are many restrictions, imposed by the Department of Homeland Security, on approaching military or commercial vessels. Most important, you must keep at least 100 yards away from all naval vessels and paddle at minimal speed within 500 yards. You may risk both fine and imprisonment if you approach closer. This same 100-yard rule should also be applied to docked container-ships, freighters and tankers underway, and ferries.

Know the Tides and Currents

In Pacific Northwest waters, staying in tune with tides and tidal currents is as important as keeping an eye on the weather and the marine traffic. Adverse currents can slow or stop your progress, but more important are the hazards of rough water created by currents and possibly made far worse by weather.

Tidal currents, the horizontal movement of water, stem from tides, the vertical movement of water. Paying attention to tide cycles is helpful for picking the safest traveling times.

Tides in the inland waters of the Northwest are generally "mixed semidiurnal," which simply means that there are two daily cycles of high and low tides. Typically, one low is considerably lower than the other of that cycle as Figure 1 indicates. The exact shape of the daily curve changes during the month, and at times the smaller cycle may become little more than an afterthought—just a small deviation in the primary cycle.

The strength of a current is roughly proportionate to the size of the ongoing exchange or the difference between high and low tide. Thus, in Figure 1, the flood current between lower low (l.l.) water and higher high (h.h.) will be

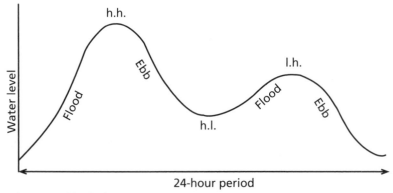

Figure 1. Tide Cycles

The author paddling a stand up paddle board on the ebb in Deception Pass State Park (Christy Cox)

swifter than that during the exchange from higher low (h.l.) to lower high (l.h.) later in the day. Since the order of this mixed semidiurnal pattern varies from day to day, the tide graphs included in some tide tables such as the *Tidelog* (see Resources), for example, are helpful for getting an overview of the day's current strengths.

Another important factor is the duration of exchanges. Though the average time lapse between high tide and low tide is about six hours, the current-flow interval in some places can be as much as nine hours on very big exchanges or little more than an hour on very small ones during which there may be hardly any current.

You should also be aware of the bimonthly cycles in tide and current size caused by the alignment of the moon in relation to the earth and the sun.

Every fourteen days a period of "spring" tides, nothing to do with the season, and bigger-than-usual currents occur when the moon is either full or new. This happens when the moon is aligned either between or on the far side of the earth in relation to the sun.

In between spring tides are periods of "neap" tides and currents, which are smaller than average, occurring during quarter moons when the moon is out of alignment with the sun and Earth.

These cycles exert their biggest influence on outer coast tides and currents. They have less effect on inland tides, though they do affect inland currents to some extent.

More important in Northwest noncoastal waters is the declination of the moon's orbit from the equator, which follows fourteen-day cycles independent of the spring-neap progressions. The difference between the sizes of the two daily tides and their accompanying currents will be greatest when the moon is at its maximum north or south declination. Since the moon's orbit is elliptical, those periods of the month when it is closest to the earth, "perigee," produce larger tides and stronger currents, particularly on the inland waters.

In short, all of these factors can cause dramatic differences in tides and currents, particularly when they coincide. As a consequence, current speeds can be more than twice what they are on another day at the same stage of the tide. So take a close look at your monthly tide tables to keep track of such trends and note that the two daily cycles are somewhat independent of each other. Many tide and current tables include calendars noting the astronomical conditions so that you can see their effects.

Times of no current are called "slack water" or, in some documents, "minimum flood or ebb current," because the water may not completely stop flowing. The length of the slack is related to the strength of the currents before and after it. Slack water times do not necessarily coincide with high or low tide. The characteristics of each waterway greatly affect the differences between tides and currents. Hence, mariners use current tables to predict slacks and times of maximum current. These are far more useful for travel planning than tide tables, though paddlers find the latter useful for timing launches and haul-outs.

Predicting Northwest Currents

Predictions for tidal currents are found in two types of documents or online: current tables, and current charts or atlases. (See Figure 2 for an example of a current chart.) Current tables are available from a few sources. The National Oceanic and Atmospheric Administration (NOAA) has tidal current tables online for Washington State available to download as a PDF, XML, or TXT file. See also *Saltwater Tides, Washburne's Tables,* and software by Xtides. (See Resources). The Canadian Hydrographic Service (CHS) publishes its own tables, which are also available online as a PDF or in print through a retailer. These are very similar in format to the NOAA tables. For additional information: www.charts.gc.ca/index-eng.asp.

Current tables are composed of two parts, allowing predictions of slack water and maximum currents at specific places. The first part is a calendar of times

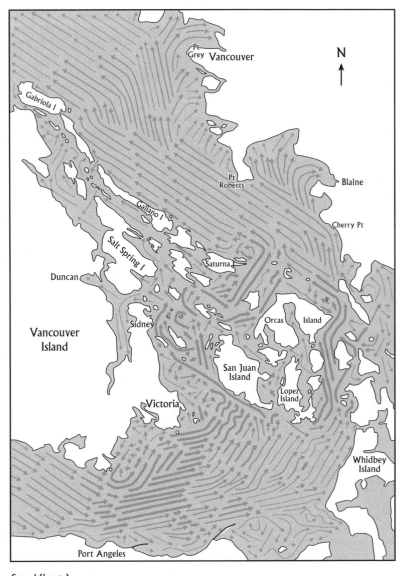

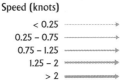

Speed (knots)

< 0.25	
0.25 – 0.75	
0.75 – 1.25	
1.25 – 2	
> 2	

Figure 2. Example of a Puget Sound Current Chart

for slack water and maximum current with predicted speeds for major reference points. In Washington's inland waters, for example, these are Admiralty Inlet, Tacoma Narrows, Deception Pass, Rosario Strait, and San Juan Channel. Following these are correction factors for many local places based on the major reference points and showing how local currents will differ from those in time and speed.

Current charts or current atlases show schematic pictures of current flows at different stages of the tide. They are easier to use than current tables and are best for getting an overall picture of the flows during a particular time period when route planning. In some areas such as the San Juan Islands' east/west channels, where flows are far from intuitively obvious, current charts and atlases can be a great help. Another advantage is that these are perennial rather than annual. However, they are less accurate for predicting slack-water times. For critical places, such as Deception Pass, use the current tables.

For Puget Sound, Hood Canal, and Admiralty Inlet, NOAA has two sets of current charts that are used in conjunction with the annual current tables. For the San Juan Islands and the Gulf Islands, the Canadian Hydrographic Service's *Current Atlas: Juan de Fuca Strait to Strait of Georgia* accurately locates both current streams and the large eddies that occur in this complex area. It also shows how current streams vary both in strength and location depending on the size of the tidal exchange. The major difficulty with this book is finding the right chart to use. To do so, you must have a Canadian tide table and make some calculations about the tide times and exchange size. As an alternative, consult the annual publication *Washburne's Tables* (see Resources), which takes you directly to the right chart for any hour of any day without the need for a tide table, calculations, or daylight saving time corrections.

Hazards from Currents

The majority of Northwest sea-kayaking accidents have resulted, at least in part, from currents usually aggravated by bad weather. The most common dangers are those caused by the interaction of wind and currents.

When wind-generated waves encounter an opposing current—one moving against the wind—the waves are slowed down or, if the current is strong enough, prevented from advancing at all. The waves become steeper, larger, and may break heavily. The result is a much rougher and more difficult sea for small craft to handle. A channel that has only moderate seas when the current is flowing in the wind's direction may turn into something untenable for kayaks after the current change.

Consequently, kayakers should plan to cross open water when the current and wind are moving in the same direction. Though the wind direction cannot be anticipated with certainty, currents typically can be predicted. It is important to note that in nautical publications, wind and current directions are customarily expressed in opposite fashion to each other: winds in the direction from which they are coming, but currents in the direction toward which they are going.

A kayaker died while crossing from Tumbo Island in British Columbia to Patos Island in the San Juan Islands, a stretch of water known for its strong currents. Though the 50-knot winds that caught the party in mid-channel alone could have caused the fatality, the heavy breaking seas were made worse by a large eddy that resulted in currents contrary to the winds during a time when the general flow was with the wind's direction. This eddy could have been identified only with the Canadian *Current Atlas*.

Tide Rips

In certain situations waves are forced to break in quite localized areas called "tide rips." Most tide rips occur where land obstructions or underwater shoals impede or change the current flow, causing the moving water to accelerate because it is being squeezed around a point, through a narrows, or over a shallows (Figure 3). Waves may be able to advance against slower currents up to that place, but when they cannot get farther they expend their energy in breaking and become concentrated and trapped in rips such as at eddy lines that result in turbulence.

Where currents intersect, they form an eddy line at their edges. If the difference in current speeds is great enough, waves are unable to cross this barrier and a rip composed of stalled, multidirectional waves forms adjacent to it. The effect is reminiscent of the intersecting waves found near a vertical shoreline where waves are being reflected back through the incoming ones. The waves become irregular and pyramid-shaped. They leap up and disappear

Tide rip off Point Wilson near Port Townsend

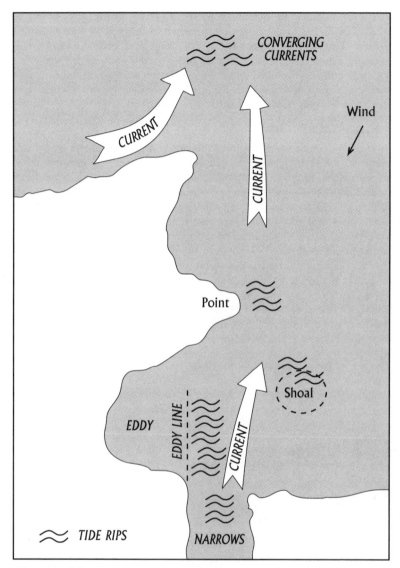

Figure 3. Tide Rip Areas

unpredictably. If you are paddling in these conditions, your kayak or SUP cannot find equilibrium on such a rapidly moving surface, so the boat or board's movement is jerky. You get splashed a lot with the possibility of losing your balance and capsizing.

Sometimes you encounter rips on calm, windless days. Where do the waves come from? They may stem from very low, widely spaced waves that are barely perceptible until they become trapped and intensified in the tide rip area. Or currents flowing over an irregular bottom may transmit the bottom features to the surface as standing waves—waves that stay in one place—simply another variety of tide rip. Occasionally rips are the result of a large eddy being swept downstream from the place where it was created and persisting with adjacent rips for quite some time and distance.

The rough water in rips may also be created or intensified by the wakes of ships or even pleasure craft. We have seen very minor rips turn into nasty ones after a powerboat passed by. Ship wakes can make such situations far worse.

It is difficult to predict with certainty where rips will be located even if you know the direction and speed of currents; there is just too little information on charts about bottom features. However, the downstream sides of points or islands, shoaling areas, underwater reefs, and places where currents are fastest or currents intersect (such as where they rejoin after flowing around a large island) are all good candidates. In the San Juan Islands, for instance, colliding currents from Spieden Channel and San Juan Channel regularly form dangerous rips. The particularly fast water at San Juan Channel's south entrance usually has rips that are at their worst on ebbs against southerly winds.

From a distance tide rips can be heard as a low roar. Seeing them from the low viewing point of a kayak is harder, particularly on windy days when distant rips are camouflaged by wind waves. If you find yourself heading for a rip, assess your drift in the current and then try to take evasive action while there is still time. Determining your direction of drift can be done with ranges: compare something in the middle ground like a buoy or a rock to a feature in the background such as a hill or tree. Observe their movement in relation to each other. Frequent checking of two ranges at right angles to each other—one ahead and one to the side—will help keep track of what the current is doing to you and how effective your paddling is in countering it. **Note:** A tide rip is different than a surf rip, which is a sand channel on a beach that draws water like a river out to sea, pulling unsuspecting paddlers with it.

Paddling in Rips

If you cannot avoid the rip, head straight through it. Remember that you are moving with the current, whereas the rip is stationary. You will soon pass through it. With most rips there is more noise and splashing than real threat to your stability. A suggested defense is to paddle rapidly, each stroke serving as a mini-brace to help maintain equilibrium and direction. This method also works for SUPs where a shorter cadence provides stability.

Often, when a current passes along an irregular shoreline or around a point, the flow breaks off from the main current near shore forming an eddy of still water or even a back eddy—water moving in the opposite direction of the current for a short distance. Such eddies usually form on the downstream side of points, islets, or other obstructions. Sometimes the eddy system will extend out alongside the obstruction as well. Sharply defined eddy lines between the current and the still or backward-flowing eddy are often accompanied by swirls, turbulence, or possibly whirlpools. The southeast side of Pass Island in Deception Pass on a strong flood current is a good example of this situation.

Eddy Lines

Eddy lines can sometimes upset small craft such as kayaks. The primary cause is inertia: crossing from current to eddy or vice versa involves a rapid transition into water going a different direction. Consequently, the rule is to lean and brace downstream. Also, the tremendous turbulence and up- and down-welling in some eddy lines can focus forces of strong torque on a kayak's hull, possibly causing the kayak to capsize.

Crossing powerful eddy lines is best done quickly and at right angles. Keep paddling at a rapid pace so that strokes can serve as braces. SUP paddlers should use this information and get as low as possible and use a short cadence while crossing the eddy line.

Using Eddies to Go Upstream

Usually, wherever currents are found, there also are eddies along the shore made up of either still water or localized currents moving upstream for some distance. The more irregular the shoreline, the more extensive the eddy system. A good example is along the south side of Deception Pass where paddlers can use the irregular shoreline to move upstream on a strong ebb. The boundaries between the main current stream and an eddy may be marked by turbulence or changes in the texture of the water's surface. These may be difficult to see in slower currents. Within the eddy itself, which may cover an extensive area, water can move in many different directions. Most eddies are actually circling water. A good strategy is to move around when passing through large eddies to find the most favorable currents, using cues such as the direction in which the kelp lies.

More than likely you will be forced to paddle hard to progress upstream from one eddy to the next, usually when you must round a point where, for a short distance, the current sweeps along the shore as fast as in midstream. Such "eddy hopping" requires some positioning, careful boat handling, and perhaps a burst of everything you have for a short, hard pull. Use the still water generally found just downstream from a point to build up some speed and inertia, then break out into the opposing current as far upstream and as close to the point as possible. Head as directly upstream as possible as you enter the main current; otherwise the boat's bow will be pushed out and you will find yourself heading perpendicular to where you intended to go, rapidly losing ground. If this occurs, rather than trying to recover, just continue to turn downstream, reenter the eddy you just left, and try again.

going paddling

This section contains information to consider when you prepare for a paddling outing. It discusses general information such as selecting trips, preparing clothing and gear, finding launch sites, carrying kayaks or SUPs onto the ferries as a foot passenger, and some thoughts about paddling during the off-season on these inland waters. In addition, you also need to evaluate whether your physical condition and skills are appropriate for the trip you have in mind and whether the distances are appropriate for the time you have and the amount of energy you are willing to put out.

Choosing a Trip

New paddlers have difficulty identifying trips where the conditions are within their paddling limits. Saltwater trips are more difficult to classify than those on rivers where conditions can be fairly accurately predicted. The water can be

Madronas line a rocky shore on the west side of Indian Island.

mirror smooth on the best of days and a raging sea in the worst of conditions. There is no sure way to avoid the latter. Overconfidence comes easily on those glassy days, and many paddlers have gotten more than they bargained for by taking on challenging routes after better-than-average weather on early trips. It is wise to start out slowly and experience a range of weather conditions in protected situations before testing your skills in more exposed places.

Carefully review the ratings and descriptions for each route in this guidebook when choosing a trip. Also learn trip-planning skills by paddling with experienced paddlers, or through one of the many local clubs or commercial classes frequently offered.

Finally, make note of the mileage provided for each paddling route. Paddling distances are in nautical miles (nms), not the standard land miles you normally think in. A nautical mile equals 1.15 land miles. But please note that all driving directions are in land miles.

Trip Ratings

With some trepidation, I have rated saltwater paddling routes in this book by the degree of hazard potential. Though much needed, this was as slippery a task as getting a footing on a kelp-covered rock.

All routes are rated with a *Protected*, *Moderate*, or *Exposed* rating, which reflects the numerous discrete and sometimes ethereal elements that are the sea environment. Unlike easily rated rivers with predictable conditions that are related to a particular rate of flow, sea conditions change by the minute as winds and currents change in intensity independent of one another. Ratings are based on potentials for trouble that may express themselves only rarely, but with perhaps dire consequences: tide rips that spring up from nowhere when the tide changes or a sudden wind that delivers difficult sea conditions during a crossing.

There is a real danger that new sea kayakers or SUP paddlers, lulled by a placid first trip, might be drawn into traps laid by changing weather or tides with few escape routes. Weekend trips where the demands to be home by Sunday night and the lack of a long but easy alternative route may lead to "going for it" on a nasty crossing. Sucia Island and its neighboring islands are frequented by weekend neophyte kayakers, yet the trip-rating criteria led me to rate this trip *Exposed*. (A kayaking fatality has occurred in this vicinity.) The ratings suggest the potential for trouble based on circumstances and paddlers' experiences. How you use them depends on your abilities and judgment.

You might evaluate your own ability to counter the potential sea forces according to your awareness, strength, and survival skills on the water. Awareness is your ability to anticipate and avoid hazards—for example, to spot a dangerous tide rip far downstream and assess which way to paddle to avoid it. Strength is your ability to paddle hard against wind or current to escape a bad situation. Survival skills on the water are your boat-handling reflexes: balance, braces, and rolls. These abilities enable you to keep going in spite of the sea's

Rating	Description
Protected	A trip designated as *Protected* is suitable for novice kayakers possessing basic boat-handling skills and rescues, as well as rudimentary familiarity with nautical charts. Daily distances are 7 nautical miles or less. Routes mostly follow the shore with no crossings over 1 nautical mile. Waters are largely protected by nearby landforms, and sea currents never exceed 1 knot. Tide rips are unlikely.
Moderate	A trip designated as *Moderate* is suitable for kayakers who have well-established boat-handling skills, have some previous saltwater paddling experience, are aware of current and weather patterns, and can use current- and weather-prediction resources for planning. Since this rating may commit you to paddling in wind and choppy seas, you should be able to stay on course and keep upright through balance and bracing in these conditions. Daily distances may be up to 10 nautical miles on waters where crossings of 1 nautical mile or more are required. Wind and current could cause dangerous seas. You may need to cross marine shipping lanes. Currents may attain 2 knots or so for short distances with tide rips possible, especially in opposing wind conditions. *Moderate* + indicates the presence of a localized hazard that can be avoided by timing your travel or by choosing an alternate route.
Exposed	A trip designated as *Exposed* is suitable for experienced sea kayakers who have a thorough understanding of weather and currents and can interact with those elements. They also can handle their boats in rough water. The potential for very rough seas is greater on these routes and long open-water crossings may require paddling for some time in these conditions. You may need to cross major marine shipping lanes. Daily distances may be 10 nautical miles or more with travel in exposed seas 1 nautical mile or more from the nearest shore. Currents may exceed 2 knots and tide rips are likely. Trips of this class become very risky during the off-season and should be undertaken only with ample buffer time to await safe weather.

energies around you with the hope that conditions eventually moderate or you reach calmer water.

Trips have been rated primarily on the potential for trouble from either weather or currents with consideration of the availability of "escape" routes. These ratings take into account the amount of protection provided by land in windy conditions and the distance from shore that paddling each route requires. The ratings also consider currents and the hazards they can introduce, and hazards from marine shipping traffic. Daily paddling distances determined by either a minimum loop distance or the least distance between campsites may be longer for trips with a more challenging rating.

Even the lowest rating presumes some kayak experience—solid instruction, ability to perform assisted and solo rescues, and a saltwater trip with one of the many clubs or commercial outfitters is recommended for your first time or two in a kayak. A first-time kayaker should start by learning basic boat-handling skills, possibly in a pool, lake, or sheltered harbor that is likely to be warmer and smoother than the open Puget Sound.

These ratings are effective from late spring through early fall. Each trip moves up one rating during the off-season, October through April (see "Paddling During the Off-Season" below).

Surf kayaking at Crescent Beach, Salt Creek Recreation Area

Trip Planning

Trip planning requires the consideration of many factors, including personal kayaking skills, navigation, group dynamics, and much more. It takes time to acquire these skills, but many are translatable from other activities such as bicycling and hiking. What follows is a brief overview of three trip planning topics specifically important to kayak touring.

Nautical Charts. National Oceanic and Atmospheric Administration (NOAA) charts are issued for Washington waters, and the Canadian Hydrographic Service issues charts for British Columbia waters, although there is overlap. These charts are sold in many nautical-supply retailers around the region and are available online. SeaTrails charts are designed for kayakers, are waterproof, and have popular crossing distances detailed, as well as WWTA sites, public and private shoreline areas, and hazards. Maptech charts are essentially basic navigational charts but are waterproof and already folded small for easier use.

Two and sometimes three chart alternatives with different scales of coverage are available for any locality in Pacific Northwest. The least expensive coverage is 1:80,000 charts, available in large, single sheets or in folios containing three sheets printed on lighter paper. The folios are called small craft (SC) charts and three of them—18423 SC and 18445 SC, and the Canadian Hydrographic Service's 3310—cover all the waters discussed in this book. The detail at this scale is adequate, with the Canadian one a bit better at 1:40,000, for cruising. In addition, the light paper and small pages make them easy to fold into a chart case. These small craft charts are usually more thorough in identifying parks than the single-sheet equivalents.

Larger-scale charts such as 1:25,000 give you a more intimate and detailed view of the shorelines but are more expensive and bulkier, resulting in more frequent turning and refolding. Though the scales of 1:40,000 or larger are preferred for the wilder shores of British Columbia and Alaska in order to spot good landing sites, the 1:80,000 chart is serviceable in Washington. In Washington and southern British Columbia, landownership is more relevant to getting ashore than shoreline composition and foreshore extent (the area between high and low tide), which shows how far you might have to carry your boat if the tide is out.

Daily Distance. The distance you cover on a daily basis depends on how much time you are willing to spend in the boat. This factor is far more important than your paddling strength or the boat's speed. In general, most people cruise between 2.5 to 4 knots (nautical miles per hour). With stops to look around, rest, and stretch your legs, an average of about 2 knots for the day as a whole is about right (time between getting underway in the morning and hauling out for the evening divided by miles traveled). About 12 nautical miles per day seems a comfortable distance for most people in average paddling conditions, barring strong head winds or currents. Using the current can make a dramatic difference. Paddlers who paddle with a favorable current can reach up to 5 knots, and thus cover a 10-mile distance with fairly leisurely paddling in a relatively short amount of time. Using the currents, paddlers have traveled the 21-mile distance from Anacortes to Friday Harbor in a few hours. SUP paddlers using a fourteen-foot or longer displacement hulled board can travel as much as 35 miles a day in a favorable wind and/or current.

Weather Allowances and Alternative Routes. One of the most dangerous situations into which paddlers get themselves is the need to be someplace at a certain time. This self-induced pressure prompts them to paddle during unsettled weather in exposed places. For some trips, this book includes route options offering safer but longer ways back to your launch point or to somewhere from which you could hitch a ride back to your car. The existence of such options is incorporated in the trip ratings for this book.

The more exposed the route and the fewer route options there are, the more time should be allowed for bad weather contingencies. How much time depends on the season and the current regional weather pattern. A large, stable high-pressure area over the Northwest in July probably holds the least likelihood of being weather-bound. In January, however, weather patterns are too changeable to count on forecasted conditions for even a day in advance. During the summer months you may want to consider the forecast for the period you will be paddling and choose a trip rating accordingly. During the off-season, periods of bad weather should be assumed. Either build extra time into the itinerary or choose less exposed trips. Because of the increased hazard potential between September and May, all trip ratings in this book should be considered one rating more hazardous during that time.

Become a Better Paddler

If you're seeking to increase your paddling level or want to go on the *Exposed* trips in this guide but lack skills, consider joining a local paddling club or taking a class at a paddling shop. Both options provide training and experienced trip leaders to safely take you on such trips. Several paddling shops offer guided skill-building tours to destinations such as the San Juan Islands. Paddling clubs are also a good way to connect with other paddlers at your same skill level.

You also should consider taking a class on how to recover from a capsize and how to rescue others in rough water. Such skills will be valuable on trips in remote areas thus resulting in a better experience.

Increase your skill level in rough water and on long trips by taking a surf kayaking and/or white-water kayaking class. Cross training will allow you to be at ease in rough water and in situations where the weather changes unexpectedly far from shore. To increase your stand up paddling skills, practice paddling in rough water, upwind, and learn to surf and paddle in moving currents or whitewater. Boards that are fourteen feet and longer make more sense for distance paddling and carrying overnight gear. Make sure you pick a board that feels comfortable to you in rough water. These skills will allow you to travel farther to more places.

This kayaker's wide-brimmed hat protects both his face and neck from the sun.

Clothing and Gear

Northwest water is cold all year. Wearing the appropriate clothing for the air and water temperature will allow you to extend your paddling season and enjoy each trip more.

What to Wear

Always dress appropriately for each trip. A common practice is to dress for the water temperature in case of unexpected immersion. This applies especially if you are going to be paddling in rough water, through fast moving currents, in surf, at night, or during open water crossings. If the air temperature is hot but the water is cold, consider dressing in layers so you can remove or add clothing easily if necessary. Kayakers with a reliable Eskimo roll often cool off with a quick roll.

Several clothing options are available that can provide adequate warmth without hindering movement while paddling. Dry suits keep you mostly dry and allow for your choice of layering underneath depending on the conditions. Always use insulating synthetic clothing under, such as polar fleece or polypropylene products. Full surfing wetsuits have come a long way in recent years, there is a range of affordable styles made of warm, flexible neoprene in varying thicknesses. Other clothing options include farmer john/jane armless neoprene wetsuits, wetsuit pants, paddle jackets, and insulating rash guards.

Neoprene booties, gloves, and hoods are recommended for providing insulation on rough water trips, during immersion, and for cooler weather. Booties and gloves also protect your feet and hands from the Northwest's barnacled and gravel shores.

Consider carrying some or all of the above items with you in a dry bag in your kayak in case you get chilled or take an unexpected swim.

Winter Clothing. Clothing for the off-season, in fact any season, should be able to shed water and wind. The heavier precipitation and stronger winds mean you will want to wear a paddle jacket, dry top, full wetsuit, or dry suit most of the time. A good barrier against the substantially greater wind-chill factor, even in light breezes, is important for your safety as well as comfort. Gloves that guard against both wetness and cold air are also important. Head protection is extremely important; this is where a majority of the body's heat is lost. A wool, synthetic, or neoprene cap or hood serves most paddlers very well. Wearing neither, one, or both together allows adjustment to a full range of temperature and wetness conditions. Neoprene booties are essential for keeping your feet warm and also protecting them from barnacled rocks. A bootie with ankle support is wise for preventing foot injuries if you'll be doing a lot of walking on shore. Bring a warm jacket and hat, stored in a dry bag, to stay warm when you stop paddling at the end of the day or during shore lunch breaks.

Lifejackets or Personal Flotation Devices (PFDs)

The US Coast Guard (USCG) requires all paddlers of kayaks and other small human-powered watercraft such as paddle boards, canoes, and the like to wear a PFD. Aside from flotation in case of a swim, the more commonly used Type III PFDs add insulation to your core in cold temperatures and provide pockets to carry a VHF radio, knife, energy bar, whistle, and camera. Some PFDs have built-in short tow ropes and quick-release tow belt straps for rescues. Consider a PFD with reflective strips to provide more visibility in busy boating areas.

Inflatable Type V PFDs are also available for paddlers who prefer a minimalist feeling on the water. In the case of a sudden capsize or a head or shoulder injury, a paddler who is panicked may not be able to inflate the vest properly. If you use this type of PFD, practice using it by pulling the cord and putting it on while in the water. Clean the PFD with fresh water after each use and replace the PFD's CO_2 cartridges every few months; saltwater corrosion can cause the device to malfunction.

Many stand up paddlers are choosing to put their PFDs on their board. At the time of writing this edition, this practice is legal, but make sure your PFD can be easily removed in case of an emergency and always wear your leash to prevent losing your board and PFD.

What to Carry on Every Trip

Paddling guides often carry a "hypo" kit for their customers. These provide paddlers with a variety of important clothing and other items to make sure the paddlers stay warm and comfortable on a trip. Consider a similar kit for your trips. Items in these kits often include a VHF radio, energy bars, chemical heat packets, prescription medications, hydration tablets, a first-aid kit, extra warm synthetic clothing, neoprene hoods and gloves, and a compact emergency blanket or bivy sack. Also carry emergency signaling devices such as handheld rocket flares, a signaling mirror, and smoke canisters for daytime use.

Make sure you are able to keep yourself hydrated properly by carrying bottles of water or a hydration bladder attached to your PFD. Research whether your destination has water or where you can find it along the way. Also bring sunblock, lip balm, sunglasses with a strap, sun hat, marine chart, tide and current tables, compass, GPS, and a waterproof white light for night paddling.

A tow rope is essential for you to tow a friend or another paddler who is in trouble, or for others to tow you in case of an injury, capsize, seasickness, fatigue, or other unexpected situation. Some kayaks have attachments for tow ropes but most paddlers carry them in a fanny pack or waist pack or on quick-release straps on their PFDs. Tow ropes can also be used to dry gear in camp.

If you plan to stand up paddle offshore, outfit your board to carry extra warm clothing, camping and fishing gear, and water. Always wear your leash and PFD in case of a fall or if a storm front catches you off guard. Consider carrying an extra break-down SUP or kayak paddle in case of a loss or breakage. Kayak paddles give you a chance to sit down and are more effective in paddling upwind for long distances. Boards that are fourteen feet and longer make more

Launch beach at Posey Island State Park

sense for distance paddling and carrying overnight gear. Make sure you pick a board that feels comfortable to you in rough water.

Logistics

Pre-planning can make your trip safer and easier once on the water. Check the relevant charts and research not only your trip but also information on the launch location, parking, and ferries.

Launching and Parking

Bring your wallet with small bills and credit cards as one of your essentials on every trip, since almost every public or private launch and parking area requires a fee. Annual passes may be purchased from several agencies including Washington State Parks and Department of Fish and Wildlife.

Finding a place to launch your kayak and leave your car while you are gone can be something of a problem. Some shorelines are well endowed with public facilities providing both access to the water and convenient parking. Others, particularly in certain parts of the San Juan Islands, are limited in public shore access, parking areas, or both. Shaw and Orcas islands have the least public access and parking, and private property is the probable option—at a cost.

The Washington Water Trails Association has a guidebook to its trail system both in print and online. The guidebook provides access, location, directions, a description of the specific type of launch (whether beach, road-end, ramp, or float), amenities at or near the site (such as water availability, restrooms, groceries, or other), any fees involved, and other useful facts. Whether planning a trip to a Cascadia Marine Trail site, other destinations, or just a day trip, these are handy resources that can alleviate a lot of headaches.

Respecting Private Property

Etiquette at access locations is very important. In the busy summer months, many launches become overwhelmed with human-powered and motorboat traffic. Parking can be tight and even unavailable, thus forcing paddlers to park in residential areas, sometimes blocking driveways. A few popular residential boat launches in this book include Boston Harbor, the Randall Drive Northwest ramp in Gig Harbor, and North Beach on Orcas Island. To avoid hassles, arrive early, carpool if traveling in a group, or use a less popular ramp if there is one available nearby. Boston Harbor Marina has asked paddlers to park end-to-end in the street lot west of the boat ramp.

Maps such as SeaTrails mark which areas are public and private. Respect private property especially in boating-heavy regions such as the San Juans where there are few public access areas. As much as paddlers feel they are less obtrusive than powerboaters, large groups of kayakers can be a hindrance and have been reported landing and even camping on backyards in the San Juans. Many islands in the San Juans and Gulf Islands are private and sometimes well signed, others are not. Check marine charts and with locals to confirm where public access is along your route.

Loading on the Orcas Island ferry, San Juan Islands

Transporting Kayaks, Canoes, and SUPs on Ferries

Both the Washington and British Columbia ferry systems allow foot passengers to carry kayaks, canoes, and SUPs aboard, preferably on a cart or dolly. Washington charges the stowage rate, equivalent to the motorcycle rate, for the boat. Their statewide information number is 888-808-7977; www.wsdot .wa.gov/ferries.

British Columbia also charges a stowage rate, but it differs from their motorcycle rate, so you need to check for the specific ferries you will travel. Their information number is 888-223-3779; www.bcferries.com/.

In Washington, a couple with two kayaks car-topped on one vehicle under 20 feet in total length including overhang and less than 7.5 feet in total height can save money by driving on. In the San Juan Islands or Vashon and Bainbridge islands, the one-point toll collection or westbound fee structure, collected on the mainland, means a free ride if you paddle out to any of these islands and ferry eastbound back.

The savings are not as significant as the flexibility that carrying a kayak on board allows in choosing paddling routes. For example, you can have a fine day excursion paddling from the town of Winslow on Bainbridge Island to Bremerton if you use the Seattle–Bainbridge and Bremerton–Seattle ferries to start and finish (see the Eagle Harbor to Bremerton chapter). In the Gulf Islands and to a fairly limited degree in the San Juan Islands, you can leave your car on the mainland, ferry to one island, paddle to another, and ferry or paddle back to the car.

Opportunities to launch a kayak carried aboard the ferry in the San Juan Islands are limited to Friday Harbor and possibly Orcas Island. Orcas Landing has intermittently allowed launching from a private dock near the ferry landing for a fee but has suspended it due to congestion caused by kayakers loading inefficiently. Check with the ferry office at the Orcas Island terminal. Access to the beach next to the ferry dock at Shaw and Lopez islands is not allowed.

Carrying a kayak on board also provides a significant bad weather fallback, particularly in the San Juan and Gulf islands, where paddling to a closer or less exposed terminal and ferrying may be safer than paddling back to your car.

Some paddlers always carry a stowable kayak cart in case bad weather prompts them to take a ferry back rather than paddle home.

During the summer months large numbers of foot passengers with kayaks make the San Juan Islands ferry run particularly hectic. The ferry staff recommends a few things to make it easier for everyone.

First, arrive at least one hour early. This will give you time to find parking and get your boat and gear ready to board. The biggest problem that carry-on kayaks pose for the ferry staff is the multiple trips that kayakers make to get their gear aboard, which delays loading cars. The staff asks that you consolidate as much as possible and/or use a boat cart to minimize the trips. Consider using a mesh backpack to carry your loose gear to minimize trips.

Because of the tremendous growth in use of the San Juan Islands ferries in recent years—and because walk-on kayak traffic has increased dramatically—kayaks now compete with cars for spaces on the ferries. Westbound from Anacortes the crews are able to fit kayaks into "void spaces," those not used by other vehicles, well enough that kayaks readied for boarding ahead of time will stand a good chance of getting aboard. But eastbound from the islands these void spaces cannot be filled readily. Since each island has an allotment of vehicle spaces on each ferry, kayaks must be counted into these and wait their turn to fill them. You will not be required to line up with the cars; kayaks can be staged near the ramp.

Kayakers who carry on their boats need a put-in within walking distance of the ferry terminal where they disembark. In many cases, but not all (including Shaw Island in the San Juans), there is someplace to do that. However, at some there may be a fee for the privilege. Fees are described in trips that involve those ferry terminals.

Entering Canada or the United States

If you regularly paddle into Canada from the United States, consider getting a CANPASS for Private Boats. This preapproved pass requires only one phone call thirty minutes prior to arriving at your Canadian destination. If you don't have the pass, immediately go to the nearest designated telephone reporting marine site and call 888-226-7277. Be prepared to provide details of your trip, how many in your group, and each paddler's declaration. Find a list of telephone reporting sites by calling the same number prior to your departure. The site is operated by the Canadian Border Services Agency. (See Resources.)

To enter the United States from Canada, contact the number of the customs office closest to your destination prior to landing. You can also contact the US Customs and Border Protection (CBP), the main number is 800-562-5943. Be prepared to report your date of birth, the citizenship of all persons with you, your passport number, type of watercraft, homeport, current location, and a return contact number. See Resources for information on finding these sites. The NEXUS Program is similar to the CANPASS for those crossing the border frequently.

Paddling During the Off-Season

For many, paddling in Northwest inland waters during the off-season is just as appealing as during the summer. In fact, there is much about it to be preferred. During the winter months, there are fewer boats with which to share the waterways. A quiet wildness comes from the scarcity of boats and from having whole marine park islands to yourself, something you would never expect in your wildest dreams of summer. Other boaters met are kindred spirits who appreciate the advantages of winter boating to the extent that they are foolish enough to be out there too. Boaters are more inclined to say a few words as they pass one another, acknowledging some sort of bond.

Then there are the many seabird species that are rarely seen in the warmer summer months. There are the overcast November days when the air and the sea are languid, almost paralyzed, from dawn to dusk. Silence is broken only by the distant conversations of floating seabirds or the gentle breathing of a passing harbor porpoise.

However, the question of imminent weather is seldom far from the winter paddler's mind. Winter in these waters is a stern, no-nonsense time of year. You do things on nature's terms or suffer the consequences.

The changeability and strength of the winds during the winter months are major hazards to contend with. Upgrading the trips to a more severe rating for the off-season is entirely justified for this reason alone.

Weather is simply more unpredictable during the off-season. Fronts and low-pressure systems follow each other in much closer succession. Conditions are more extreme and changeable. And you must paddle in rougher and more uncertain situations than you might prefer. There is also the pressure of time: twilight lurks never far away. Cloudy, low-pressure days can get dark sooner than clear days. With the stronger winds and the more fully developed seas, tide rips can occur where they rarely do in less windy times. And those admittedly reassuring passing pleasure craft that eagerly watch for the chance to rescue during the summer are now snug in their moorings while winter wilderness isolation is all yours.

Beaches, particularly gravel ones, become steeper. The characteristically bigger waves tend to move the beach material more, piling it up at the current water level so that there is a definite berm or steep drop-off. Driftwood is often found floating offshore from extreme high tides or from wind-generated waves pounding the shore. Rivers may flow faster after heavy rains, creating a stronger outflow of current at its mouth, which can affect your route. Daily wind patterns from the summer no longer hold either, particularly less wind in early morning. These summer cycles are largely generated by the heating of landmasses and subsequent convection currents. But the low angle of the sun in the winter gives it far less heating power. Thus, the land often remains as cold or colder than the sea and generates negligible convection.

Off-season camping likewise requires the acceptance of some austerities in return for your own private reserve of gorgeous winter wildlands—perhaps bartering an evening under cover in a continuous downpour for a frosty morning walk along a marine park pathway that shows no recent footprints. The challenge of setting up a warm and comfortable evening's nest in spite of what is going on outside is a large part of the season's appeal.

Paddling at Dusk

Trying to make 10 miles a day requires using every minute of daylight during the shortest days of the year. If you hate rising before dawn and it gets light at 8:00 AM, it means getting a 10:00 AM start on the water. Assuming 2 knots for travel speed and a brief lunch stop, you should plan to reach your next camp at about 3:00 PM with an hour of fading light left in which to get ashore and set up camp. Be particularly wary of being caught on the water at dusk in the winter since a quick weather change for the worse in the dark is especially unnerving and dangerous.

Carry clip-on waterproof white LED (nonblinking) lights to attach to the rear shoulder of your PFD for night paddling. It's also wise to have one handheld waterproof flashlight to shine at a boater if the rear light isn't enough. Keep this light on a short string so you don't lose it. Keep an ear out for boats that don't have running lights.

Going Ashore

Kayakers are amphibious creatures, at home on both sea and land, with the ability to make the transition easily and frequently. In many other parts of

the country, going ashore often puts you in somebody's front yard or private preserve. By contrast, the Pacific Northwest is well endowed with public lands and camping sites hospitable to boaters if you know where they are located. Included is the Cascadia Marine Trail, a "string of pearls," which is a network of dedicated campsites for users of hand-carried, nonmotorized, beachable watercraft throughout Puget Sound and the San Juan Islands.

Many of the trips listed in this book are two days long or more, so you will need some camping gear and outdoor skills for these. Though this book offers no primer on camping, a few peculiarities of kayak camping

Starfish on beach, Wallace Island, Gulf Islands, British Columbia

along these inland waters are worth noting, including things that kayakers can do to minimize their effects on these wildlands and their wildlife while ashore or paddling nearby.

Camping Access and Fees

Most public lands are available for use by everyone, but some, particularly national wildlife refuges, are not. State parks provide the most extensive opportunities for both day-use and camping throughout Washington's inland waterways. Although most of Washington's park sites are developed, some of the marine (boat access only) state parks are totally undeveloped and overnight camping is not permitted. However, with a few exceptions, camping is allowed at the many small island parks where sanitation such as a vault or solar composting toilet is provided. Most of these also have picnic tables and fire rings, but no drinking water. Some are also included within the Cascadia Marine Trail System.

Establishing your own campsite in the woods, also known as dispersed camping, is not permitted in any of Washington's state parks. This is to prevent spreading the impact that camping has on wildlands. It is also to avoid conflicts with other management goals, such as, for example, eagle habitat management in the San Juan Islands.

Wherever you plan to park and launch, be sure to bring plenty of dollar bills because almost all agencies charge a fee for day-use or overnight parking. Annual permits are sometimes available. At the time of writing this edition, the Discover Pass had been recently implemented to cover access to state parks and several other smaller parks and boat ramps in the region. Almost all marine state parks charge a fee collected through self-registration stations. A few state parks with more highly developed campgrounds are popular with kayakers. These developed sites, usually with restrooms and running water, charge more. Most of these parks also have a Cascadia Marine Trail site near the water available for a per-night fee (see the Cascadia Marine Trail section below). Generally this book will not mention specific parking or camping fees—but do expect that there will be fees.

Where to Camp

The following is a brief description of the different jurisdictions and what kayakers can expect in each:

Gulf Islands National Park Reserve. Policies and facilities are like those of Washington's state parks, with "full-service" campgrounds used by kayakers in the Gulf Islands at Sidney Spit. Other island parks are less developed—a few have hand pumps for drinking water and some have none. Camping is allowed at designated sites, though fires are prohibited unless an official fireplace is provided and no fire bans are in effect.

Washington Department of Natural Resources (DNR) Recreation Areas. The DNR manages some of the best-kept secrets along Washington shorelines, primarily because they are not labeled on most nautical charts.

Many DNR camping locations are also designated Cascadia Marine Trail sites. The DNR's recreation areas are picnic and campsites that provide most of the same basic amenities as those of state parks. Facilities are simple (a pit or solar composting toilet and typically no water) and maintenance is infrequent, as the DNR covers a large area with a tiny staff.

Not all undeveloped DNR lands are open to camping. As an example, four-fifths of Cypress Island is undeveloped DNR land, but only two sites at Cypress Head and Pelican Beach are open to camping. You can expect to be evicted by island staff if you camp elsewhere.

The DNR also manages the state's public tidelands, which are scattered throughout Puget Sound and the San Juan Islands. More than half of the tidelands in the latter are public, but few in Hood Canal are. Public tidelands are rarely identified by signs, but booklets and maps showing their locations are available from the DNR (see Resources). Almost all of the public tidelands extend only as high as the mean high-tide line unless the uplands are publicly owned too. In general, these are not very useful for kayakers except for a quick leg stretch or some clam digging. Remember, you will be trespassing if you wander above the high-tide line.

The Cascadia Marine Trail. The Cascadia Marine Trail system augments public waterfront campgrounds by providing a dedicated network of simple campsites located an easy day's travel from the next for sea kayakers and captains of other human- and wind-powered, hand-carried boats. It ranges from south Puget Sound to the British Columbia border.

Since the system's inception in January of 1993, the volunteer organization, Washington Water Trails Association (WWTA), has facilitated the creation of over fifty campsites stretching over 140 miles. About half of the campsites are located within Washington State Parks, with the remainder in DNR, county, and city parks.

The Cascadia Marine Trail was honored in 1996 with an international Ecotourism for Tomorrow award and in 2000, when it was named one of sixteen National Millennium Trails by the White House.

Benefits of membership include full access to the WWTA trails network online and in a downloadable PDF form. For additional information: www.wwta.org.

Trail fees: Fees for the use of campsites and trailheads vary depending on whose jurisdiction they fall within. These fees, along with any additional site-specific fees, are usually noted on signage at the site, by contacting the supervising land manager, or within the Cascadia Marine Trail guidebook (and online).

The majority of campsites along the trail system fall within Washington State Parks. The standard campsite fee is $12 for six people per site. Overnight campsites managed by the Department of Natural Resources, however, are open to all. No camping site is specifically designated for nonmotorized boaters.

Campsite fees under other jurisdictions vary, and for planning purposes it is best to contact the land manager directly to determine the required payment.

Cascadia Marine Water Trail signpost on Blake Island

Trail Standards and Guidelines. Maintaining and continuing development of the Cascadia Marine Trail system depends on the good will and cooperative spirit of state, county, and city agencies, port districts, Native American tribes, land trusts, and private citizens. To ensure their support, WWTA asks that its members, users of the trail system, or any other user of a human- or wind-powered, hand-carried boat to practice low-impact, "leave no trace" camping techniques and appropriate camping etiquette.

BC Marine Trails Network. Launched in the spring of 2011, the BC Marine Trails Network includes thirty access/launch and camping sites in the Gulf Islands as well as more sites along the West Coast of Vancouver Island. For additional information: www.bcmarinetrails.org.

Where Not to Camp

National Parks. Washington State has one national park on its inland shoreline, the San Juan Island National Historic Park, commemorating the so-called Pig War of 1859 between Britain and the United States. There are two units, both on San Juan Island: American Camp at the southern end and English Camp on the northwest side. The park has historical reconstructions and interpretive programs, and facilities for picnicking, but not for camping. Camping is also prohibited on the park's undeveloped lands.

National Wildlife Refuges. The Nisqually, Protection Island, San Juan Islands, and Dungeness national wildlife refuges all control shorelines along

Washington's inside waters. The Nisqually refuge allows boating close to shore and walking onshore as long as nesting sites are not disturbed. Areas may be closed during sensitive times of year. The Dungeness refuge limits landings to one site, available through advance reservation only. No shore access is available at Protection Island. The San Juan Islands refuge includes eighty-three islets, rocks, and reefs in that area, as well as some larger islands such as Matia and Turn islands. Many of these are also part of the National Wilderness Preservation System. No landings are allowed on most of these eighty-odd places without permission of the US Fish and Wildlife Service. It requests that you stay at least 200 yards from these refuge islands. Matia Island and Turn Island have portions leased to the Washington State Parks Department. You may camp in these park areas and walk the trails on the rest of the islands, or land on most of the beaches as long as birds' nesting sites are not nearby.

Such islands are particularly inviting to kayakers, but this is a case of protecting birds' and seals' rights to peaceful nesting and haul-outs. The US Fish and Wildlife Service will not compromise these goals to provide public recreation. You will be cautioned to keep away where units of the San Juan Islands refuge are encountered on routes in this book. They are well marked with signs to that effect.

Private Property. Public access is disappearing quickly in our region. The San Juan Islands have very few access points compared to other areas nearby and even fewer camping opportunities. For years, paddlers have camped illegally on backyards of waterfront residences in the islands, a situation that creates a negative image of the activity and can affect attempts to gain more public access in the future. Maps such as SeaTrails have shaded areas showing private and public waterfront property for the Puget Sound, San Juans, and nearby waterways.

Camping Etiquette

Camping has its own set of requirements and responsibilities. And though we are known by our mode of travel, we need to come ashore each evening to make our temporary home. Though the effect of each sea kayaker is minimal, there are now enough of us that some problem patterns are emerging and will increase with kayaking's popularity unless each of us is aware of the impact on the environment.

Water. To be surrounded by water without a drop to drink is the Ancient Mariner's dilemma. It is shared by sea kayakers unfamiliar with camping along Northwest inland waters. The majority of campsites along these shores have no drinking water, and those that do, such as Jones Island State Park, often run out midway through the summer or shut it off between fall and spring.

Unless you are going somewhere where you know there will be water, carry your own or bring filtration equipment if there is a running stream nearby. Take along enough to tide you over should you have to stay longer because of bad weather, and so you won't be forced to beg water from people on yachts or head for home in dangerous conditions.

Three quarts of water per person per day usually is enough if you are careful with it. Wash dishes in saltwater followed by a sparing rinse with fresh water to prevent corrosion. You can also add saltwater to fresh water for cooking. A half-and-half combination is about right for water that will be poured off such as for boiling noodles. One part saltwater to two or more parts fresh water is a good ratio when the water stays in the food such as in cooking rice.

A collapsible two- to three-gallon jug fits well in most kayaks. Soft hydration bladders are also common for storing large amounts of water in your kayak. Some paddlers use flattened two-liter soda bottles that fit easily in between gear or under deck bungees and don't roll inside or on top of your boat.

Fires and Stoves. Though most public campsites have fire rings or grates, firewood is not always available. It is also a better practice, environmentally, to use a backpacking stove. The downed wood provides a home for small creatures in the ecological web of things and, ultimately, once broken down returns needed materials to the soil. In most places driftwood is the only option, and during the busy months all pieces have usually been collected. If you do build an open fire, do so only where fires are permitted.

Beach fires are generally not allowed, both because of the unsightly scars they leave and because they can get out of control and spread to the uplands.

Loading sea kayaks at the Cascadia Marine Water Trail site on Skagit Island

Wildfires are a particular fear in drier places such as the San Juan and Gulf islands during the summer. If you must build an occasional small fire, do so in a designated ring, and never leave it unattended.

Dispersed Camping. Another problem is independent or "guerilla" camping in nondesignated sites. While common in areas where there are no designated campsites, many paddlers camp outside of established campsites in busy months when overcrowding occurs. This can destroy plant life and scar the landscape so many come to enjoy.

The problem is that Washington's coastline is simply too popular to provide the isolated camping that many kayakers seek. There are opportunities for legal, independent camping on undeveloped DNR lands and in some British Columbia parks, but they are rare and often not very attractive. The rule is to stick to designated campsites and, when in doubt, ask.

Garbage. Boat it in, boat it out. Kayakers can also cultivate their own best interests by being the most inexpensive and inoffensive user group. Be prepared to take all the trash whether left by your party or others and avoid using the garbage cans that are provided if you can take your garbage home. Many marine state parks now have a pack-it-out garbage program to combat the high cost of removing the mountains of trash left by boaters at the island parks. If you plan ahead you can repackage your food before you set out to lessen the burden on remote trash removal systems.

Human Waste. As marine recreation has grown, so has the stress on the land from improper disposal of human waste and the need for the acting land managers to provide adequate facilities to deal with this natural phenomenon. Use only established tent sites and do not deposit feces anywhere but in a toilet facility or, as is now commonly practiced on some water trails in other parts of the nation, pack it out in a suitable container. Serious health problems from the contamination of groundwater and edible marine food sources are best prevented in the first place.

Campground Behavior. Help your group use camping areas in a compact way, and extend a friendly welcome to other users of the trail who arrive after your party. Strive to preserve the serenity of the camping area and be considerate to others, particularly from dusk to morning. Encourage others, through example and/or gentle correction, particularly members of your own party, to maintain appropriate, courteous behavior. Leave and respect what you find. Avoid trampling vegetation and respect any wildlife you may encounter, including intertidal life.

Solitude. One important ingredient to satisfactory camping, solitude, may be the most difficult to find during the summer months and particularly on major holidays. During such peak times, try to aim for places less attractive to overnight boaters: sites without docks, moorings, or protected anchorages. Look to some of the lesser-known DNR sites, especially those with no overland access and poor landings for boats. Or head to the glorious south Puget Sound while everyone else crowds the San Juan Islands.

Harbor seals abound in Puget Sound.

Wildlife Etiquette

Marine mammals (particularly seals) and birds are most vulnerable when they are bearing and rearing their young. Mother seals may abandon their pups if they become separated from them or if the pups are handled by humans. Seal pups do not know enough to fear humans, and there have been reports of pups trying to climb aboard kayaks! Stay clear of mothers with young and paddle away from pups if they approach you. Maintain an adequate distance of 100 yards from seals, sea lions, and birds on land as prescribed by the Marine Mammal Protection Act. Report abandoned or dead seals to the Washington Department of Fish and Wildlife or the Marine Mammal Stranding Network. In Canada contact the Cetus Society or the BC Marine Mammal Response Network.

Whales. The Whale Museum in Friday Harbor on San Juan Island has created a "Code of Ethics for Kayakers." This code is designed to make paddlers aware of where they belong in saltwater environments and also provide guidelines to prevent disturbing marine wildlife such as whales. Paddlers are required to stay 200 yards from whales and 400 yards from their direct path. San Juan County Park requires paddlers to watch a video about respecting and understanding such guidelines before launching at their site. For additional information: www.bewhalewise.org; www.whale-museum.org.

Birds. Birds are particularly sensitive when they are incubating their eggs. Bald eagles are of special concern to wildlife managers, as they may abandon their eggs if there is too much human activity in the vicinity of the nest. This

Summer trip across the extensive kelp beds of Freshwater Bay near Port Angeles

is a major reason that camping is either prohibited or confined to one area in popular eagle-nesting areas such as Patos Island. Eagles are incubating between late March and late May, so be especially unobtrusive on shore or while paddling along shore in eagle country at that time.

Visitors to Cypress Island's Pelican Beach should note that the trail to Eagle Cliffs is closed from January through mid-July to protect peregrine falcon nesting sites in the cliffs area. This closure also affects going ashore on the beaches below Eagle Cliffs.

Raccoons. Cuteness is the sole virtue of the ubiquitous raccoon. You can expect a visit from these bold and persistent critters at any time, day or night. Their ability to cart off large food packages is notorious.

James and Jones Island state parks are home for the commando elite of raccoons, well known for their bravado and larcenous skills continuously honed on park visitors. The tenacity and deviousness of this cadre is unequaled in all the San Juan Islands. They never desist from their mission and apparently never sleep. Neither will you. Hanging food is protection only if done cleverly enough to foil these excellent climbers. Another solution, if you have enough stowage space, is to store food in the animal-proof plastic containers commercially available or, as an inexpensive alternative, containers in which foods like Greek olives are shipped. These containers will hold several days' worth of food. Paddling guides suggested tying zippers together and wrapping all loose gear in two layers of tarps with bungee cords or rope to prevent the animals from finding an access hole.

A final note to aid a half-decent night's sleep: bring everything that clanks or rattles such as clean cookware into the tent with you, or suffer through listening to the raccoons examining it all night.

Emergencies

We all hope that an emergency never happens, but we should all be prepared just in case. It is wise to have at least the basics of first aid and cardiopulmonary resuscitation (CPR) training in our repertoire of skills. Classes in these disciplines are taught on a fairly regular basis by local chapters of the American Red Cross, through community service organizations such as the local fire department, and by outdoor recreation groups and clubs.

In addition, the importance of taking classes and practicing to become proficient in performing fundamental sea-kayak rescues, such as the T-assisted rescue and paddle-float self-rescue, cannot be stressed enough. We never plan to take a swim on a trip, but being prepared with a clear mind and practiced response for that off-chance swim can literally be a lifesaving skill.

Stand up paddlers should know how to tow another paddler and provide others with a method to tow themselves. Waist-worn kayak tow ropes are ideal for this purpose. Stand up paddlers should also be prepared to rescue people in other types of watercraft such as kayakers.

Beyond the unmistakable reality that the best help is the immediate aid of your paddling group, you can obtain assistance from a variety of sources when on or near the water. Who to call will depend on the nature of the emergency, your location, and the communication means available to you.

When asking for help, you should be prepared to provide relevant information including:

- Nature of the emergency: injury (exact description), overboard, missing person, etc.
- When the problem occurred and how long people may have been in the water or suffering an injury
- Exact location or direction and distance from recognizable landmarks
- Description of persons and boats involved
- How many people and what equipment, including survival gear and first-aid supplies, are at the scene
- What equipment is needed
- Method of evacuation needed
- Local weather and sea conditions, including currents and wave action
- Names and addresses of members in party and whom to notify

Location

Knowing your precise location can be difficult at times, especially due to the nature and stress of the emergency situation. But it is essential if help is to reach you in time. For an exact location, a global positioning satellite (GPS) receiver is ideal. Some cell phone systems can provide the location of the caller to 911. However, batteries and electronic equipment seem to have a predisposition to fail in saltwater environments. For that reason there is no substitute for waterproof nautical charts and a compass to continually track your progress and position.

Communication

In many cases, a telephone is the primary means of communication. In all emergencies when feasible, call 911 for assistance. The dispatcher can contact the appropriate agency for aid. The county sheriff is the standard emergency responder in most areas of Puget Sound and the San Juan Islands. The US Coast Guard is tasked with providing emergency aid on the water.

As common as cell phones are, do not rely on them totally, as you may be out of transmission range. A VHF-FM radio is invaluable for this reason alone. Handheld waterproof floating VHF radios are available, which are perfect for keeping handy in your PFD or immediate reach.

But remember: Don't just carry a radio, know how to use it and keep it accessible at all times. Beyond these communications means, you should carry flares and other emergency signaling devices and know when and how to use them for maximum effectiveness.

Emergency Contact Numbers

US Coast Guard
206-217-6410
Mobile: call 911
Emergency: CG prefers VHF-FM channel 16.
www.homeport.uscg.mil/seattle

US Customs: General
877-CBP-5511
If you are outside the United States, 202-325-8000.
www.cbp.gov

US Customs: Port Angeles
360-457-4311; 360-565-7300

US Customs: Friday and Roche harbors
360-378-2703; 360-378-2080

Seattle Harbor Patrol
206-684-4071
16 on VHF-FM radio

County Sheriff
911 dispatcher will contact

Paralytic Shellfish Poison Hotline
800-562-5632

1 Hammersley Inlet

The skinniest of major Puget Sound inlets, Hammersley is a saltwater river ride if you time the currents right to transport you from one end to the other. There is the possibility of making a fairly easy round trip by coordinating your return with the tidal exchanges, enjoying a snack and exploring the shoreline at your turnaround while you await the current's reversal. Hammersley Inlet was completely overlooked by Peter Puget's expedition and not discovered for another fifty years, possibly due to the overlapping points of Cape Horn and Cape Cod near the inlet's entrance, which mask its true character. Once this inlet was found, the fertile uplands quickly became and still are a primary source of timber.

Duration: Full day to overnight.

Rating: *Moderate* or *Moderate +*. During large tidal exchanges the current can flow at a swift 5 knots. Areas of tricky current and tide rips can be avoided.

Navigation Aids: SeaTrails WA 205; NOAA charts 18445 SC or 18448 (both 1:80,000) and 18457 (1:10,000). The Narrows current table with adjustments for Hammersley Inlet.

Planning Considerations: Use the current tables to carefully plan the timing of your trip in either direction, traveling on the flood west to Shelton, and on the ebb east to the Arcadia launch. In this slender inlet it is much more fun and exhilarating to paddle with the current than against, which is impossible at high exchanges. Cape Horn, jutting out from the north shore about 0.5 mile from the inlet's entrance, helps develop a strong tide rip that is avoided by staying to the south shore. Also note that tricky eddies may form at other smaller protuberances along the inlet. If you paddle out to Hope Island, be aware of the strong current that builds on the west side of Squaxin Island and the long fetch of Totten Inlet, which is able to produce stiff southerly winds.

Getting There and Launching

Four public launch sites provide access, three in and near Shelton at the inlet's west end, and another one at the Arcadia boat ramp just to the south of the inlet's entrance on Puget Sound.

Shelton: The launch on Shelton's working waterfront is along Pine Street (State Route 3 to Bremerton) just north of the old downtown.

Looking east over Hammersley Inlet from Walker County Park

Once you pass under a railroad bridge, take the first immediate right into the Oakland Bay Marina. At this public access gravel and dirt launch site you'll find plenty of parking. For additional information about the marina: www.portofshelton.com/marina.html.

Jacoby Shorecrest County Park: This launch is on the crook of the inlet's elbow across from Shelton. From SR 3 at the north end of Oakland Bay, head south on East Agate Road 3.4 miles, then turn right onto East Crestview Drive and go 2.4 miles. Turn left on East Parkway Boulevard and then right onto East Shorecrest Park Way and you'll reach the county park, which has a paved boat launch.

Walker County Park: This small wooded Mason County park (closed in winter) is on the south shore of the inlet almost across from the Jacoby Shorecrest ramp. Drive SR 3 south out of Shelton and, as you reach the top of a long hill, turn left onto Southeast Arcadia Road. Travel for 1.5 miles and turn left onto Southeast Walker Park Road. In another 0.5 mile you enter the park. A brief walk from the parking lot gets you to the beach on the right side of the park. Cascadia Marine Trail campsites and overnight parking are available by prior reservation only. Call 360-427-9670 ext. 535. Year-round caretakers live

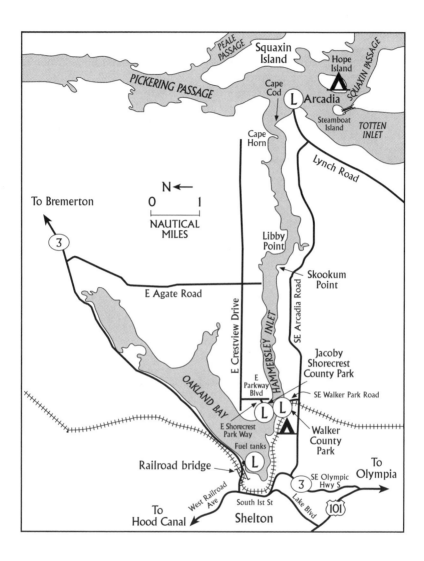

across the driveway from the toilets. The park is small and may be noisy with day users. For additional information about the park: www.co.mason.wa.us /parks/walker_park.php.

Arcadia Boat Ramp: To reach this paved boat ramp, drive just over 7.5 miles from Shelton along Southeast Arcadia Road. At Lynch Road turn left and proceed to the launch. The ramp is owned by the Squaxin Tribe and was improved in 2011. Park one block away from the ramp on the road's south side in the large gravel lot. There is one toilet.

Route

Your direction of travel is highly dependent on the current's flow and your timing. The one-way route is just under 7 miles if you travel from Shelton to Arcadia or vice versa. If you prefer to avoid Shelton, Jacoby Shorecrest County or Walker County parks are pleasant alternatives with picnic tables and sanitary facilities, and will shorten the route about 1 mile.

Starting in Shelton, you immediately recognize this as a logger's town. The Simpson Mill dominates the waterfront, and numerous logs floating on Oakland Bay are normally corralled within booms. The logs are often tended by one-man, lime-green work boats that are best described as pint-sized tugboats. It is fun to watch them push and prod the logs into obedience, but remember to stay a safe distance.

Looking to the north you see the wider expanse of Oakland Bay. Oysters are farmed in its uppermost beds. East lies narrow Hammersley Inlet.

As you paddle down the inlet for the next 4 miles, the shoreline is dominated on both sides by agreeable homes old and new, of various shapes and sizes, many hugging the beach. There is no public access, so be prepared to stay in your boat. The inlet maintains a fairly even but cozy width of less than 500 yards along most of its length.

As you course the remaining 2.5 miles of the inlet after Libby Point, it gradually reverts to a more natural state, primarily due to the higher, steeper banks that discourage building. Nevertheless, houses appear sporadically at the tops, and a few have made inroads down the sides. Generally, the land feels a little wilder here and the paddling is pleasant with plenty of shorebirds and waterfowl, often harbor seals and sometimes eagles if you travel during a quieter time of the day or in the winter season.

Just before entering into Pickering Passage from Hammersley Inlet, you pass the jutting prominence of Cape Horn. It helps create a strong rip tide at high tidal exchanges. It is a place to practice paddling technique or to be avoided depending on your skills and intentions for the day.

As you leave the inlet, Squaxin Island appears directly across Pickering Passage, to the southeast is Hope Island, and to the south lies Steamboat Island with its obvious long, low bridge connection to the mainland. Bear south along the western shore of Pickering Passage to reach the Arcadia Boat Ramp in under 0.2 mile.

If your plan is a round trip or overnight, the best spot to relax or camp before the return is the Cascadia Marine Trail site on Hope Island, which is 6 miles from Walker County Park. (See the Hope Island trip.) However, this requires paddling across Pickering Passage and adds another 2.5 miles to your round-trip journey. Traveling in the other direction, either Jacoby Shorecrest County Park or Walker County Park is the much more comfortable alternative for a picnic compared to the barren launch at Shelton.

2 Eld Inlet

This is a pleasurable place to paddle with no real destination, or to explore the little mid-inlet coves and southern tidal estuaries. Only one boat ramp, a driveway through the yard of a private home and boat building shop, provides direct trailered boat access on Eld Inlet. This factor helps encourage greater tranquility than found elsewhere. The other access point, at Frye Cove County Park, is only suitable for hand-carried boats.

Duration: Part day to full day.

Rating: *Protected* or *Moderate*.

Navigation Aids: SeaTrails WA 205; NOAA charts 18445 SC (1:80,000), 18448 (1:80,000), and 18456 (1:20,000). The Narrows current table with adjustments for Eld Inlet entrance.

Planning Considerations: The timing of any trip into the southern tidal estuaries requires careful planning so you explore them only during a high tide. Extending your trip into these shallow channels too long into ebb means likely dragging your craft through deep mud. The current can also be a factor, especially as the channels drain, which creates fast flowing waters.

Getting There and Launching

There are two launch sites for hand-carried boats: a very small commercial boat ramp open to the public and Frye Cove County Park.

Commercial Boat Ramp: From US Highway 101 take the Hunter Point/Steamboat Island Exit and drive north 1.1 miles on Steamboat Island Road Northwest. Turn right onto Gravelly Beach Road Northwest, proceed another 1.6 miles to Gravelly Beach Loop Road Northwest, and turn right. There is a sign at that intersection directing you to the boat ramp. In another 0.6 mile you will come to the boat ramp, a marine repair shop, and boat builder clustered on the same property. The ramp is concrete with a float along the side. There is no portable toilet and very limited parking. Weekend parking is actually a little better, as the boat builders need the spaces during work days. Overnight parking is allowed by permission of the friendly facility owners, who charge a small launch fee to help maintain the facilities.

Frye Cove County Park: Once on Gravelly Beach Road Northwest, continue past the turn to the commercial boat ramp another 2.5 miles to the junction of Young Road Northwest and the other end of Gravelly Beach Loop Road Northwest. Turn right onto Young Road Northwest and proceed 0.7 mile and turn right onto 61st Avenue Northwest (also known as Giddings Road). In

0.5 mile, at the end of 61st Avenue Northwest where it intersects with Boardman Road Northwest, is the park entrance to the right. Follow the park road to the main parking area. Wheels are recommended for carrying your boat down Cove Trail, a steep rocky path, about a quarter mile to the small beach at the head of Frye Cove. Add 200 yards to access the beach during low tides. The park itself is delightful. It is well maintained and has a nice view out over Eld Inlet. The park has restrooms, picnic tables, clamming on the beach in season, and a great lawn for lazing on. For additional information about the park: 360-789-5595.

Routes

Young and Frye coves: *Protected.* Great for novices, either of these snug little coves makes for a tranquil paddle of an hour or so. It is best to time a trip for higher tides so the coves' inner reaches are accessible. Pass by trees dripping with mosses and lichens, and small creatures foraging along the sheltered banks.

Mud Bay: *Moderate.* The distance to the head of the Mud Bay inlet and back is 8.5 miles. The route offers pleasant views of homes nestled in a wooded shore and backed to the south by gentle mountains. It is an easy paddle with no current to speak of until you approach the southern reaches and tidal channels passing beneath US 101. The ebb and flood of the tide creates a fairly strong current that is difficult to paddle against, especially in the restricted passages near the highway during a large ebb. However, the southern reaches are the ideal conditions for waterfowl and wading birds. It is likely you will see heron, kingfisher, and numerous other winged hunters in these shallows.

Eld Inlet still produces a reasonable share of oysters, and you may see the markers

Eld Inlet and Frye County Park at low tide

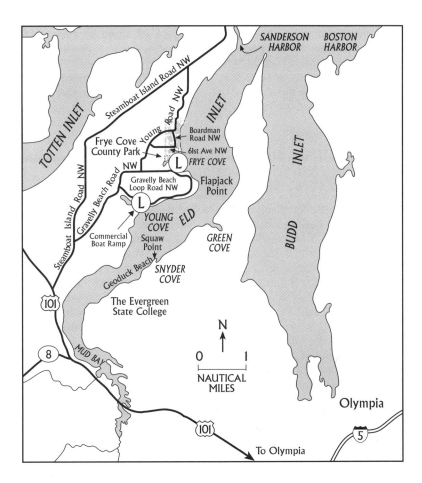

that define growers' beds in the shallows and shoals here and there. However, the major harvests of old have long since dwindled. You will see evidence of this once productive past intermittently along the shore as you pass the remnants of piers and pilings of oyster shacks, which you can identify by the mounds of sun-bleached oyster shells surrounding them.

Geoduck Beach: *Moderate.* Directly across from Young Cove is Geoduck Beach, the western boundary of The Evergreen State College campus. This wonderful stretch of shoreline is fully wooded except for a couple of buildings. The buildings and the beach comprise the college's Marine Study/Ecological Reserve. Landing is prohibited to protect the marine and shore life for research, but simply paddling this edge of sandy shore and tall forest is pleasure enough. If you must walk the beach, save it for another day—the approach is by land, on maintained trails from the bluff above.

A fulfilling round trip is to launch from Young Cove, exploring it first, then paddle south across Eld Inlet to the southern end of Geoduck Beach. Follow the beach north, then recross Eld Inlet rounding Flapjack Point to Frye Cove. Stop for a rest or picnic at Frye Cove County Park, then return south to your start by following the western shore and once again rounding Flapjack Point. The total distance is about 7 miles.

3 Henderson Inlet: Woodard Bay Natural Resources Conservation Area

Henderson Inlet offers a serene place to paddle, especially when compared to other, more trafficked inlets of south Puget Sound. This is partly due to the absence of public beaches or boat ramps excepting a limited launch place for hand-carried boats and because a fair amount of undeveloped and protected shoreline remains. A reclaimed gem along the western shore, Woodard Bay Natural Resources Conservation Area, has been transformed from a Weyerhaeuser timber storage and transport facility to a lush oasis of wildlife, managed by the DNR. Waterfowl, seals, great blue heron, and numerous other shoreline and marine creatures call this home, consistently providing a prime wildlife viewing destination. However, access is tightly restricted to protect sensitive wildlife habitat, so pay close attention to current regulations.

Duration: Part day to full day.

Rating: *Protected* or *Moderate* +. Within Woodard and Chapman bays and the south end of Henderson Inlet, the paddling is gentle and sheltered. Kayaking around Johnson Point exposes you to the possibility of tide rips and strong winds depending on currents and weather.

Navigation Aids: SeaTrails WA 204, 205; NOAA charts 18445 SC and 18448 (both 1:80,000). The Narrows current table with adjustments for Dana Passage.

Planning Considerations: If the Woodard Bay Natural Resources Conservation Area is your planned launch, be aware that shoreline access is only permitted from April 15 through Labor Day to protect a varied and exceptional mix of wildlife. The alternative launch, from the marina on the east side of Johnson Point in the Nisqually Reach, requires paddling in possibly bumpy and exposed waters when the current is fast, the wind is blowing, or a combination of the two. It is easiest to paddle around Johnson Point into Henderson Inlet and back again by timing your trip with the respective flood and ebb. Be sure to watch the tide levels as Woodard Bay can dry completely on lower tides.

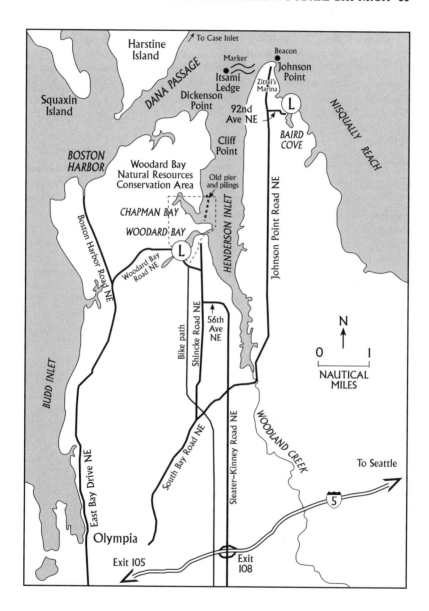

Getting There and Launching

Two launch sites provide access: one a public site within Henderson Inlet at the conservation area, the other is Zittel's Marina on the east side of Johnson Point in the Nisqually Reach.

Woodard Bay: This launch provides the most direct access to Henderson Inlet, but, as stated above, it is closed right after Labor Day until April 15 to protect wildlife. From Interstate 5, exit at Olympia (Exit 105) and drive north on East Bay Drive Northeast just over 2 miles. The road then becomes Boston Harbor Road Northeast, and you drive an additional 2 miles. Turn right onto Woodard Bay Road Northeast and follow it for just under 2 miles (watch for a right turn after 1 mile rather than going straight on Libby Road) to a bridge that spans Woodard Bay. Just before the west end of the bridge turn left into the DNR lot, which provides parking next to the grassy launch slope. Signs in the lot warn of break-ins, make sure extra gear is secured to your car or out of sight. Note: Access to the water is on your left over a five-foot-high metal gate that blocks vehicle access to the nature trail. Maneuvering over the gate can take some effort if you're solo. Be careful on the short steep embankment leading to the beach. Low tides can make for a muddy entry. If you decide to walk over the bridge on the main road, watch for cars speeding down each hill on both sides.

Johnson Point: The boat ramp at Zittel's Marina near the end of Johnson Point can be reached from I-5 by turning off at Exit 108. Drive north on Sleater-Kinney Road Northeast for 3.25 miles, turning right onto South Bay Road Northeast. In about 0.5 mile the road turns into Johnson Point Road Northeast where it bends under the head of Henderson Inlet. In approximately another 5 miles turn right on 92nd Avenue Northeast. Follow it to its end at the marina. A fee is charged to use the boat ramp. Parking and toilets are available. Note: Parking can be tight during fishing season.

Routes

Woodard Bay Natural Resources Conservation Area: *Protected.* The paddling distance is a round trip as short as 2.5 miles from Woodard Bay to Chapman Bay and back again, or longer as self-determined. Launching at Woodard Bay allows easy exploration of the two bays included within the conservation area and is an ideal trip for novice kayakers. High tide is best for launching, as the bank is a potential slippery mud slide at lower waters. Paddling at high tide also allows you to explore the bays to their fullest extent. Summer water temperatures can get very comfortable in the bay.

After launching, begin by investigating Woodard Bay with the option of paddling southwest under the car bridge back into its farthest reaches. On a flood tide, enjoy a mild tidal rapid as the water squeezes through the narrow opening below the bridge into the back bay.

From Woodard Bay paddle to the open water of Henderson Inlet, rounding to the north the peninsula separating the bays. Paddlers are asked not to enter Chapman Bay to protect sensitive habitat. Return to your launch point by retracing your route.

The conservation area is the perfect place to immerse yourself in the intimate sanctuary these two bays provide for marine wildlife. The bays are well sheltered with a thick blanket of tall trees and natural vegetation guarding their perimeters. In places, the overhanging branches and fallen trees drip with lichens and mosses, dappled with sunlight highlighting their various greens, producing an almost southern feel of bayou. From either bay when the skies permit, the white cone of Mount Rainier can be spied sitting atop the forest canopy on the opposing shore of Henderson Inlet.

You may spot smaller upland, perching, and clinging birds flitting within the branches and shrubs, while heron, eagle, or hawks deck the upper branches. Waterfowl grace the bays' surface, including ducks, waders, and gulls. Seals and jellyfish are two of the marine creatures likely to be encountered lurking within the water.

Woodard Bay to the Head of Henderson Inlet: *Protected* or *Moderate*. An option for wildlife exploration and close-in shoreline viewing is to paddle south to the head of the inlet. This is a round trip from the Woodard Bay launch point of 5.75 miles or more, given how deeply you explore the bay and its shoreline convolutions. It is

Overhanging trees are common on Woodard Bay.

best to visit at higher tides to gain maximum entry into the tidal lands. If winds are strong from the north, seas can build over the long fetch and make the return trip a difficult one. Remember also that there is no public access along these shores, so you must be comfortable in your boat.

Here you can wander in the little channel formed from Woodland Creek emptying into Henderson Inlet and explore remnants of log booms left from the timbering days. Seals often inhabit these booms and breeding also takes place. Remember to maintain an adequate distance of 100 yards from seals or other wildlife as prescribed by the Federal Marine Mammal Protection Act and DNR's posted instructions.

Johnson Point to Henderson Inlet: *Moderate* or *Moderate* + (depending on current and wind). The approach to Woodard Bay Natural Resources Conservation Area from the marina ramp adds 4.75 miles (one way) to the trip. The tidal flood and ebb passing between Johnson Point and the Key Peninsula, along with the long fetches of Case Inlet and Nisqually Reach, means you must plan your travel to and from with the current's direction and an eye to the winds. Ideally you would like a flood in the morning, high tide at midday, and an ebb in the afternoon for a full day round trip. Of course, a one-way trip in either direction is also easily accomplished with a shuttle.

Zittel's Marina is a pleasant place, as it is well kept and has a small store for last-minute provisions. You might even want to investigate among the docks or poke around a bit in Baird Cove.

As you leave the marina, you will see Mount Rainier looming up from the southeast across Nisqually Reach. Look to the right of the big volcano and you may also see a somewhat smaller one, Mount Saint Helens. Proceeding north around Johnson Point, you will be facing the Olympic Mountains strung out across the far horizon.

The tower beacon just off Johnson Point is where cormorants often perch to dry their wings. As you head west around the point into Henderson Inlet, be aware that Itsami Ledge is midwater between Johnson and Dickenson points, marked by another light. If conditions are right, it can produce sharp waves. It is easily avoided by staying along the gravel shore of Johnson Point.

Once you enter Henderson Inlet, you have two basic options. You may head diagonally across to Woodard Bay Natural Resources Conservation Area, passing by Cliff Point jutting from the opposing shore, or paddle south along the eastern shoreline to the bottom of the inlet, admiring modest and grand structures alike as you go. There are a couple of interesting little coves to explore as well.

4 Nisqually Delta

The Nisqually Delta (or Nisqually National Wildlife Refuge) is one of the finest estuaries in Puget Sound, and a good place for paddlers who like to exploit their craft's shallow water abilities and explore brackish back channels as few other boaters can. Needless to say, this is a prime place for birders. In 2009, the Nisqually Tribe removed 8 miles of dike, including the Brown Farm Dike, opening the delta and freeing the river to flow naturally for the first time in a century. For additional information: www.fws.gov/Nisqually/visit.html.

Duration: Part day.

Rating: *Protected.*

Navigation Aids: SeaTrails WA 204; NOAA chart 1844S SC (1:80,000); Seattle tide table (add 30 minutes).

Planning Considerations: Most channels are negotiable at midtide or above; high tide opens up many others. A Washington Department of Fish and Wildlife conservation license or Discover Pass are required to use the Luhr Beach Public Access site. Nisqually Delta can be unpleasant in wind because of steep seas in the shallows and the chance of getting wet at the unprotected launch site. Waterfowl hunters are present in the Department of Fish and Wildlife portions of the delta from mid-October to mid-January.

Getting There and Launching

From Interstate 5, take Exit 114 (Nisqually). Go south on Martin Way and follow it for just under 1 mile to Meridian Road Northeast—veer right through the roundabout. Turn right here and follow it for almost 3 miles to 46th Avenue Northeast. Turn right again and go 0.25 mile to D'Milluhr Road Northeast on the left with a sign pointing to public fishing. Follow it downhill for about 0.5 mile to the parking area.

The Department of Fish and Wildlife's ramp at Luhr Beach has a moderate-size lot and a beach next to the ramp for launching. At high tide there is limited launching space on the rocky beach, which becomes sandy at lower tides and offers more space. To park here you will need a Department of Fish

Kayakers launching from Luhr beach into Nisqually Delta

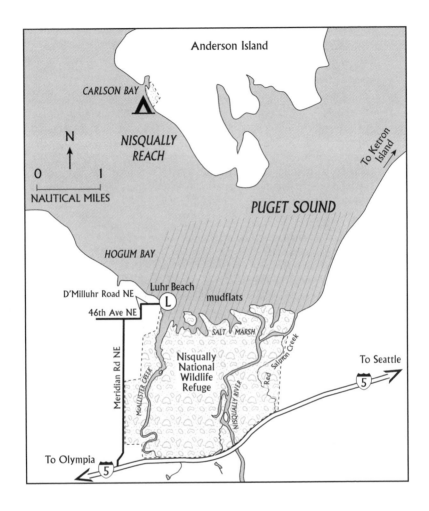

and Wildlife permit or Discover Pass, which can be purchased at most sporting goods stores that sell hunting licenses. Next to the parking area is the Nisqually Reach Nature Center, which is open on selected days of the week depending on the season.

Routes

Choose your own route and distance. This area is managed by the US Fish and Wildlife Service and the Washington Department of Wildlife. The federal Nisqually National Wildlife Refuge includes the lower delta's tide flats and the meadows and woods of old farmland in the central portion above the dike that extends between McAllister Creek on the west and the Nisqually River on the east. State Wildlife lands include most of the lower salt marshes and most of the land along McAllister Creek.

Lower Delta: *Protected.* If you arrive near high tide, you may wish to explore the myriad channels that wander across the salt marshes in the lower delta. At highest tides you may be able to pick your way through shallow channels, though a spring tide is required if you are to make it all the way across the delta by this inner route. Otherwise, head north to the lower flats to find your way to the eastern side of the delta, where you can head upstream on the Nisqually River or explore the connecting channel to Red Salmon Creek, farthest to the east. At the very northeast corner of the flats, still within federal refuge boundaries, is a sand jetty of old pilings and a beached concrete barge that makes a nice lunch and sunbathing stop. A few miles to the north is tiny Ketron Island (not on map) which has no facilities and a few private homes.

McAllister Creek: *Protected.* If you care to venture inland, McAllister Creek at the western edge of the delta offers the possibility of many miles of small stream paddling, using the last of the flood tide to assist you on the way in and then riding the ebb back out. The creek can be paddled easily to well inland of the freeway overpass. In autumn, salmon can be viewed under your boat in the creek. Settler James McAllister was the first white man to be killed in the 1855–56 Indian war. Medicine Creek, a tributary to McAllister was the location of the Medicine Creek Treaty where Governor Isaac Stevens tricked the Native American chiefs of the region to relocate their people to reservations in the South Sound.

Luhr Beach to Anderson Island: *Protected.* An alternative route that can include an overnight is to paddle to Anderson Island only 1.5 miles across from the boat ramp. Bear west on Anderson to Carlson Bay which is 4 miles from Luhr Beach. The Cascadia Marine Site on Carlson is by reservation only and is located on the end of the sand spit in the bay. Restrooms are on the spit in the park.

5 Hope Island (South)

Hope Island is a state park with beaches, meadows, forest trails, and the remnants of a farm homestead. Access from various sides of the South Sound is easy using the Hammersley Inlet, Boston Harbor, or Pickering/Peale Passage routes described here. Hope Island can be incorporated into a single-day trip around adjacent Squaxin Island or a multiday circumnavigation of nearby Harstine Island. Other camping possibilities are the two Cascadia Marine Trail sites at Jarrell Cove State Park (7.8 miles) and Joemma Beach State Park (7.6 miles) on the Key Peninsula.

> **Duration:** Part day to overnight. There is a campsite for the general public and six for Cascadia Marine Trail users.

Rating: *Moderate* or *Moderate +*. The Boston Harbor route requires an open-water crossing and exposure to possible tide rips in Dana Passage. Currents on the Peale Passage route may exceed 1.5 knots at times.

Navigation Aids: SeaTrails WA 205; NOAA charts 18445 SC or 18448 (both 1:80,000). Chart 18456 (1:20,000) covers the Boston Harbor route. Use current tables for the Narrows with adjustments for Dana Passage on the Boston Harbor route, or with adjustments for Pickering/Peale Passage.

Planning Considerations: Use the current tables to avoid maximum flows in Dana Passage on the Boston Harbor route. On the Pickering/Peale Passage route, travel to Squaxin Island on the ebb and return with the flood current. On the Pickering/Peale Passage route, travel south on the ebb and return on the flood.

Getting There and Launching

This area sits astride a portion of Puget Sound where island destinations are separated by only a few miles of water and easily accessible by boat, though are hours apart by highway. Residents of the west side of Puget Sound can start from Latimer's Landing at the Harstine Island Bridge near Shelton and paddle the Pickering/Peale Passage route, or launch at the Arcadia boat ramp just to the south of Hammersley Inlet. Those coming from the east will find Boston Harbor near Olympia most convenient.

Latimer's Landing at the Harstine Island Bridge: To reach the landing, turn onto East Pickering Road from State Route 3 about 8 miles north of Shelton (there is a sign for Harstine Island). Follow this road approximately 5 miles to the bridge. The county landing includes a public ramp, dock, and parking lot located just north of the bridge's western end. The lot by the ramp is for day use only. For overnight parking, use the lot about a quarter mile up the road. Be cautious of swift currents here. The dock can be busy with fishermen, so leave your boat on the shore until you're ready to launch.

Arcadia Boat Ramp: See the Hammersley Inlet trip.

Boston Harbor: Take Exit 105B (Plum Street) from Interstate 5 in Olympia. Drive north after exiting the freeway; the rest of the route is essentially straight ahead. After passing through several intersections for approximately 1 mile, you will see water on the left. Plum Street becomes East Bay Drive, which eventually becomes Boston Harbor Road. Continue another 7 miles to 73rd Avenue Northeast and turn left. The boat ramp is on the west side of the Boston Harbor Marina building on the right. Arrive early on weekend mornings to get a parking spot in the free gravel lot parking west of the boat ramp. The marina suggests that paddlers park end-to-end to save space if coming in a large group. With a Discover Pass, you can park in the paved parking lot across from the marina building for up to three days. Also park end-to-end here if possible to save space. If you find street parking in the neighborhood, please be respectful

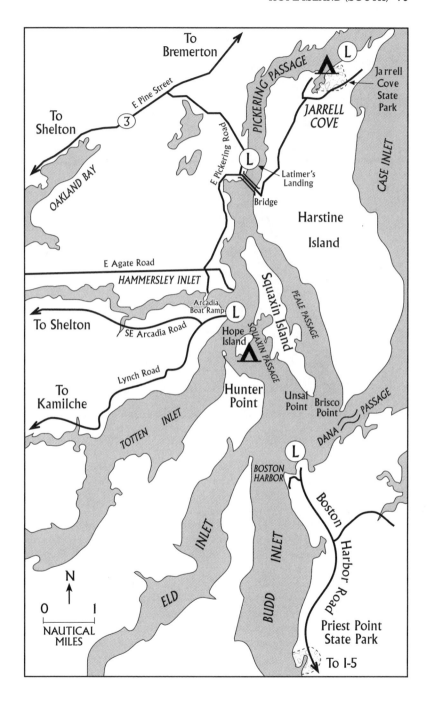

To
Bremerton

PICKERING PASSAGE

L

JARRELL COVE

Jarrell Cove State Park

E Pine Street

To Shelton

3

E Pickering Road

L

Latimer's Landing

Bridge

OAKLAND BAY

CASE INLET

Harstine

Island

E Agate Road

HAMMERSLEY INLET

Arcadia Boat Ramp

L

To Shelton

SE Arcadia Road

Hope Island

Squaxin Island

SQUAXIN PASSAGE

PEALE PASSAGE

Lynch Road

To Kamilche

Hunter Point

Unsal Point

Brisco Point

DANA PASSAGE

TOTTEN INLET

L

BOSTON HARBOR

Boston Harbor Road

ELD INLET

BUDD INLET

Priest Point State Park

To I-5

N

0   1

NAUTICAL MILES

A kayaker stands below the day-use site for Hope Island (South).

of residents. A restroom is available across the street from the marina. The marina has a café, food and boating store, kayak rentals, and moorage.

Routes

Pickering/Peale Passage (Latimer's Landing to Hope Island): *Moderate.* One-way distance is 4 miles. Currents can exceed 1.5 knots along this route. Using favorable currents can make a significant difference for travel, although alongshore eddies can be used to travel against the currents in most places. Tide rips are possible, especially when the current opposes the wind direction.

The flood currents coming around both sides of Harstine Island meet in the vicinity of northern Squaxin Island.

To travel from Latimer's Landing to Hope Island via the west side of Squaxin Island, catch the flood current starting soon after the turn to the flood for Pickering Passage off Graham Point, and return when the current begins to ebb at the same location. If you are circumnavigating Squaxin Island, note that Peale Passage has quite a different schedule, flowing north during most of the flood cycle and south during the ebb. Consequently, plan to head up the east side of Squaxin Island about two hours before the turn to the ebb at Graham Point, so as to ride the flood up Peale Passage and then the new ebb the remainder of the distance.

South of the Latimer's Landing, the shores in Pickering Passage alternate between houses and steep tree-lined banks, but the shore of Squaxin Island is a fine oasis of natural beauty. Paddling close to its shore, you can imagine yourself exploring Puget Sound two centuries ago with British explorer Captain George Vancouver.

An alternative camping option is to travel north from Latimer's Landing 2.5 miles to Jarrell Cove on Harstine Island, which has a Cascadia Marine Trail site. (See the Jarrell Cove State Park chapter.)

Squaxin Island is an Indian reservation. Do not go ashore without permission. Squaxin's shoreline has escaped development except for an oyster-rearing operation in the bay midway down the island. Occasional decaying shacks are the only signs of the island's sparse settlement. More evident residents are river otter, blue heron, or even a coyote trotting along the beach.

Hope Island State Park is a 106-acre island that supported a working homestead until the 1940s. This addition to the park system includes meadows, orchards, and an old windmill on the west side, as well as extensive trails leading through the forests on the island. At lower tides, you can hike the approximate 2 miles around the island on the beach. A caretaker's cabin is located above the beach on the flatter west side of the island. This area is also the Cascadia Marine Trail campsite, with several sites for general usage on the south side of the little cove here. There are vault toilets, but there is no water system. Make sure to bring your boat up to the site as there is no beach at low tide.

Boston Harbor to Hope Island: *Moderate +.* The one-way distance is 3.8 miles. Dana Passage currents can attain almost 3 knots at times, and rips can be lively here, especially with an opposing wind. Watch for heavy boat traffic in the summer.

The strongest currents can be avoided by crossing directly from Boston Harbor to Squaxin Island. This route, however, involves crossing 2 miles of open water. Also, an ebb current flows southeast from Unsal Point on Squaxin Island most of the time, averaging a little over 1 knot at its peak, making this route most practical for the return.

To avoid open water and the strongest currents, cross Budd Inlet from Boston Harbor, then Eld Inlet entrance where currents there may reach 1 knot at times. Next follow the shoreline north and then west through Squaxin Passage, where the current may exceed 1.5 knots, flowing west during the flood. If you are circumnavigating Squaxin Island, expect either a longer open-water crossing from or to Unsal Point, or take a detour east to Dana Passage for a shorter crossing to Harstine Island at Brisco Point. Currents in Dana Passage may reach several knots, and tide rips can develop. Try to cross when the current is slack or at least flowing in the same direction as the wind. Note that Peale Passage flows north on the flood.

6 Jarrell Cove State Park

Located along the western shore of Harstine Island, this 11.5-acre state park is a low-key destination that can be accessed easily from Tacoma or the Bremerton area via the Key Peninsula.

Duration: Part day to overnight.

Rating: *Moderate.* Requires a 1.5-mile open-water crossing. Currents along the route are weak.

Navigation Aids: SeaTrails WA 205; NOAA charts 18448 or 18445 SC (both 1:80,000).

Planning Considerations: McMicken Island is day use only and watch out for poison oak. Watch for heavy boating traffic on both approaches in summer.

Getting There and Launching

Joemma Beach State Park: This trip originates at the state park and Cascadia Marine Trail site on the Key Peninsula, 8.5 miles from Jarrell Cove. From State Route 302, turn south in Key Center onto the Gig Harbor—Longbranch Road and follow it to Home. About 1 mile south of Home, turn right on Whiteman Road (there are signs for Joemma Beach here and at the next junction). After another mile, bear left at the fork, and then turn right a little less than 0.5 mile beyond onto Bay Road South. This road turns to gravel and then forks. Take the right-hand road and follow it downhill to the recreation area. Generally, there is ample parking in a lot just above the beach. Do not leave valuables in your parked car. There is also a Cascadia Marine Trail campground in the park.

Route

Follow the peninsula's shore north to a point opposite McMicken Island before crossing; on the return leg follow the Harstine Island shore south and cross opposite Joemma Beach, which involves a slightly longer crossing. The shoreline north of Joemma Beach is pleasantly natural, with a pebble beach below high bluffs, the remains of an old pier, and a shallow lagoon with water that warms to bathtub temperatures during the summer, and, at upper tidal stages, a miniature tide race at its entrance. Harstine Island's shore offers a similar setting. Buffingtons Lagoon, less than 1 mile south of McMicken Island on Harstine, is another pleasant detour, though accessible only at high tide. Keep in mind that tidelands on both of these shores are private, so stay in your boat.

McMicken Island is particularly attractive to boaters who like the isolation afforded by low levels of development. There is no dock or any drinking water, but there are two vault toilets. Be alert for poison oak. Fires are not allowed on the island. Landings and access to the island are practical only on

View from the Cascadia Marine Trail site on Jarrell Cove

the southwest side due to the steep bluffs above the narrow beaches elsewhere. Behind this pebble and shell beach is a meadow with the handiest picnic sites. The fenced-in area and buildings behind the meadow are private land. A trail network circles through the dense forest north of the meadow, with occasional views out over the bluffs.

Leaving McMicken and heading north, the Harstine shoreline beyond the island is DNR for the next mile or so. Enjoy Harstine's sandy shores and relative solitude. Turn in Spencer Cove and paddle toward Dougall Point, which becomes more residential. The point at low tide is sandy with some current swirls and eddies depending on the tide direction. Head south along the island to Indian Cove, a protected inlet with a marina. The remaining medium bank shore leading to Jarrell Cove has sand and gravel beaches with views across

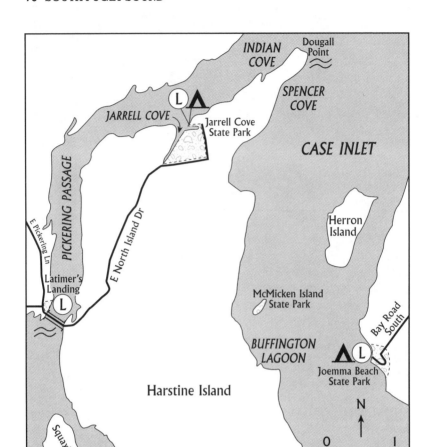

Pickering Passage. Pickering's flood current flows south and can reach 2.75 knots of current. Take advantage of the gentle push and enter Jarrell Cove.

The state park and Cascadia Marine Trail sites are on your left (north side) as you enter the cove. A kayak rack is provided above the water, look for the three tent sites in the trees and in an open area behind the rack. The restroom and other facilities are above in the main campground.

The cove cuts nearly a half mile into the island providing boaters and paddlers with a very protected gunkhole. A side inlet on the north side curves around Jarrell Cove State Park. Explore the cove and its peaceful calm waters. A few beach homes appear amongst pocket beaches and mini coves. Swamp-like overhanging trees angle over the water.

Jarrell Cove can also be accessed by Latimer's Landing and Boston Harbor to the south. See the Hope Island chapter for more information.

7 Carr Inlet: Horsehead Bay, Cutts Island State Park, and Kopachuck State Park

If you live south of Seattle, this is a short, easy trip, ideal for those with limited saltwater experience, or for families. Distances between stopovers are not long, and there are plenty of shore attractions and beaches with warm water for wading and swimming during the summer months. The route can be altered or shortened if weather is inclement. Camping is available at Kopachuck State Park or the Cascadia Marine Trail site located there. The beach is expansive at low tide and is known for ample sand dollars.

Duration: Part day.

Rating: *Protected* or *Moderate.*

Navigation Aids: SeaTrails WA 204; NOAA charts 18445 SC or 18448 (both 1:80,000), 18474 (1:40,000); Seattle tide table (add about 30 minutes).

Planning Considerations: Consult the tide table before starting out, as low tides make for long hauls to the water. Poor planning may lead to getting stuck in the mud in nearby inlets.

Getting There and Launching

Launching alternatives are boat ramps on Horsehead Bay and nearby Fox Island, or a short drive from the parking lot to the beach in Kopachuck State Park.

Kopachuck State Park: From State Route 16, follow Rosedale Street Northwest 2.32 miles and take a left on Ray Nash Drive Northwest. Go 2.27 miles to 58th Street Northwest and turn right into the park. At the time of writing signs for the park were hard to see from the road if coming from the north. Bring a cell phone to call the ranger at Kopachuck State Park for driving access to the beach for dropping off boats. To contact the ranger: 253-265-3606.

Horsehead Bay Boat Ramp: From SR 16, take the Wollochet Drive Northwest exit. Follow past Artondale. Take a right on 40th Street Northwest, then a left on 92nd Avenue Northwest. Then a right on 36th Street Northwest. Follow 36th Street Northwest past the intersection of Horsehead Drive to the boat ramp. A turnaround area is located just above the ramp. Limited parking is available along the west side of Horsehead Bay Drive. All property around the ramp is private.

Fox Island/Towhead Island Boat Ramp: From SR 16, take the Wollochet Drive Northwest exit. Follow past Artondale. Take a right on 40th Street Northwest, then a left on 70th Avenue Northwest, then right on Warren Drive Northwest. Veer left onto the Fox Island bridge. Exit to the right at the boat ramp before you reach Fox Island, this is Towhead Island, which is connected

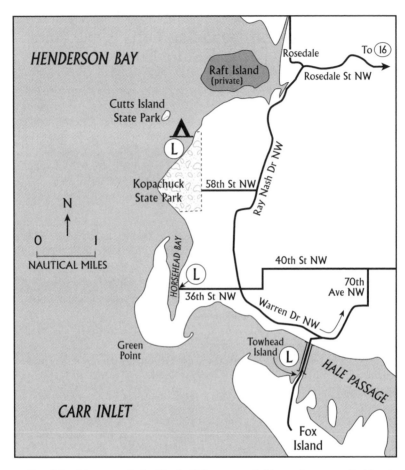

to Fox Island by a sandspit. No facilities are available at the ramp. Parking is limited; arrive early on weekends or during fishing season.

If you want to avoid the 0.35-mile carry from the parking lot to the beach, you can drive down the gravel service road above the beach to unload and load your boat. There is a gate across the road. If it is locked, call the park ranger; the ranger's cell phone number is listed on the bulletin board by the gate. You can also call ahead to the park office: 253-265-3606. If you want to walk down with your boat, the gravel service road is smooth enough for boat carts. The Discover Pass is required for park use.

Routes

Horsehead Bay to Cutts Island and Kopachuck state parks: *Protected.* Launch alongside beach homes and docks in this narrow inlet and head north toward Kopachuck State Park, a distance of 1.2 miles. An impressive sand

View of Cutts Island from the Cascadia Marine Water Trail site in Kopachuck State Park

spit exposed at low tides juts out to the west entry of the bay. Don't land as all property in this inlet is private. As you near Kopachuck, Cutts Island will appear in the distance.

Fox and Towhead islands to Cutts Island and Kopachuck state parks: *Moderate.* Currents in Hale Passage can be as much as 3 knots, stronger on the ebb. Base tidal predictions on The Tacoma Narrows. Watch for busy boating traffic on Hale Passage as you launch. The bridge may also create limited sight distance. Paddle along Fox Island to the sand spit at the island's end and cross north toward Green Point where Hale Passage meets Carr Inlet. Resembling a horse head, Horsehead Bay is a result of a geological tombolo, a spit that has been built up by wave or tidal action over time and becomes attached to a neighboring island. At lower tides, wide sandy beaches lie around Green Point. Large mansions soon become obscured by a medium bank bluff offering you some privacy from the curiosity of homeowners. The extensive sandy spit on the north tip of Horsehead Bay points to the southern edge of Kopachuck State Park. Cutts Island will appear in the distance offshore just past Kopachuck.

Tiny Cutts Island seems larger than it really is. Steep bluffs, which increase in height toward the south end, partition the use of the island to either strolls in its madrona and fir woods above or beach hikes below. At the north end is a pebble and shell spit that extends almost to Raft Island during the lowest tides; this is steeper and easier on boats than the rockier beaches to the south. Also known as "Deadman's Island," this is where coastal peoples buried their dead in canoes placed in the forks of island trees. Watch out for poison oak. This attractive little island cannot sustain camping or fires, and both are prohibited.

Kopachuck State Park, barely 0.5 mile from Cutts Island, brings you back to the intensity of road-accessible recreation. On a warm sunny day there are picnickers along the beach and kids splashing in the water. End the day here with a barbecue at one of the shoreside picnic sites, or perhaps a car-camping overnight in the campground at the top of the bluff. You may also camp at the Cascadia Marine Trail site if you have launched from another location.

The Cascadia Marine Trail site at Kopachuck is located above the beach on the north side of the park just off the main access road leading to the beach. The carry from the beach to the site and its kayak storage racks are a very steep 75-yard haul. A fire ring and picnic shelter are available at the site. Restrooms and water are located 500 feet south of the site in summer and at the day-use parking lot above in winter. Fees are $14 per night, with a maximum of eight people.

8 Tacoma Narrows

Famous for the 1940s film of the collapsing Tacoma Narrows bridge, also called "Galloping Gertie," the Narrows is known for its tidal bottleneck effect. With Puget Sound squeezing through its mile-wide channel, currents can move swiftly. In places 400-foot-tall bluffs rise from both sides of the Narrows sometimes creating a wind tunnel. The modern Narrows bridge has two spans 500 feet above the water. A Cascadia Marine Trail site is located on the west side below the bridge at Narrows Park.

Duration: Part day to overnight.

Rating: *Moderate* or *Exposed*.

Navigation Aids: SeaTrails WA 203, 204; NOAA charts 18440 (1:150,000); 18448 (1:80,000); Tacoma tide table and The Tacoma Narrows current table.

Planning Considerations: Time the currents so they give you a push through the Narrows. Not doing so will be a slog while bucking current. Avoid the Narrows when the currents oppose the wind which can create dangerous conditions. Watch out for boating traffic.

Getting There and Launching
Gig Harbor Launch: See the Gig Harbor chapter for more information.

Owen Beach, Point Defiance Park, Tacoma: From Interstate 5, exit at State Route 16 and drive 5.6 miles west (Narrows Bridge exit). Exit right to North Pearl Street (SR 163) and follow 4.9 miles north. Enter Point Defiance Park and follow signs to Owen Beach. Owen Beach has plenty of parking, restrooms, picnic tables, and an easy-to-access gravel beach.

View of the Tacoma Narrows Bridge from Narrows Park

Narrows Park: If going west across the bridge on SR 16, exit at 24th Street Northwest. Go over the freeway then left on Jahn Avenue Northwest (also 95th Street Northwest), left on Stone Drive Northwest, then a right on Lucille Parkway Northwest, and follow down the windy forested road to the park.

Titlow Beach Park, Tacoma: From SR 16, exit at Jackson Avenue south, then take a right on 6th Avenue. Follow this to the park. A full service park, Titlow has restrooms, a boat ramp, and picnic tables.

Route

Contrary to what you may think, the currents don't necessarily run smoothly through the channel. On the east end of the bridge there's an underwater shelf that blocks current flowing south forcing the water to run in a counterclockwise direction near the north end of the Narrows. You can see the effect up above from Point Defiance Park. Note that ebb tides run stronger on the east side, and floods are strong on the west side. The south end can have currents over 5 knots.

Launching from Owen Beach, take the flood southwest into the Narrows. Cross to the west side for more efficient flow south, watching boat traffic as you go. Enjoy the canyon-like feeling of being in the Narrows below the forest-covered slopes. On the east side you'll see the unique Salmon Beach community. The homes are on pilings above the water and supported by a long wooden stairway up the hill. Burlington Northern tracks suddenly

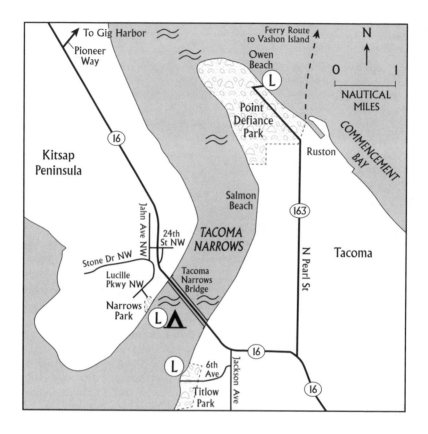

appear on the south side of Salmon Beach. The train tunnel runs from the Tacoma community of Ruston under Point Defiance Park to just south of the park.

As you near the bridge, stay clear of the concrete pillars holding the bridge. Eddies can form behind them creating a section of bumpy water. As you pass the bridge, Narrows Park will come into view on the right (west). The Cascadia Marine Trail site is just past the house on the shore in the trees. It has eight sites, a chemical toilet, water in summer, and no fees. Fires aren't allowed. The site has a 1200-foot-long gravel beach and impressive views of the gigantic bridge to the north.

Titlow Beach Park begins less than a mile south of the bridge on the east side. The park has a full service marina and is a good take-out or launch for the Narrows. Consider running a shuttle between Owen Beach and Titlow or time your trip to take the ebb back north. Total mileage from Owen Beach to Titlow using the west side flood is 10.4 miles one way. With the current assisting you on large tidal exchanges the trip could feel like 5 miles!

9 Gig Harbor

In 1867, Yugoslavian immigrant Samuel Jerisch and two partners rowed a flat-bottomed skiff from British Columbia to what is now Gig Harbor. Samuel and his wife, Anna, began the fishing industry here, which later grew to a successful commercial fleet. The protected harbor has a narrow entry and is considered by boaters to be a perfect gunkhole. A quick jaunt from Tacoma's Point Defiance Park, the Narrows, Vashon Island, and Colvos Passage, Gig Harbor is centrally located to many paddling destinations.

Duration: Part day to full day.

Rating: *Protected* or *Exposed.*

Navigation Aids: SeaTrails WA 203; NOAA charts 18440 (1:150,000); 18448 (1:80,000). Use Tacoma tide tables and The Tacoma Narrows current table.

Planning Considerations: The inner harbor is very protected yet busy in summer with recreational boaters. Paddling outside of the harbor can be moderate during large tidal exchanges from the Narrows and Dalco Passage. Visit the Tides Tavern by the waterfront for a great view of the bay.

Getting There and Launching

Gig Harbor: From State Route 16, take the Pioneer Way exit going north. Follow 2.24 miles into Gig Harbor. Take a left on Harborview Drive and look for Skansie Brothers Park and the Jerisch dock on your right next to the Gig Harbor Marina. Use street parking, which can be busy in summer. The park has restrooms, a public dock, a little beach, and PFDs to loan. For additional information: www.cityofgigharbor.net/.

Gig Harbor Public Boat Launch: From the Gig Harbor waterfront continue on Harborview Drive and follow it around the harbor. Take a right on Vernhardsen Street, then an immediate right on Randall Drive Northwest. Follow Randall to the boat ramp. Located in a residential area, the ramp has no facilities and overflow parking is on the street. The day-use-only ramp and side streets get very busy in summer during fishing season.

Alternative Launch: Owen Beach, Point Defiance Park in Tacoma, see the Tacoma Narrows chapter.

Routes

Gig Harbor: *Protected.* Centrally located, Gig Harbor has many paddling opportunities. The harbor itself is a pleasant place with beach homes and recreational boats lining the shores. Explore both ends and dip into the small inlet below Vernhardson Street. Paddle to the harbor entry and enjoy a dash of

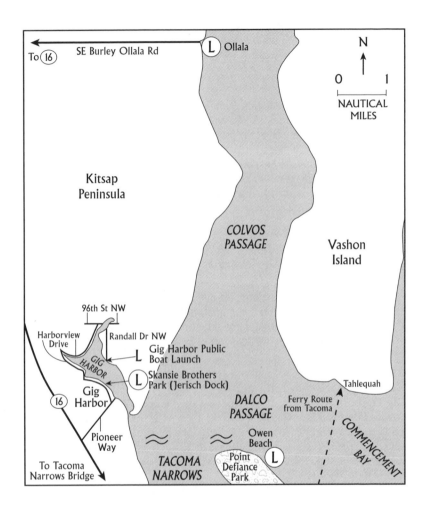

light current on pulling through on larger tidal exchanges. The entry may be a blind corner for boaters coming in and out of the harbor.

Point Defiance Park: *Exposed.* For longer moderate routes, consider crossing from the outside of the harbor over to Point Defiance Park in Tacoma. A 3.12-mile paddle to Owen Beach on the north side, this is a great trip crossing currents coming in or out of the Narrows to the south. You may encounter swirls and a push or pull depending on the tidal direction. This trip is for intermediate to advanced paddlers.

Olalla: *Protected.* Run a shuttle to Olalla, a tiny waterfront community 11 miles north up the Colvos Passage from Gig Harbor. The currents in the Colvos almost always run north.

Stand up paddlers enjoying Gig Harbor

In 1881, a Native American approached settler L. P. Larson and offered him a "Mamook olallie," meaning strawberry. In the early 1900s strawberries ripened here three weeks earlier than those sold at Seattle's Pike Place Market, thus were in great demand. Take SR 16 north 12 miles to exit on Southeast Burley Olalla Road. Follow this 6 miles to Olalla. Park in the gravel lot on the south side of the road above the estuary. Launch or take-out at the boat ramp below. Aim for higher tides as the bay empties out to a mudflat. There is a small store above the beach for basic supplies.

Alternative trips nearby: A short drive from Gig Harbor brings you to the head of Henderson Inlet and Fox Island (see the Carr Inlet chapter).

10 Commencement Bay

Here you will find a pleasant contrast to expectations of a polluted industrial wasteland. Commencement Bay has a bit of everything. There are the
wooded bluffs of Point Defiance, the "downtown" feel of the Thea Foss
Waterway with its yachts and workboats, the melancholy quiet along the slag
shores of the abandoned Asarco smelter site, and the intense activity of loading and off-loading ships in one of the busiest ports in the Northwest. Within
the bay and adjacent waterways is enough to fill many days of exploration.

Duration: Part day to full day.

Rating: *Protected* or *Moderate.* The *Moderate*-rated Commencement
Bay Loop requires crossing about 2 miles of open water.

Navigation Aids: SeaTrails WA 203; NOAA charts 18445 SC
(1:80,000), 18474 (1:40,000), or 18453 (1:15,000).

Planning Considerations: As Commencement Bay is a port of
commerce, always stay alert to the locations and movement of other
watercraft.

Getting There and Launching

Launch sites around Commencement Bay are scattered unevenly.

Thea Foss Waterway: In downtown Tacoma, the waterway is accessible via
the floats at the city dock. Located behind Johnny's Seafood, between private
marinas north of the 11th Street bridge, the waterway is marked with a sign on
Dock Street. Parking may be scarce.

Thea's Park: This park at 405 Dock Street, just at the north end of the Thea
Foss Waterway, has a ramp, sandy kayak launch, restrooms, and approximately
twenty-five parking spaces. Just a short walk down the street, at Foss Marina,
you can rent kayaks and paddleboards.

Tacoma to Point Defiance Shoreline: There are many alternatives to
choose from on the shoreline between Tacoma and Point Defiance. The closest
to the city is Commencement Park, located at the point where Schuster Parkway
becomes Ruston Way, a little less than 2 miles from downtown. There is a good
sand and gravel beach here. Similar parks are located at intervals along Ruston
Way between Commencement Park and the old Asarco smelter site.

Point Defiance Park: You can set off from Owen Beach inside the park,
(closes at sunset). To reach it, continue into the park, past the zoo and
aquarium, and drive along the bluffs to a side road that drops down to the
right to the beach. Usually, in summer months, a local concessionaire rents
recreational kayaks and paddleboards from a trailer.

North Side of Commencement Bay: The Dick Gilmur Memorial
Shoreline offers access to the north end of the bay. Rustic homes on stilts, small

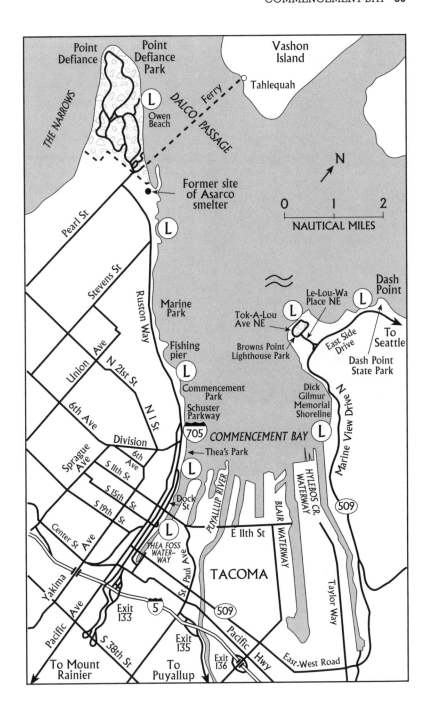

View of downtown Tacoma below the 11th Street bridge from the Thea Foss Waterway launch

marinas, and views across the bay to downtown Tacoma make this a great place to paddle.

The Dick Gilmur Memorial Shoreline access has parking limited to four cars, no restrooms, and is closed at dusk. A smooth gravel ramp leads to the sandy beach. Navigate around the wooden boom to open water. For additional information about this launch: www.portoftacoma.com/Page .aspx?cid=5203.

Browns Point: Farther northwest along the north shore of Commencement Bay is picturesque Browns Point Lighthouse Park, part of the Tacoma Metro Park System, an appropriate launch for a loop tour of the entire bay and the closest access from north of Tacoma. Watch for tide rips off the point on a strong flood. From Tacoma, follow Marine View Drive North (SR 509) west from downtown Tacoma 3 miles to Le-Lou-Wa Place Northeast. Turn left, then go about 0.75 mile, curving around to the right as the road becomes Tok-A-Lou Avenue Northeast. Parking is limited but there are restrooms. Also, though there is no camping in this park, you can make reservations to stay in the park as a lighthouse keeper. Boats must be carried about 100 yards down a grassy hill to the steep gravel beach. Note that the park and lot close at dusk. For additional information: www.pnehs.dreamhosters.com/lighthouse/.

To reach Browns Point from the Seattle area, take Exit 143 (Federal Way) from Interstate 5. Go west on 320th Street for 4.5 miles until it intersects 47th Avenue. Go right for 0.5 mile and then left on Dash Point Road. Follow this road for 3 miles, passing Dash Point State Park, after which it becomes East Side Drive. Proceed to Le-Lou-Wa Place Northeast. Turn right and go 0.75 mile to the park.

Routes

South Shore Local Paddling: *Protected.* Choose your own distance. Pick any of the launch sites described along Ruston Way to Point Defiance Park.

One possibility is a short trip from Owen Beach west toward Point Defiance, following the gravel beach beneath steep wooded bluffs that restrict access to the beach except for occasional trails. The current here usually flows west, which is strongest during the flood, and can be quite swift near the point.

Also consider paddling between Owen Beach and one of the parks along Ruston Way, perhaps in conjunction with a car shuttle. Many new restaurants have sprung up along the shoreline, offering dock space to lure passing boaters in for a meal. This route also skirts the former site of the Asarco smelter, beginning with its reeflike tailings of slag and cinders. This forms a steep and jumbled shoreline that is surprisingly pleasant and interesting: seaweeds grow profusely and waves have eroded sea caves large enough to paddle into cautiously.

A third and more urban alternative on Commencement Bay's south shore is the paddle from Commencement Park southwest into Thea Foss Waterway, with a round-trip distance of up to 4 miles. As an option, a much shorter exploration of the waterway can be made from the city dock at Thea's Park, perhaps on a Sunday morning when parking is easiest to find. You pass bulk carrier freighters being loaded as you enter the waterway and the buildings of downtown Tacoma come into view. Thea Foss Waterway is the hub of recreational boating in the bay, so there are plenty of yachts to view in the many marinas along both shores. Commercial fishing boats have their own floats on the northeast side of the waterway.

Commencement Bay Loop: *Moderate* (due to 2-mile crossing). Loop distance is about 7 miles, plus any exploration into the waterways, but can be shortened to about 5 miles by cutting across parts of the bay at any point. You can start from Commencement Park on the south shore or from Browns Point Lighthouse Park on the north, depending on the direction from which you approach the area. This description begins at Browns Point.

Begin with the crossing from Browns Point toward downtown Tacoma via Commencement Park if you care to make a stop there first—these are the only public facilities along the route. This course should take you past ships that usually are at anchor there. You'll also paddle past the Tacoma skyline and the Museum of Glass. Perhaps after a look into Thea Foss Waterway, start northeast across the old Puyallup River estuary, now among the most active maritime industrial areas in the region. There may be a fairly strong current outflow as you cross the Puyallup Waterway.

Beyond are the Blair and Hylebos Creek waterways, where large container ships and car carriers unload. At the mouth of the Hylebos Creek Waterway is a small military station with US Army Corps of Engineers vessels. The north shore is mostly private marinas, one of which has interesting old ships positioned to form a breakwater.

MIDDLE PUGET SOUND

11 Maury Island

A narrow isthmus connects Maury Island to Vashon Island providing an age-old portage. The most challenging route here combines the quiet charm of Quartermaster Harbor with a more arduous paddle along the "island's" south coast to produce a circumnavigation that will leave you feeling you have seen a great deal as well as had a good day's exercise. For a more relaxed alternative, dabble in the harbor. If you wish to start from south of Seattle, launching from Saltwater State Park involves a more demanding crossing, traversing shipping lanes and possible tide rips.

Duration: Part day or full day.

Rating: *Protected, Moderate,* or *Exposed.* The *Moderate* route may require committing to several miles of paddling in wind and choppy water. The *Exposed* area has potential tide rips and shipping traffic.

Navigation Aids: SeaTrails WA 203; NOAA charts 18445 SC, 18448 (both 1:80,000), or 18474 (1:40,000); Seattle tide table (add 15 minutes).

Planning Considerations: Windy weather can make the east side of Maury Island unpleasant; the shallow beaches make offshore seas steep and landings wet and rough. If you are going to circumnavigate, plan for high tide to make the portage at Portage and to avoid the extensive tide flats on the Quartermaster Harbor side. Swift currents flow around Point Robinson. Check your current tables when paddling here or when crossing from Saltwater State Park.

Getting There and Launching

Maury Island routes can be reached via Vashon Island by launching at either Portage, Jensen Point Boathouse, or Dockton County Park. It can also be reached from the east shore of Puget Sound from Saltwater State Park, which requires a 2-mile crossing.

To reach Vashon Island from Seattle, take Exit 163 from Interstate 5 and follow the West Seattle Bridge. In West Seattle, this becomes Fauntleroy Way Southwest and leads to the Fauntleroy ferry terminal. Exit the ferry at Vashon Island and drive south to the town of Vashon.

To reach Vashon Island from Tacoma, follow Ruston Way to Pearl Street, then turn right down the hill to the Point Defiance ferry landing. Take the ferry to Tahlequah, and follow the Vashon Island Highway Southwest north to the Quartermaster Harbor area.

View from Maury Island toward Seattle overlooking Quartermaster Harbor, Portage, and Puget Sound

Dockton County Park: To reach Maury Island from the town of Vashon, follow Vashon Highway Southwest south about 3 miles to Southwest Quartermaster Drive, where you turn left for Maury Island. For Dockton County Park, continue past Portage, where Southwest Quartermaster Drive becomes Dockton Road Southwest, about 3.5 miles. Parking is ample with restrooms and a beach below a short sea wall. There's no services in the town of Dockton.

Portage: This launch is a popular beginning and end for a Maury Island circumnavigation. There is limited parking along both of the two roads that cross this isthmus, which are connected by Portage Way Southwest. The carrying distance between high-tide lines is approximately 200 yards on pavement. Watch out for speedy traffic here. A high-tide launch or take-out on the Quartermaster Harbor side is particularly desirable, since it becomes a large mudflat at low tide. The Shomamish people who were native to Vashon Island used the portage not only to save time in traveling through the area by canoe, but they also raised 300-foot-wide nets made from bark and plant fibers to catch birds flying low over the portage. The east side of Portage is known for a bunch of exercise bikes set above the beach across from the old building.

Jensen Point Park/Burton: Continue ahead on Vashon Highway Southwest to Southwest 240th Street, turn left, and then right onto Bayview Road. Turn right into Jensen Point at the sign for the park. There is usually

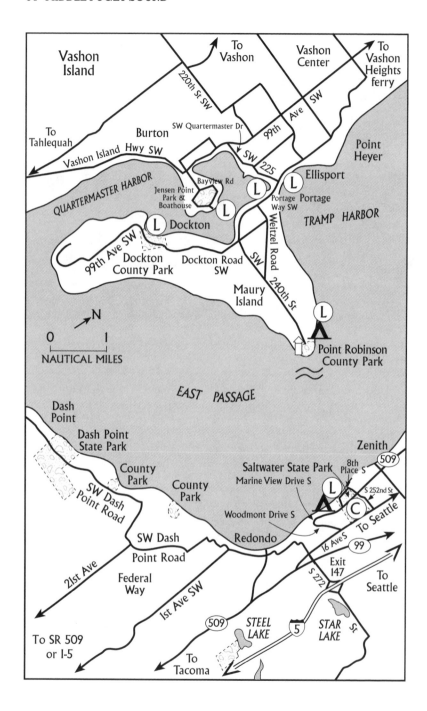

plenty of parking. The park has a ramp, toilets, and a beach that gently slopes into Quartermaster Harbor. The Vashon Island Parks District has constructed a smart little boathouse—Jensen Point Boathouse—that provides human-powered boat rentals and storage for the local rowing club's fleet. Managed by Vashon Island Kayak Center, it has sea kayak and other small-craft rentals, and lessons are offered to the public on a regular basis. For additional information: 206-463-9257 or e-mail kayak@vashonparkdistrict.org.

Saltwater State Park: From I-5, take Exit 147 and go west 0.8 mile on South 272nd Street. Turn right at 16th Avenue South and proceed 0.7 mile. Turn left onto Woodmont Drive South. In 0.6 mile, bear sharply right onto Marine View Drive South (SR 509). At 1 mile, turn left onto South 252nd Street for one-half block, then turn left onto 8th Place South, which leads to the park's entrance. Saltwater State Park has vault toilets and easy access to a sand and gravel beach. Despite its nearly 300 parking spots, the lot may fill quickly on summer weekends. Unless you are camping, parking is for day use only. There is a Cascadia Marine Trail campsite near the beach, and regular state park campsites along the forested hills at the east end of the park.

Routes

Quartermaster Harbor: *Protected.* Choose your own paddling distance. Quartermaster Harbor is a fine place for a leisurely paddle year-round. It features warm waters with the opportunity to swim during the summer and the quiet of still, overcast days in winter. The Burton Peninsula effectively breaks up the fetch, so seas are not likely to develop extensively. Both Jensen Point Park and Dockton Park are good for a picnic, though Dockton offers more shoreside seclusion with its longer beach. Tables and restrooms are available at both.

Maury Island Circumnavigation: *Moderate.* The total paddling distance is 12 miles. The long shallow bight of Maury Island's south side is an unusual mix of wildness amid the development of the central Puget Sound area. Though about half of the shoreline is occupied by residences, some are only accessible via long wooden stairways from the bluff above. The remainder are grassy or wooded bluffs that invite a climb for a magnificent view of East Passage, Commencement Bay, Tacoma, and Mount Rainier in the distance. On the southwest corner of Maury in Manzanita, there is a rock native peoples have said is where killer whales play.

A large part of this shoreline and the bluffs behind are occupied by huge, controversial gravel and sand pits below 300-foot cliffs. However, these do not detract in the least from the overall attractiveness or interest of the area. Grass, alder, and madrona are rapidly reclaiming most of the pits, while rusty, derelict conveyor systems descend through the brush to rotting terminals where barges once loaded. There are no public uplands or tidelands along this shore, so respect private property rights.

The south and north shores of Maury Island can turn into rough paddling in southerly or northerly winds, so you might want to plan a circumnavigation to cover the portion most exposed to prevailing winds early in the day. Though currents for East Passage are described as weak and variable, tide rips are known to form off Point Robinson, and are perhaps at their worst when ship wakes cross them. (See the Saltwater State Park to Point Robinson route below for information and cautions about Point Robinson.)

Saltwater State Park to Point Robinson: *Exposed.* The total paddling distance is 5 miles. The crossing from Saltwater State Park, about 2 miles at the narrowest point, is easy in moderate weather. Currents in the area are listed as weak and variable, though they do accelerate around Point Robinson as water is compressed around it. Rips are possible. The primary hazard on this crossing is marine shipping bound to and from Tacoma. The traffic lanes separate to either side of the mid-channel buoy; northbound ships pass to the west. Wakes from ships and the many pleasure boats that ply this channel can create quite choppy seas. Surf at Point Robinson from a passing ship's wake can be quite large, a thrill to those who like to surf but a hazard to others. Look well before landing or launching, particularly at Point Robinson where ships pass close by. Pull your boat well up onto the beach when ashore.

The beach at Point Robinson and the grassy area behind the US Coast Guard's lighthouse are open to the public during the day. The lighthouse began operating in 1887. The lighthouse houses are available for rental through the Vashon Parks District.

Up the hill, northeast of the lighthouse, is a Cascadia Marine Trail campsite. Access to the site is on the northwest side of the lighthouse in the trees below the hill. Signage is minimal. There is a boat storage rack by the beach, but the carry to the campsite is a long distance up stairs and across a grassy field. Consider carrying a mesh backpack to transfer your gear to the site.

12 Blake Island

Come to Blake Island for either a pleasant day trip or for one of the most unusual kayak-camping experiences on Washington shores. Pitch your tent at Tillicum Village, take a shower in the heated restroom, then stroll over to the longhouse for a salmon dinner followed by Native American dancing. Too civilized for you? Choose the Cascadia Marine Trail site on the north-west corner or the even more primitive campsite on the southern shore.

Duration: Full day to overnight.

Rating: *Protected, Moderate,* or *Exposed.* Tide rips may be encountered on the *Moderate* route; the *Exposed* route involves 4 miles of open water across shipping lanes, with the potential for rough seas in southerly or northerly winds.

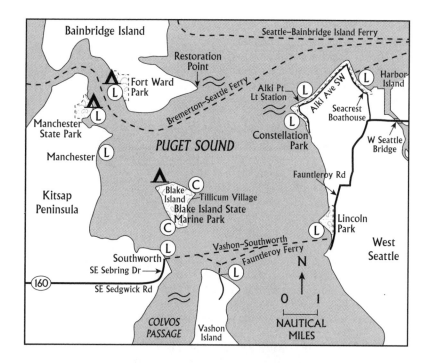

Navigation Aids: SeaTrails WA 202, 203; NOAA charts 18445 SC or 18448 (both 1:80,000), and 18449 (1:25,000); Seattle tide table.

Planning Considerations: Call ahead if you want a salmon dinner at Tillicum Village (see the West Seattle to Blake Island route description for specifics).

Getting There and Launching

From West Seattle, launches can be made at either Alki Beach, along Beach Drive Southwest, or Lincoln Park.

Alki Beach or Alki Point Light Station: Take Exit 163 from Interstate 5 and follow the West Seattle Bridge to the Harbor Avenue Southwest exit, then follow the road north (right). In 1.3 miles, the first launch is at the Seacrest Boathouse or at Alki Kayaks on Harbor Avenue Southwest. Kayak and SUP rentals are available here as well. Continue around Duwamish Head to where it becomes Alki Avenue Southwest. Continue west along Alki Avenue Southwest to the designated launch site between 54th Place Southwest and 55th Avenue Southwest, or proceed farther to access at the far west end of Alki Beach or just south of the Alki Point Light Station, along Beach Drive Southwest at Constellation Park. Public restrooms are available at 58th Avenue Southwest and 63rd Avenue Southwest, respectively. On-street parking is extremely difficult to find in the summer, so be prepared to launch early before the crowds arrive to avoid a long walk. Consider parking in residential areas if Alki Beach is too crowded.

Lincoln Park: It has the unique advantage of being near the Fauntleroy ferry landing, so you can return on the ferry if necessary. Park in the south lot and follow the path at the park's southern boundary about 150 yards down to a defunct boat ramp and the sand and cobble beach. Restrooms are close by. Note that the park closes at night.

For ferry access to Vashon Island and Southworth, take the West Seattle Bridge and follow the signs to the Fauntleroy ferry.

Vashon Island: To launch your kayak use the small ramp just east of the north-end ferry dock. Parking next to the ramp is private, so unload and move cars as soon as possible to the ferry parking area up the hill. There is no beach on either side of the ramp at higher tides, and you must be prepared to launch quickly from the ramp itself at those times without delaying other users. Do not try to get to the beach from west of the ferry dock: this is private land.

Southworth: You can unload and load your boat at the dead end of Southeast Sebring Drive, parallel to the ferry entrance. Please be courteous as private homes closely border this put-in and there is no parking. Park in the twenty-four-hour lot on the slight hill above the dock.

Manchester: Access to Manchester is from Port Orchard or Southworth. Park in the dirt overnight lot across from the restaurants. You can use the boat ramp if not busy or the small hand-carried boat launch to the right of the boat ramp. Restrooms and a small park are near the boat ramps.

Alternative launches include Fort Ward Park on south Bainbridge which has a Cascadia Marine Trail site; Manchester State Park across from Fort Ward, which also has a Cascadia Marine Trail site.

Routes

West Seattle to Blake Island: *Exposed.* The paddling distance is over 3 miles one way from either West Seattle launch point, across open water with heavy shipping traffic. Currents in this area usually are less than 1 knot; they are strongest on the ebb. Be prepared to use one of the alternative routes or

Decorative prows of Tribal Journeys canoes

to return to West Seattle by ferry if the weather takes a turn for the worse. You can monitor boat and shipping locations on channel 14 with your VHF radio to assure a crossing free of traffic.

Vashon Island to Blake Island: *Moderate.* The paddling distance is approximately 1.5 miles each way, with about 1.25 miles across open water. Currents in this area rarely exceed 1 knot, but rips can occur between the two islands, particularly near the Allen Bank off Vashon Island. Colvos Passage is unique in that the current flows only on the ebb (moves north) and becomes weak and variable at other stages of the tide. Hence, this area becomes roughest on northerly winds when the ebb current opposes it. Stay clear of Southworth and Vashon ferry traffic.

Southworth to Blake Island: *Protected.* The paddling distance is approximately 1.9 miles each way, with about 0.75 mile across open water. Currents here are weak and variable as long as you stay west of Colvos Passage and head for the more westerly shore of Blake Island.

Manchester: *Protected.* Paddling distance is 2.2 miles to Blake Island. Watch for busy pleasure-boating traffic in summer.

Some say Chief Sealth, whom Seattle was named after, was born on Blake Island in 1786. The island was originally logged in the 1850s and was later home to a wealthy Seattle lawyer, William Pitt Trimble. It became a park in 1974 and is visited by nearly 300,000 people a year. A quick escape from the city, the 475-acre island has remained a favorite among paddlers and boaters alike.

Blake Island is roughly triangular, with a paddling circumference of about 5 miles. Most of its shoreline consists of low bluffs above rocky beach, but there are sandy beaches and a shallow high-tide lagoon at the west end. Once ashore, you can hike an extensive network of paths and trails.

There are three camping areas, all of which bear a camping fee year-round. On the northwestern corner of the island is the Cascadia Marine Trail site with three tent spaces and a general public camping area with water, normally shut off during winter months, and restrooms located up the hill. The landing there is a nice sandy beach. The primitive camping rate is charged for the public sites. Boaters tend to camp in the sites around the corner from the Cascadia site and can be quite noisy on summer weekends.

On the southern shore are two more campsites, which charge the same rate but have no water. A pit toilet is located about 100 yards east along the trail. Of the two, the eastern site is situated on a small embankment above a rocky beach with madronas hanging over the site. There are only two tent sites at this spot.

The eastern point, Tillicum Village, is more developed and crowded with boaters and boat-in campers during the summer months. A breakwater encloses a boat basin with floats for the boaters who come here year-round. The campground is between the boat basin and the stony beach to the south. If you are camping here, land on this beach unless there is a strong southerly wind and waves; in that case use the beach in the boat basin. Most of the campsites here have little or no southerly wind protection. Campsites here cost the higher full-service rate because of the heated bathrooms with coin-operated showers and other amenities.

Nearby are semi-enclosed shelters for group picnics; they also can be used for cooking and shelter during the day if not already reserved. A large central fireplace can make them cozy in cooler weather.

The most interesting element is the Tillicum Village longhouse, featuring Native American–style baked salmon followed by demonstrations of traditional dance. The clientele is primarily people arriving by tour boat from Seattle, but boaters may reserve a place for themselves by signing up at the longhouse at least one hour prior to mealtime. Service is daily during the summer and on weekends during the off-season. For additional information: 206-443-1244.

13 Eagle Harbor to Bremerton

This is one of the most interesting and long-range day trips in Puget Sound, and the ability of foot passengers to carry kayaks aboard ferries allows 10 miles of one-way paddling. Leave your car in Seattle, walk your boat aboard the Bainbridge Island ferry, paddle through Rich Passage and Port Orchard to Bremerton, then take the ferry back to the city. State parks along the way make nice picnic stops with old military installations to explore. To make this into an overnight, stop at one of three Cascadia Marine Trail sites: Fort Ward on the south end of Bainbridge Island, Manchester State Park on the south side of Rich Passage, or add a 2-mile side trip to Blake Island (see the Blake Island chapter).

Duration: Full day.

Rating: *Moderate.* Involves current with possible tide rips and heavy boat and shipping traffic in Rich Passage.

Navigation Aids: SeaTrails WA 202, 203; NOAA charts 18445 SC or 18441 (both 1:80,000), 18446 (1:25,000); Admiralty Inlet current tables corrected for Rich Passage.

Planning Considerations: Ferry schedules dictate timing here, but runs are frequent. A favorable current in Rich Passage is desirable as it can reach 3 or 4 knots. The flood flows toward Bremerton in Rich Passage.

Getting There and Launching

This trip includes two ways to get to Bainbridge Island from Seattle: directions for wheeling your kayak or SUP on the ferry and driving directions for car topping your kayak or SUP.

If you are coming from downtown Seattle with your carted kayak or SUP on the ferry, weekends are the preferred days for this trip because parking close to the Seattle ferry terminal at Colman Dock is easier, especially early on Sunday morning. At the time this edition went to press, the State Route 99 Alaskan Way Viaduct was being demolished to make way for a tunnel that will change parking availability in the near future. Check street parking and nearby garages for overnight parking. Be aware that there is a small kayak "storage fee" to wheel your boat aboard. Arrive one hour early and ask ferry personnel for directions on loading.

Eagle Harbor: After leaving the ferry terminal with your carted kayak, turn left on the first street beyond the toll booths signed Eagle Harbor Condominiums. At the bottom of the hill, take a left at the Waterfront Trail before the condos. This leads to a small beach just south of the ferry terminal. Total carrying distance is about 300 yards. Respect private property at the put-in, as the put-in shares a fence with the condos. There is no parking for this launch.

If coming by car off the ferry, follow traffic up the hill above the ferry dock and take a left at the light onto Winslow Way. Drive through the downtown corridor and take a left on Madison Avenue, then next left onto Bjune Drive Southeast. In less than 0.1 mile turn right onto Shannon Drive Southeast and follow it down to the ramp and circular parking area by the water. These are temporary parking areas to unload your boat and gear. Three-hour parking is located above the park on Bjune Drive Southeast and Brien Drive Southeast. Overnight parking is available in the ferry lot a few blocks away. There is no overnight parking in downtown Winslow.

Kayaker's view of the destroyer USS Turner Joy *in Bremerton*

Blakely Harbor/Blakely Harbor Park: Another option for day-use launching is on Blakely Harbor, just south of Winslow. There are two public beach access spots here each a short distance from each other. One has a 50-yard carry and the other a 100-yard carry. There is a restroom, parking lot, and nice beaches. Low tides may make for a longer muddy carry as the bay empties out a bit.

Bremerton: In downtown Bremerton, there is water access via a natural-looking boat ramp in the Port of Bremerton Marina just north of the ferry. There's a turnaround to drop your boat and gear adjacent to the ramp and restrooms on 2nd Street below Washington Avenue. Overnight parking is available above in two pay lots. There's abundant starfish below by the ramp below the docks.

Another option is to launch at the boat ramp north of the Manette Bridge in Evergreen City Park on Park Avenue and 14th Street. Parking can be tight on sunny summer days. The park has restrooms and picnic tables. Port Washington Narrows flows by the park, usually with a few knots of current. Flood and ebb currents are stronger at the narrow's north end with speeds up to 4.5 knots on a flood and 3.1 knots on an ebb. Plan your launch to use the currents to get to your destination.

In East Bremerton, Bachman Park provides a small put-in and a few parking spots. Access the park by taking Manette Bridge from downtown Bremerton. Take the first right at East 11th Street and follow to Trenton Avenue. The park is two blocks farther near the end of the street. Look for the gazebo and picnic tables.

Across Sinclair Inlet, launch east of the Port Orchard marina along Bay Street, (State Route 160). There's also a boat ramp just east of Annapolis on Beach Drive East by the commuter ferry dock. There's plenty of parking but no restrooms.

Route

Paddling distance from Eagle Harbor to Bremerton is 10 miles. Add 4 to 6 miles for a side trip to Blake Island State Park depending on which part you visit.

Eagle Harbor is a worthy destination in its own right, and you may want to return on another day to explore it (see the Eagle Harbor chapter). But for this route, watch ferry traffic and cross to the south side and out of the harbor, passing the sandy, fenced-in site that was once the location of the world's largest plant for creating creosote-treated pilings. There's a restored public sandy beach just south of the point, one of several Eagle Harbor beaches once tainted by creosote chemicals. Head south from here, passing modern homes packed along the shore. Watch out for ferry wakes here that can create sizeable surf waves along the shore. Stay close to shore as ferries cruise parallel to this shore before turning into Eagle Harbor.

You'll soon pass Blakely Rocks at the opening of Blakely Harbor. In 1863, one of the largest logging mills in the region opened in the harbor, shipping

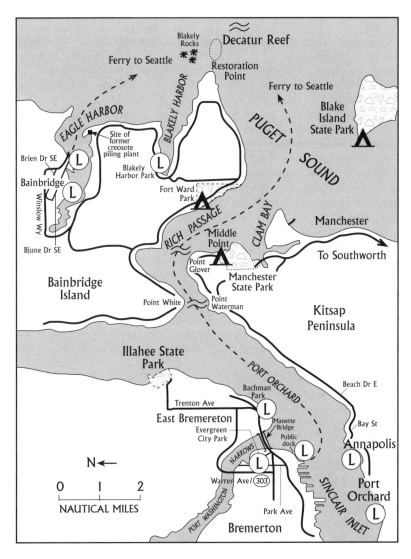

lumber throughout the world. In 1881, the Hall Brothers opened a shipyard, building seventy-seven vessels in twenty-two years. In 1889, the "Great Mill," the largest in the world, was built on the site employing over 1000 workers. Remnants of both operations exist at the end of the bay. There is a day-use park with two put-ins and restrooms on the north side of the bay adjacent to the old ruins. Stately homes now line the shorelines on both sides of the bay.

Continue to Restoration Point, being careful to stay out of the way of the ferries that run fairly close to this shore for some way before turning east toward Seattle. Off Restoration Point is Decatur Reef, a long rocky spine that can produce breaking waves or tide rips. Swing wide around the navigation marker if conditions inside of it warrant. Note the white sandy beaches on the north side of the homes by the point. Rumor has it the sand was shipped in from the Caribbean to supply the mansions in the exclusive neighborhood located there.

Both Fort Ward Park and Manchester State Park provide a Cascadia Marine Trail campsite, boat ramps, picnic tables, water, and restrooms, as well as interesting things to explore in the vicinity. The two parks are located across Rich Passage from each other. Look for the pier and picnic tables at Fort Ward just beyond the salmon aquaculture pens along the north shore. This is the location of the Cascadia trail site, also next to Battery Vinton, a pre–World War I era coastal defense gun battery. The boat ramp farther to the west is a good launch spot, also with restrooms.

Manchester State Park, on the south shore west of Middle Point, also has military origins, with gun emplacements and a large brick picnic shelter that originally housed torpedoes. Beach your boat at either side of this shallow bight (the center dries to a muddy foreshore). Be wary of boat and ferry wakes. Views along this route are mostly of beach homes and a few pocket beaches. Look for signs of the Cascadia Marine Trail site to the left of the house. The sites are in the forest.

Rich Passage makes a dogleg to the south and narrows just beyond the two parks, and currents become much swifter. Keep in mind that you could encounter an incredible array of large or small vessels coming through here— even huge aircraft carriers coming or going to the naval base at Bremerton.

Currents themselves are not likely to be dangerous unless interacting with adverse winds or ferry wakes; use them to your advantage while keeping an eye out for large vessels like the Bremerton ferry that must keep up some speed in order to stay in control in this flow. If you should encounter an opposing current, there are eddies north of Point White on the north shore and smaller ones along the south shore by Points Waterman and Glover. The latter may be preferable since you can continue along shore, avoiding marine traffic into Port Orchard, where the currents weaken.

There is public access at the pier northwest of Point White on Bainbridge. Cross to the East Bremerton shore 1 mile or so beyond the eastern end of Rich Passage.

The Bremerton Shipyard is an impressive sight with its rows of mothballed aircraft carriers and destroyers. The USS *Turner Joy,* a retired destroyer is open for tours and is located in the marina just north of the ferry landing. But remember that it is a military installation, and you must keep a minimum of 500 feet from the perimeter of all naval vessels, piers, and other naval facilities. Consider a bite at the Boat Shed, a classic waterfront restaurant in East Bremerton under the Manette Bridge on Shore Drive. You can paddle to the restaurant and tie up to their dock.

Rich Passage, looking east past Point Glover and Point White

14 Eagle Harbor

This excursion is for sea kayakers who love looking at all sorts of boats, exploring pockets of wildlife, and viewing picturesque waterside structures old and new. They are all on Seattle's doorstep, yet far from the urban bustle.

Duration: Part day.

Rating: *Protected.*

Navigation Aids: SeaTrails WA 202, 203; NOAA charts 18445 SC (1:80,000 with 1:25,000 Eagle Harbor inset) or 18449 (1:25,000); Seattle tide table.

Planning Considerations: Higher tides allow exploration of the back bay and side coves in Eagle Harbor, which dry at lower tides.

Getting There and Launching

If you are driving from the Bainbridge Island ferry dock, turn left at the first traffic light onto Winslow Way, right if you're coming south on State Route 305, and into downtown Winslow. After 0.3 mile, going through the "downtown" shopping area, take the first left onto Madison Avenue at the four-way stop, then the next immediate left onto Bjune Drive Southeast. In less than 0.1 mile turn right onto Shannon Drive Southeast and follow it down to the ramp at the water.

Public parking for Eagle Harbor Waterfront Park is located along Bjune and Brien drives Southeast. Most parking is limited to three hours in daylight hours only within the park. Longer term parking is difficult to find elsewhere in Winslow. Do not park in the trailered boat parking lot, or suffer a stiff fine. The park is a lovely picnic stop with many options in Winslow for supplies and take-out food.

You may also wheel your kayak onto the ferry at Colman Dock in Seattle. When you exit the ferry, take the first left (before the light) onto a road signed for Eagle Harbor Condominiums. Follow it down a slight hill a very short distance. You may take either the left or right Waterfront Trail footpaths. The left footpath leads past the condo complex to public beach access right next to the ferry terminal. The right footpath leads to Eagle Harbor Waterfront Park and along to the public ramp and dock in about 0.1 mile. Either footpath, with a combination of hard pack and asphalt surfaces, are easily negotiated.

A final option is to rent a sea kayak from the barge moored at the public dock. With prior planning, you might even arrange for them to store your kayak if you paddle there for an overnight bed-and-breakfast stay.

Route

Choose your own route and distance. From Eagle Harbor Waterfront Park, there are things to see in any direction. Just east are the state ferries' maintenance facilities, where out-of-service ferries dock. Here is a chance for a close-up look at the old veterans and the larger new ferries. Before approaching the ferries, look carefully for activity suggesting that one of them may be about to move. Never paddle in front of a ferry while it is underway.

Eagle Harbor is very popular with pleasure boaters due to its location and protection from wind. Several marinas, one directly across from the ferry docks and the others just west of the park, hold a wide assortment of fantastic yachts.

Along the shore are the remnants of past industry, including, at the harbor's south entrance, a former plant site, now an empty lot that once produced creosote-treated pilings to build the Panama Canal. Around the corner on the outside of the harbor is a pleasant public beach accessed from the land via Northeast Eagle Harbor Drive.

A handful of other relics remain from the past—sheds and warehouses on pilings, some abandoned and some still in use. A tiny, shallow cove across from the ferry dock is particularly picturesque for its shoreline structures as well as its seclusion.

The very back of the harbor is quieter and less popular with boats because it dries on lowest tides, but it is worth exploring when the tide is in. Midway back in the harbor are eroding warehouse-pilings that are all that remain of the vigorous berry-farming industry that once thrived in the vicinity. You can often spot eagle, osprey, heron, and other birds dependent on a productive water environment.

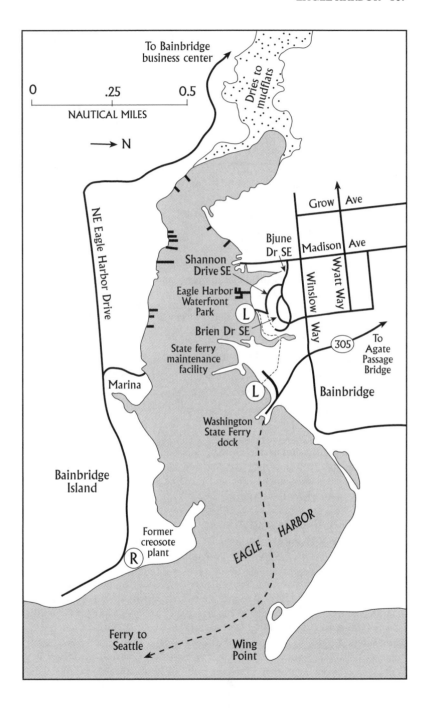

15 Elliott Bay

Shipyards with naval frigates or an Alaska ferry in dry dock create an engaging scene, one that is in constant motion and change. There are also routes deep under the waterfront's piers and the opportunity to make a stop along Alaskan Way South for fish and chips. You are sure to find plenty if you like seaport cities. A longer outing could be made by exploring south around Harbor Island and the Duwamish Waterway (see the Duwamish Waterway chapter), or around Magnolia and West Point to Shilshole Bay (see the West Point, Shilshole Bay, and Golden Gardens chapter).

Duration: Part day.

Rating: *Moderate.* Ship and ferry traffic is heavy, landings are not allowed along much of the waterfront, and the circle route involves crossing 2 miles of open water and busy traffic.

Navigation Aids: SeaTrails WA 202, 203; NOAA chart 18450 (1:10,000) or 18445 SC (1:80,000, see 1:40,000 inset); Seattle tide table.

Planning Considerations: High tide is more pleasant, but some riprap shores provide small low-tide beaches where landings are not possible at higher tides. There's no launches in the immediate downtown corridor. Watch for ferry and other boating traffic.

Getting There and Launching

There are two launch sites in downtown Seattle, one in Magnolia, eight in West Seattle on the south side of the bay, and one downtown marina. As the city grows, every year new launches become available as others disappear. Double check our locations here to make sure they still are available.

Downtown Seattle and Magnolia:

Myrtle Edwards Park: The launch is in the northern entry to the park close to the Magnolia Bridge. The park skirts the waterfront and connects downtown to the Magnolia neighborhood. It is a popular biking and walking trail. The park offers access to the northern reaches of Elliott Bay as well as Discovery Park. From Elliott Avenue West, turn east one block south of the Magnolia Bridge following signs to the cruise ship terminal and Port of Seattle. On the bridge, take the left fork. After the bridge crosses Elliot Way and curves around, take a right on Amgen Louis Dreyfus Road. Then another immediate right on West Galer Street, which takes you to the park and the Elliott Bay Trail. Unload your gear in the circular pull-out above the beach, then park farther down in the main lot. Watch for high speed bicyclists along the bike

Stand up paddler on Elliott Bay

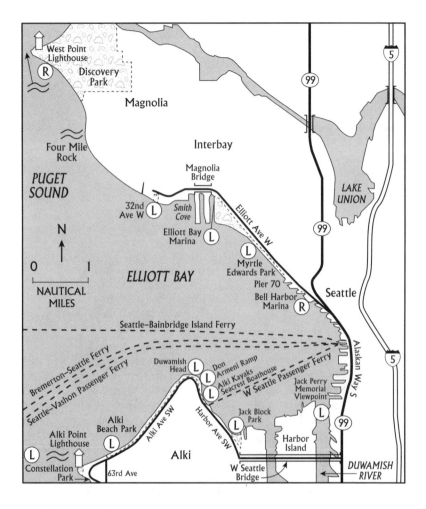

path. Restrooms should be available in the lot; if not, there are vault toilets along the bike trail a few hundred yards south and around the bend at the Elliott Bay Fishing Pier. Make sure to lock your car.

32nd Avenue West in Magnolia: This launch provides access near Smith Cove at the north end of Elliott Bay. From downtown Seattle drive north on Elliott Avenue West and bear right onto the overpass for the Magnolia area (15th Avenue West). From the overpass follow West Garfield then West Galer streets a total of 0.9 mile to Magnolia Boulevard West. Bear right on Magnolia Boulevard West and follow it 0.4 mile before turning left on West Howe Street. Take the next immediate left onto 32nd Avenue West, following it downhill to the water. There is usually parking available in the dirt pull-out alongside the road. The small lot by the beach is for residents of the walk-in waterfront homes to the west. The beach is rocky with concrete slabs.

Jack Perry Memorial Viewpoint Public Access/Alaskan Way: Farther south, across from Harbor Island, use the launch at the Jack Perry Memorial Viewpoint located at the point where Alaskan Way South becomes East Marginal Way South, adjacent to the south side of the US Coast Guard station. There's plenty of parking and no restrooms. The park provides easy access to view freighters being loaded or access to the rest of Elliott Bay. The launch is down a gravel trail leading to the water.

See the Duwamish Waterway chapter for more launches south of Elliott Bay.

West Seattle:

Jack Block Park at Terminal 5: This park is part of a long-term project to clean up the industrial waste from decades of heavy industry along Harbor Island. The park has two impressive crescent-shaped sandy beaches, restrooms, picnic areas, and a lot of parking. Take the Harbor Island exit off the West Seattle Bridge and take a right onto Harbor Avenue Southwest. Follow about a mile and look for a large metal sculpture framing the entry to the park. Once inside the park, stay to the right and follow signs to the beach.

Continuing west on Harbor Avenue Southwest past Jack Block Park, you'll see three more launches with street parking.

Seacrest Boathouse west of Salty's is also home to Alki Kayak Tours, a full-service kayak and paddleboard facility with lessons, tours, and rentals; Alki Kayak Tours, www.kayakalki.com. Park in the lot south of the building or along the street. You can put in in the finger dock below the fishing pier or via the pocket beach west of the shop. This location has restrooms and a restaurant and is popular with divers. Parking is tight on sunny summer days.

Immediately west of Alki Kayaks along Harbor Avenue Southwest are two more put-ins. The Don Armeni Boat Ramp has parking and restrooms. Duwamish Head, where Harbor Avenue Southwest curves left becoming Alki Avenue, has on-street parking, no restrooms, but a nice viewpoint deck overlooking Elliott Bay. Enter the beach on the left side of the viewpoint down a short set of stairs.

There are several opportunities to launch off Alki Avenue Southwest if you can find parking, especially on a sunny weekend. Be watchful of the busy bike path as you carry your boat to the beach. South of the Alki Point Lighthouse is Constellation Park, another popular put-in. Street parking can be tight. Enter on the north side where the walkway slants to the beach. The beach is rocky and has a reef, which is part of a fault line. There are no facilities.

Bell Harbor Marina: Although not a launch site, this is an attractive option for a rest stop. The Port of Seattle has made provision for kayakers at the marina to moor for a few hours or overnight. The fee is insignificant, generally less than parking a car, and a special bargain when you consider there is security for your boat at all times. There is a hotel across Alaskan Way South from the marina and several restaurants nearby. Pike Place Market and the aquarium are an easy walk from there.

Route

Paddle locally from any of the launch points, or make a circle tour of as much of the bay as desired. A good option is to launch at Jack Block Park or Alki Kayaks, then paddle straight across Elliott Bay toward Pier 70 or a point farther south. There's a nice, improved rest beach along Myrtle Edwards Park with restrooms just above the waterline.

Follow the waterfront south with the option of taking a break at Bell Harbor Marina, perhaps strolling along Alaskan Way for a snack of fish and chips.

Though fun to observe, be careful of the varied private and commercial boats and ships coming and going from the numerous piers, especially in the summer months. Plan your trip when a large naval or ocean liner is docked at the marina and get a waterside view not seen by many. Just make sure to keep the proper distance between yourself and the vessel for safety and due to security concerns.

At the container terminal, Pier 47, and Harbor Island shipyards, you must stay at least 100 yards to seaward. That is still close enough to ogle the dry-docked ships with propellers, bow thrusters, and sonar domes exposed for all to see.

From West Seattle consider paddling west to the Alki Point Lighthouse and for a longer trip, south to Lincoln Park. Constellation Park is known for its tidal pools and marine life at low tides. The point off the lighthouse can be rough in strong winds. Ferry wakes create three- to four-foot-high surfing waves at Duwamish Head on lower tides—enjoyable to some, a hazard to others. Avoid the surf by paddling around the outside of the navigational marker 200 yards off Duwamish Head. The beach here is also a popular tide pool and wading area in summer during low tides.

From Myrtle Edwards Park, either paddle south to the city or west past a few shipping terminals. These were the departure points for military troops in past wars as they were shipped across the Pacific. You'll soon paddle past the Elliott Bay Marina. Watch for departing boating traffic. After the marina you'll see a boat ramp on your right, this is Smith Cove, both a launch or rest area. From Smith Cove paddle west past the walk-in waterfront homes below Magnolia Bluff. Mud slides in the early 1990s destroyed many homes along Perkins Lane, littering the beach with patios, lawn mowers, and other oddities. Soon mostly extravagant homes will appear near the waterline as the surviving part of Perkins Lane. A large erratic rock named Four Mile Rock marks where the land turns north to West Point and Discovery Park. Shallow water around Four Mile Rock has grounded a few boats. Watch for rough water and surf from strong southerlies or shipping traffic. In 1923 the steamship *Astoria* sunk a half mile off the rock.

16 Duwamish Waterway

The Duwamish River was once a curvy, slow-moving, flood-prone river providing water access and subsistence for the Duwamish people. In the Puget Sound Salish language of *Lushootseed*, Duwamish or rather *Dkhw'Doow'Absh* means "People of the Inside." Pioneers settled in the area in the 1850s and soon changed this once pristine landscape forever. Completion of dredging in 1920 straightened all but one of the original curves in the lower river. In the years following, the river became an industrial center for the city of Seattle and a home for companies such as the Boeing Company. In 2001, a 5-mile stretch was listed as a federal Superfund site. Since then, the Duwamish River Cleanup Coalition has made considerable improvements to the river, transforming sections to their natural state. The Coalition has also created public access and a few human-powered boat launches.

Duration: Part day to full day.

Rating: *Protected.* Although the paddling is easy, ship and barge traffic is heavy in this confined waterway. Novice kayakers should ensure that they have sufficient boat control to stay out of the way before venturing into the waterway, especially during the times of ebb current.

Navigation Aids: SeaTrails WA 202, 203; NOAA chart 18450 (1:10,000) or 18445 SC (1:80,000, see 1:40,000 inset); Seattle tide table.

Planning Considerations: A strong ebb current (the flood current is negligible) can make upstream travel harder and may pose problems for novice kayakers around pilings or when avoiding ship or barge traffic. Consequently, you may wish to avoid these currents during periods of an ebbing tide. At low tide the shoreline is quite muddy.

Getting There and Launching

There are several launch points on both sides of the lower Duwamish Waterway. Different sites can be used with a shuttle, making possible a one-way paddle through the entire lower Duwamish. A trip could begin, for example, at the First Avenue South Bridge and end at the Jack Block Park or the Jack Perry Shoreline Access.

Jack Perry Memorial Viewpoint/Alaskan Way Public Access: This access allows launching near the middle of the East Waterway and is also a launch point for exploration of Harbor Island and Elliott Bay. Located about 0.65 mile south of the US Coast Guard facility, just south of South Massachusetts Street, it is at the point where Alaskan Way South becomes East Marginal Way

South. Look for the Jack Perry Memorial Viewpoint sign only visible when traveling south. Access to the water is down a rocky path leading to the water. There's plenty of parking but no facilities.

Terminal 105 Viewpoint: Located off West Marginal Way Southwest less than 0.25 mile south of the West Seattle Bridge interchange, and just north of Southwest Dakota Street. This park includes parking, a picnic shelter, and portable restrooms. Those launching boats are asked to use the access point at the south end of this facility by following the path to a side channel. At low tides this launch becomes muddy: plan accordingly. Be especially careful of shipping traffic that cuts very close to the north end of the park, and a barge operation just to the north.

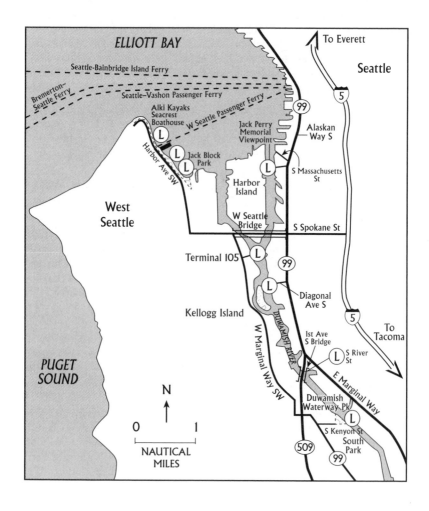

A river with many personalities, the Duwamish has both industrial and natural scenery.

End of Diagonal Avenue South: This is the closest access for visiting Kellogg Island, which is directly across the waterway. Follow State Route 99 for about 0.25 mile south of the South Spokane Street overpass and turn west on Diagonal Avenue South. Follow this street about three blocks to its end at the waterway. Public access and parking are to the left and center of a tiny bay. The carry is down a rocky embankment. Low tide can be muddy.

South River Street: Look for South River Street off East Marginal Way on the east side of the river. A wide, paved boat ramp is located under the First Avenue South Bridge.

Duwamish Waterway Park (in South Park): This renovated park has a great sandy beach and easy carry from easy-to-find street parking. The park has restrooms, picnic tables, and is accessed from the South Park neighborhood. On the intersection of South Kenyon Street and South Elgrove Street.

Alternative access points in Elliott Bay include Alki Kayak Tours at Seacrest Boathouse and Jack Block Park on Harbor Avenue Southwest.

Routes

Choose your own route in the waterway; there are shipyards, barge loading docks, cement plants, derelict ships, and much more.

Be sure to include Kellogg Island and the channel west of it. The island is close to the west side of the waterway, across from and slightly south of the Diagonal Avenue South launch point. Kellogg Island was originally much larger than Anderson Island and the approximate northern edge of the Duwamish estuary before the filling of Harbor Island and the development of the south Seattle industrial area. The waterway was dredged to the east of the original channel bend, creating the island. Kellogg Island's original height, formerly just above high tide, was raised by dredging spoils dumped on the south end. This wilderness of brambles, brush, and hidden grassy glens is worth a peek.

The shore on the west side of the old channel bend behind Kellogg Island is also a park, called Duwamish Public Access Terminal 105. The park has restrooms and a dock for easy access to the water. The Duwamish Tribal office and longhouse are across West Marginal Way Southwest from the park.

The old channel course behind Kellogg Island may dry on low tides. Though the ebb current in the Duwamish can run up to 1 knot, the flow in the old channel is slight and makes a good way to get upstream, riding back down in the main channel.

17 Lake Union

The origins of Lake Union go back 12,000 years. The lake was carved by the Vashon glacier, which also created Lake Washington. The Duwamish people called it "small lake." In 1854, pioneer Thomas Mercer predicted there would be a "union of waters" with canals connecting it to Puget Sound. Bill Boeing began his airplane company on the lake in 1915. The modern Lake Union is home to marinas, floating homes, dry docks, Gasworks Park, and a seaplane terminal. Many paddlers in Seattle have taken their first strokes there as summer water temperatures can rise into the 70s. A tour of Lake Union could be combined with excursions either east to Portage Bay, the Washington Park Arboretum, and Lake Washington, or west along the ship canal toward the Hiram M. Chittenden Locks.

Duration: Part day.

Rating: *Protected.*

Navigation Aids: SeaTrails WA 202; NOAA chart 18447 SC (1:10,000). A Seattle street map is probably as useful.

Planning Considerations: Lake Union has little protection from the wind. A strong southerly or northerly can build enough chop to make paddling unpleasant if you're uncomfortable with rough water. Watch out for seaplanes, which land in the middle of the lake and take off from the Kenmore Air terminal on the southwest corner of the lake.

Stand up paddler on Lake Union near the houseboats in the Eastlake neighborhood

Getting There and Launching

There are several public shoreline areas suited for launching and two sea kayak rental companies on the lake and another on nearby Portage Bay. Parking can be difficult to find on busy summer weekends. Centrally located in Seattle, the lake can be easily reached by Interstate 5, State Route 99, Fremont, the University District, and downtown.

South End of Lake Union–Lake Union Park: For the south shore of Lake Union, take Exit 167 (Mercer Street) from I-5. Take the first right (north) onto Fairview Avenue North and go one block, then take a left (west) on Valley Street. Get in the far right lane, and take the next right (north) to Westlake Avenue North. Within 100 yards, take a right (east) into the Lake Union Park lot. There is a sandy beach for small craft launching. If the wind is up, tuck into the small cove to your right under the foot bridge. Watch for seaplanes taking off just north of this launch. For additional information: www.atlakeunionpark.org.

West Side of Lake Union–Northwest Outdoor Center: Halfway down Westlake Avenue North between the Fremont Bridge and Lake Union Park is the Northwest Outdoor Center. A paddling shop, they offer SUP and kayak rentals and a public launch. For additional information: www.nwoc.com.

North End of Lake Union–Gasworks Park: For the north shore of Lake Union, take Exit 169 (45th Street) from I-5. Go west on North 45th Street 1 mile to Stone Way North. Turn left and follow Stone Way almost another mile to the lakeshore. Pass through the light on North 34th Street and veer left onto North Northlake Way. Gasworks Park will appear on your right in about 0.5 mile. Turn right into the main lot and park near the east end. If you're facing the park and its odd industrial features, walk your boat to the left through the trees parallel to North Northlake Way. It is about a 50-yard walk across a grassy lawn to a small protected beach lined with houseboats. For a shorter walk to

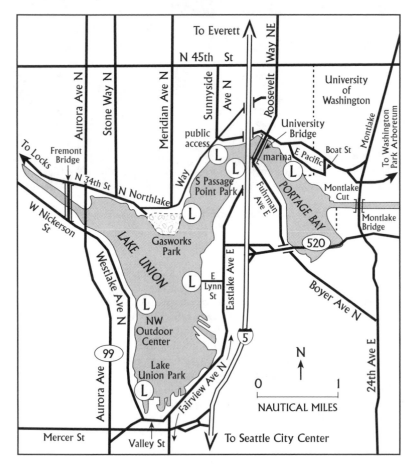

the lake, you can drop your boat at the small circular pull-out across from the Urban Surf Shop, then park in the main parking lot 25 yards to the west. **Public Access Beach Past Gasworks Park:** Going east of Gasworks Park on North Northlake Way there is a public access launch site on the right a few hundred yards past Gasworks Park. Look for the dragon boats stored below the road. Park across the street in the dirt lot. There is a restroom. This is a very protected launch that is also great for practicing skills. Urban Surf, a surf shop, is located across from both launches and can provide SUP and wetsuit rentals and other gear. For additional information: www.urbansurf.com.

East Side of Lake Union Options:

South Passage Point Park: Located directly under the I-5 bridge, this park is a great access point for launching from the east side of the lake. It's at the foot of Fuhrman Avenue East below Eastlake Avenue East. Parking may be scarce and the beach is rocky except for a small gravel beach centered under the freeway bridge.

Lynn Street Mini Park: The launch is a small, narrow beach among the houseboats, 3 or 4 feet down from the sidewalk at the foot of East Lynn Street. Access from Eastlake Avenue East. Parking on side streets may be difficult.

Route

The lake is slightly less than 2 miles in length and about 4.5 miles around if you follow the shores between the freeway bridge and the Fremont Bridge. All shores have restaurants with dock access, ranging from burgers to seafood to gourmet dining. The north shore has Gasworks Park, shipyards, and plenty of yachts to view. The west side is primarily yacht moorage. The Lake Union houseboat community comprises much of the east shore. The south end has a seaplane base, the historic lumber schooner *Wawona*, and the Center for Wooden Boats, where all manner of small wooden craft can be rented.

Lake Union's mood changes with the pulse of the city. Try it on a fair summer's evening, when the myriad sails of the Duck Dodge race frame the sunset, or on a calm Sunday morning in winter, when both city and water are quiet and you will meet few others besides hardy paddlers like yourself. On a stormy day, Lake Union is a good practice place for experienced paddlers who want to work on their rough-water paddling techniques in a reasonably safe setting.

For an extended trip, paddle under the University Bridge to Portage Bay, a busy waterway on a sunny weekend. Note that Aqua Verde Café & Paddle Club doesn't allow the general public's boats to land at their docks but does offer kayak and SUP rentals. Farther east through the Montlake Cut, the arboretum provides hours of fun paddling through heavily wooded, winding canals. West of Lake Union, you can paddle under the Fremont Bridge. Stay clear of boating traffic.

18 West Point, Shilshole Bay, and Golden Gardens

This area, west of Seattle's Ballard neighborhood, is a good place for both cautious sea outings for new paddlers during calm weather and lengthier and more challenging routes for experienced paddlers. The area includes popular and secluded sunbathing beaches, pleasure boats galore at the extensive marina, and sunset views of the Olympic Mountains. The Lake Washington steelhead run at the locks in Salmon Bay attracts a notable "chorus" of sea lions. The West Point beaches are lightly used and are backed by the woods and bluffs of Seattle's largest natural reserve, Discovery Park. The park includes a gigantic shoreside sewer treatment facility that has been landscaped to blend into the scene. From West Point the route can also be extended into Elliott Bay to connect with the launch points and routes described in the Elliott Bay chapter.

Duration: Part day to full day.

Rating: *Protected, Moderate,* or *Exposed.* The *Moderate* route may require committing to a distance of rough paddling to return to the launch site.

Navigation Aids: SeaTrails WA 202; NOAA charts 18445 SC (1:80,000), 18446 (1:25,000), or 18447 SC (1:10,000); Seattle tide table.

Planning Considerations: Winds and ships can create large breaking waves to produce rough-paddling conditions, especially around West Point, Meadow Point, and near the entry to Salmon Bay below the Ballard Locks. Lower tides offer more beaches, and many are backed by rock riprap that makes unsuitable landing places at high tide. Allow plenty of leeway for both small and large boats and ships entering and leaving the Ballard Locks.

Getting There and Launching

There are four easily accessible launch points for this trip.

Golden Gardens Park: Take Exit 172 for 85th Street from Interstate 5 and go west on Northwest 85th Street for about 3 miles. Where it ends turn right on Golden Gardens Drive Northwest and wind down the bluffs to the beach area.

At Golden Gardens, use the parking lots just behind the beach or, if they are full, park along Seaview Avenue Northwest. Launch at the beach or at the ramp just inside the marina breakwater to the south. The parking lots are closed at night.

Elks Beach: The Elks Lodge farther south on Seaview Avenue Northwest has a small beach that can be entered from the left (or south) side of their

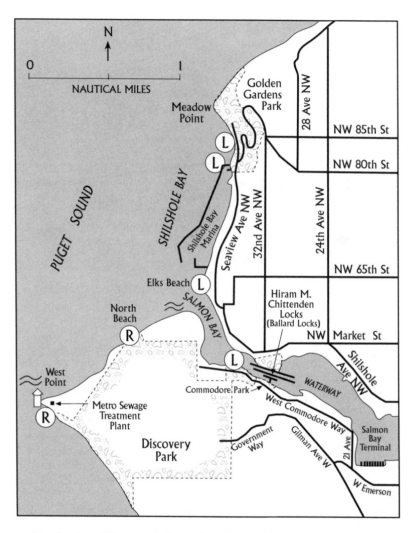

parking lot. The Elks own the beach but allow public access. Park on Seaview Avenue Northwest as the lot is for Elks members. The Elks will tow you if you load or unload in the disabled parking area or the fire lane. Don't park on the condo side of the beach as an increase of use of this beach has in recent years led to tension between the condo association and beach users. While this launch is protected, heed caution to heavy boating traffic and light outgoing current in the boating channel just outside the wooden breakwater.

Commodore Park/Hiram M. Chittenden Locks: From 15th Avenue Northwest take the West Emerson Place exit and go west toward Fishermen's Terminal. Take a right at 21st Avenue West, which will soon curve to the left

Paddlers along Discovery Park's North Beach on Shilshole Bay (Christy Cox)

and become West Commodore Way. After about a mile, look for the park on your right side before the train bridge. There's street and lot parking. Put in below the grassy slope on the left side of the lot. In lower tides the beach can be muddy. Be cautious of heavy boating traffic on the other side of the wooden breakwater. A wire cable extends across the right (south) side of the locks in front of the spillways marking a no trespassing zone. If you get too close, the Lockmaster will ask you to turn around. The spillways create a river hydraulic called a weir, or ledge, which draws water back to the wall thus entrapping anything that gets too close. It's also a sensitive area due to salmon runs that go though the locks' fish ladder from June through November, and steelhead and cutthroat trout that go from September through February. In autumn, make sure to paddle around the Muckleshoot tribe fishing nets that extend from the shore into the middle of the channel. At the time of writing, SUPs were not allowed in the locks. Kayaks and canoes are only allowed in the small lock. Free "Locking Through" classes are held throughout the year. More information is available on the website for the locks (see Resources).

Routes

Golden Gardens to Salmon Bay and Return via Shilshole Bay Marina: *Protected* to *Moderate*. Choose your own paddling distance; the full round trip from Golden Gardens to Commodore Park at the Ballard Locks is about 4 miles. Novice paddlers may prefer to stay in the bay just off Golden Gardens beach, which gets some protection from both northerly and southerly seas. However, sustained northerly to northwesterly winds can produce breaking waves just the same. As an option, explore inside the marina, being especially watchful for traffic entering and exiting at the breakwater entrance. Restrooms are available at Golden Gardens and Commodore Park.

An outflowing current is always present in Salmon Bay due to the drainage from the Lake Washington Ship Canal. Most of it can be avoided by using eddies close inshore, particularly in the shallows on the south side. Current can get up to 3 to 4 knots after several days of heavy rain. Boat traffic may be very heavy in this area, so along-the-shore routes are the safest for kayakers. Pleasure craft waiting for the locks may be numerous just below the railroad bridge. Make sure to give boaters the right-of-way when crossing the boating channel here.

Large surf from south-bound ships is possible during low tides on the Magnolia (west) side of the channel below the large concrete retaining wall. Local surfers appear here in summer months to catch the waves. Strong northerlies can also create large wind waves here that refract off the cliff at higher tides.

Golden Gardens to West Point: *Moderate* to *Exposed*. The round-trip distance is 4 to 5 miles. Keep in mind launching is prohibited from the West Point beaches, but making a rest stop is allowed by Seattle's Department of Parks and Recreation. Tide rips are possible off West Point, and the sandbar directly west of the lighthouse can produce large surf from ships some distance from the point. Be especially watchful for ships' wakes when landing along this route.

Blue skies and high pressure in summer months create strong northerlies here in the afternoon. Make sure you can paddle back to Golden Gardens or Salmon Bay in such conditions before heading out.

Popular landing spots are at the gravel and cobble beach just north of the rock riprap by the large erratic boulder, also called North Beach, and at West Point itself by the lighthouse; choose whichever side is sheltered from the wind. Restrooms are located 0.25 mile up the road from the point. For more seclusion continue about 1 mile past the point and into the bight below the bluffs, beyond where most beach walkers from West Point usually venture. Lower tides leave an expansive sandy beach here, so you will likely have to carry your boat some distance if spending time ashore. Watch for the many boulders scattered throughout this intertidal area. This area is also great for surf where smaller waves will hold up over the shallow beach for some distance.

If you follow the route within the marina on the way out, consider a straight course back across the bay toward Golden Gardens from West Point if conditions are appropriate. Strong ebbs or southerlies can create a large bay-wide eddy or gyro with a recirculating current that circles to the north then back to the point via the shoreline along Discovery Park. Sometimes paddling in a straight line to West Point isn't the most efficient way to get there. Use currents and wind protection along the shore to make your paddling experience easier.

Sea lions sometimes haul out on the buoys or riprap of the marina breakwater. At midtide a sandy beach appears on the outside of the marina breakwater providing the most secluded stop in this area, as it is not accessible by land.

19 Port Madison and Agate Passage

The northern shores of Bainbridge Island and the adjacent Kitsap Peninsula make an easy escape for locals and city dwellers alike. Though the area's shores are primarily residential with an emphasis on ritzy homes, there are two parks and a Native American museum along the winding course of a narrow inlet and the fast waters of Agate Passage. Possibilities for short or longer paddles, perhaps with a car shuttle, are numerous.

Duration: Part day to overnight.

Rating: *Moderate* or *Moderate+*. The *Moderate+* route involves crossing Agate Passage in current up to 6 knots with possible heavy pleasure boat traffic.

Navigation Aids: SeaTrails WA 203; NOAA chart 18446 (1:25,000) or 18445 SC (1:80,000); Admiralty Inlet current tables with corrections for Agate Passage.

Planning Considerations: Strong wind, particularly from the south, can make a wet launch or landing on the beach at Fay Bainbridge Park. Agate Passage currents are the only significant ones in this area, but they are strong enough to be worth planning around.

Getting There and Launching

Launch choices are Fay Bainbridge Park on the northeast corner of the island, Hidden Cove Park in Port Madison or, for the Agate Passage area, the Suquamish Museum, Old Man House State Park, or Suquamish Center. The car shuttle distance between Fay Bainbridge Park and the Agate Passage launch sites is about 8 miles.

Fay Bainbridge Park: Turn north from State Route 305 about midway between downtown Bainbridge Island and the Agate Passage bridge on East Day Road. Watch for signs to Fay Bainbridge Park. After 1.5 miles, go left onto Sunrise Drive Northeast. Go another 1.7 miles and turn right into the park. Restrooms, drinking water, and picnic facilities are provided. A Discover Pass is needed for parking.

Launching at Fay Bainbridge Park is from a gravel beach facing east onto Puget Sound. A slight bulge in the shoreline offers some protection from northerly wind waves, but the launch is exposed to ship wakes and waves from the south. This state park also has a Cascadia Marine Trail campsite at the south end of its beach, so you could also make an overnight excursion if you launch from another location.

Hidden Cove Park/Port Madison: Take SR 305 and exit east to Northeast Hidden Cove Road, one turn north of East Day Road. After about a mile, look for the park sign on your left. The park has five parking spots, no restroom, and

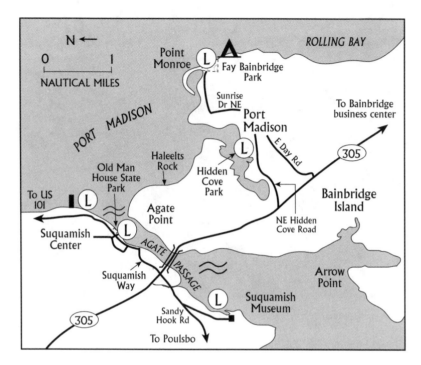

one picnic table. Launch from the old wooden float dock accessed from the right side of the park.

Old Man House State Park (Suquamish Tribe): Turn north from SR 305 about 0.25 mile west of the Agate Passage bridge on Suquamish Way. Old Man House State Park is 1.35 miles down this road at Division Avenue. Turn right there and go another 0.35 mile.

This small park has room for two cars, but fortunately it is little used. It is open to the public, but no alcohol is allowed. There are no facilities. Interpretive displays describe Native American dwellings that were located here, including Chief Sealth's. A sand beach for launching is located about 100 yards from the parking area below a grassy hill on the north side.

Suquamish Center: Continue by Old Man House State Park for another 0.35 mile along Suquamish Way and turn right where the road makes a dogleg to the left as it enters this small town. Park in the public lot in front of businesses. The walk to the beach is down a steep, paved boat ramp.

Launch next to the boat ramp on a gravel and cobble beach. Cars can be driven to the water's edge briefly to unload. Cafés and grocery stores are located nearby. Avoid launching on the long finger pier.

Suquamish Museum and Tribal Center: Turn south off SR 305 about 0.5 mile west of the Agate Passage bridge onto Sandy Hook Road, and go 0.35 mile to the entrance on the left. From the parking lot, carry boats around the left side

View of the Agate Pass bridge looking southeast

of the museum building, and take a path with wooden steps down a five-foot bank, leading to a gravel beach. It's about fifty yards' carrying distance, more at low tides. Facilities here are available during the museum's open hours.

Routes

You can choose between local paddling west of Fay Bainbridge Park or at Agate Passage, or connecting the two areas for a 5- to 7-mile round trip (or half that distance using a car shuttle for the return).

Fay Bainbridge Park: *Moderate* or *Moderate* + (dependent on wind and ship waves). You might explore the high-tide lagoon at Point Monroe. The entrance is on the west side, close to the Bainbridge Island shore, and then paddle into Port Madison to see the exclusive shoreside homes there. Once a company logging town, the bay was the home to 300 people who worked in the logging mill, or as ship builders and fishermen. The round-trip distance is about 4 miles. There are no public shorelands or facilities on this route after the park.

On Agate Point there is a petroglyph on a large erratic rock called Haleelts Rock. One of thirty petroglyphs known in the region, the carving is thought to be 1500 to 3000 years old. It's located at a bulge where the shore turns south 100 yards northwest of the former Agate Pass steamer dock (shown on charts 18473 and 18446 as a "piling"). The bridge connecting Bainbridge Island to the Kitsap Peninsula south of the point was built in 1950.

Agate Passage: *Moderate* or *Moderate* + (dependent on current). You might launch at any of the three sites described and paddle locally, or arrange a shuttle (the road distance between the museum and Suquamish Center is about 2.5 miles) and paddle along the 3 miles of shoreline through Agate Passage. The sandy beach and picnic site at Old Man House State Park make a nice stop along the way. From the water, look for the park on the west shore between the inshore navigation marker and the "2" buoy at the north end of Agate Passage. Early explorers reported seeing a Suquamish people longhouse 900 by 60 feet at this location. The building had forty apartments, each with fireplaces. Every corner post of the chief's apartment had large carved Thunderbirds. The building was burned down in the late 1800s by the US government to prevent communal living in their campaign to remove Native Americans from the area. South of the Agate Pass bridge are the Suquamish casino and hotel, which overlook Agate Pass.

Currents in Agate Passage can attain almost 6 knots under the highway bridge, but are rarely as much as 2 knots in the northern portion. You may cross between Agate Point and Old Man House State Park even if the currents are strong and unfavorable. A current flowing against either a north or south wind could make dangerous seas here, and the combination of strong currents, eddies around the highway bridge abutments, and heavy pleasure boat traffic could give less experienced kayakers problems. Most difficulties and hazards can be minimized by paddling as close to the beach as possible. However, the currents under the highway bridge can sometimes be strong enough to make slow progress against them. I surfed a sizeable tide rip in the main boating channel in front of Suquamish Center created by a flood opposing a strong southerly.

20 Kingston to Point No Point Lighthouse

An easily accessed paddle for those in the urban Puget Sound areas, the route begins in a busy harbor and quickly sheds all signs of development. Enjoy views of Edmonds, Mukilteo, and southern Whidbey Island, passing ships, and the Point No Point lighthouse, built in 1880. With three launches, you have plenty of options and routes to choose from. The route follows the North Kitsap Water Trail, which was under development in late 2011 (see Resources).

Duration: Part day to full day.

Rating: *Moderate.*

Navigation Aids: SeaTrails, WA 104 & 105; NOAA chart 18473 (1:25,000); 18440 (1:150,000); Tide Tables for Puget Sound.

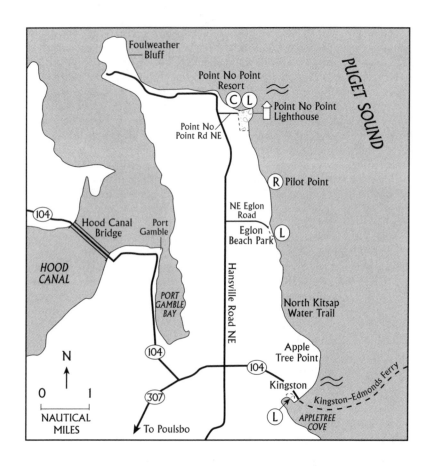

Planning Considerations: Watch for ferry traffic in Kingston harbor. The route can be exposed to wind and ship waves. Make sure to plan around the extensive tide flats at low tides from Eglon Beach north to Point No Point in spring and summer months.

Getting There and Launching

Kingston: From Seattle, take the Edmonds ferry to Kingston. Once off the ferry, take a left on Ohio Avenue Northeast, and go two blocks to the Port of Kingston ferry parking lot. A self-pay parking kiosk includes two-hour and daily/weekly parking options. The marina also provides a small boat facility with twenty-eight covered slips for small boats eight to twenty-four feet for $24 a month. A step launch and retrieval system is available for easy access to the water. For additional information: www.portofkingston.org.

Late afternoon in summer at the Point No Point Lighthouse

Eglon Beach: From the Kingston ferry, continue off the ferry and follow State Route 104 for 3 miles and turn north (right) on Hansville Road Northeast. Follow for 4.27 miles then take a right (east) on Northeast Eglon Road. Follow this windy yet scenic road to Eglon Beach Park (Port of Eglon). The park has a boat ramp and beach. Facilities include a restroom, picnic tables, and parking. The ramp is halfway between Point No Point and Kingston. Pilot Point, an undeveloped Kitsap County Park, is 1.5 miles north of Eglon Beach. The park has no street access or facilities but does offer a rest stop.

Hansville and Point No Point: From the Kingston ferry terminal, take SR 104 west for 3 miles to a stoplight. Turn right (north) on Hansville Road Northeast and go 7.4 miles. Take a right on Point No Point Road Northeast and follow it for 1 mile to the park. The park has restrooms, picnic tables, walking trails, a beach, and parking. Parking will be tight during fishing season. The park has no camping, but you can camp at the Point No Point Resort just north of the lighthouse. For additional information: 360-638-2233.

Route

Put-in from any of the three launches. If you start at Kingston, paddle to the end of the rock jetty and take a left to head north. Be very cautious when crossing in front of the ferry terminal. Best approach is to check the ferry schedule and pass by the terminal when no ferries are in the bay. If you do have to paddle by when a ferry is in dock, stay 200 yards away from the boat. Always give the boats the right-of-way if they're underway. In a few hundred yards, you'll paddle past Apple Tree Point. Watch for waves from strong northerly or southerly winds. Shipping traffic can produce waves large enough to surf at lower tides. On the north side of the point, you'll pass a high density housing development. From here on, there's only one other low bank row of beach homes then medium to high bank bluffs and empty beaches for several miles to Eglon Beach Park, and the Point No Point Lighthouse. Just south of the lighthouse, you'll see a large erratic boulder on the beach left by a glacier. At extreme low tides the beach north of Eglon extends 100 to 200 yards from the bluff. Pull out on the north side of the point just past the lighthouse. Picnic tables are above the beach. Go wide around Point No Point in fishing season. On a busy summer evening, fishermen can be lined up shoulder to shoulder on both sides of the point. Light current and rips occur on large tidal exchanges. Keep an eye out for ship wakes, which can produce breaking waves on the beach. The point isn't suitable for surfing freighter waves as the beach descends too steeply into the Sound.

21 Everett Harbor: Jetty Island and Vicinity

Just beyond the mills and marinas of Everett's waterfront, Jetty Island has both wildness and antiquity: seabirds and sea lions can be seen near the rotting barges that were beached long ago to stabilize the shifting sandbars of the Snohomish River estuary. This island also offers an excellent opportunity for a solitary beach hike in the Seattle area—winter months guaranteed. The navy's homeport facility on the east side of the Snohomish River channel south of the marina provides other big sea-going attractions but doesn't detract from the nature of Jetty Island or interfere with access to the river's channels. The waters outside Jetty Island have become popular with kite surfers seeking surfable waves on high wind days. Paddlers with the appropriate skill level can also enjoy paddling here while catching large wind waves.

Duration: Part day.

Rating: *Protected.*

The north end of Jetty Island looking toward Camano Island in the distance

Navigation Aids: SeaTrails WA 104; NOAA charts 18423 SC, 18441 (both 1:80,000), 18443 (1:40,000), or 18444 (1:10,000); Seattle tide table.

Planning Considerations: Extensive tide flats make avoiding the lower tides essential. A five-foot or higher tide level gives you access to small lagoons and backwaters on Jetty Island and makes circumnavigation of the island shorter. To be safe, paddle in on a rising tide. Currents in the Snohomish River channels can be strong on both the ebb and flood tides. Strong winds, especially those opposing currents, can create very rough water and large breaking waves on the outside of Jetty Island. Also be cautious of kite surfers who are quite numerous around the island on windy days.

Getting There and Launching

Marine Park: From northbound Interstate 5, take Exit 193 for Pacific Avenue. Turn left (west) under the freeway and go about five blocks on Pacific Avenue to Broadway Avenue. Turn right and drive four blocks. Turn left and follow Everett Avenue (State Route 529) through downtown Everett and downhill toward the waterfront, where you bear right onto West Marine View Drive

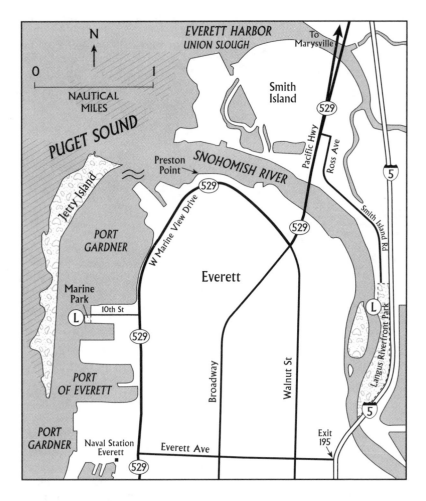

(SR 529). Follow this street for almost 1.5 miles, passing the marina on the left. Turn left onto 10th Street for the public launch ramp and marine park. Use the launch ramps and docks or, if they are very busy, the shoreline on either side. No fee is charged for hand-carried, human-powered boats. Note the closing hours for the park and be sure to return before then. AquaTrek Marine Services provides paddlers with kayak and SUP rentals as well as a full-service paddling and marine shop. They're located on the south side of the marina by several restaurants, www.aquatrekcenter.com. There is no public access at this location aside from store rentals.

Langus Riverfront Park on the Snohomish River: Enjoy a free ride down the Snohomish River to Jetty Island from Langus Riverfront Park. Located about a mile above the river mouth, the park provides restrooms, a boat ramp, a picnic area, and easy access from I-5. Avoid paddling to Jetty Island on less than a five-foot tide. Any less will leave you stranded in a mudflat waiting for rescue. Time your return to the park on the flood tide. Beware that spring snowmelt or heavy rains may increase the downstream current. To access the park from I-5 north, take exit 195. From I-5 south, take exit 198. Both lead to SR 529. Exit 529 at 34th Avenue Northeast, which takes you east. Take a right onto Ross Avenue, which will lead you parallel along the freeway past Dagmar's Landing, a dry boat storage. Ross Avenue will soon merge into Smith Island Road and take you to the park.

Route

The Jetty Island circumnavigation at high tide is approximately 4 miles. Shorter excursions to northern Jetty Island and the vicinity are attractive in themselves. For the circumnavigation, plan the direction in accordance with the Snohomish River channel flow direction, which is stronger than that on the west side of Jetty Island.

From the launching ramp at Langus Riverfront Park, counterclockwise around the island, follow the main Snohomish River channel upstream, passing extensive log storage facilities on the right. Across the channel is Jetty Island. Its shore here is used for log storage too, but less actively. Eventually, the water opens up to the left as you round the north end of Jetty Island and head counterclockwise around the island. A rip and back eddy occurs on the inside of the northeast end on the ebb tide.

The elevations of seabed and land barely differ in this river outwash area. Jetty Island itself is hardly more than a long sandbar covered with salt grass, Scotch broom, and an occasional tree. Over the years, wooden barges have been beached to control the movement of sand and silt. Walk inland toward the navigation marker tower at the north end of the island and you will find the old timbers and iron drift pins and bolts of barges that were beached and burned here long ago and are now completely surrounded by land.

Better-preserved barges are located about 0.5 mile north of Jetty Island. They are beached in a line that extends, along with countless pilings, most of the way across to Tulalip's shore to the north. The western edge of Jetty Island is an unbroken beach, with shallow waters warmed enough by the summer sun for a swim at high tide. At low tide, it becomes a sandy tide flat a mile or more wide. More hulks of old barges are found here and there along the beach.

A large colony of sea lions resides in this area during the late winter and spring, usually from February to May. At lower tides they move offshore, often floating in large clusters. The southern end of the island narrows to become a stone jetty for the last 0.5 mile. If currents are strong against you for the paddle back upstream, you may want to shorten the loop by portaging across the island north of the stone jetty. This is a distance of 100 yards or less, depending on tides and logs stored on the east side.

Low-tide mudflats at the mouth of the Skokomish River on Annas Bay

Once in the river channel, you have the choice of following the wilder island shoreline or crossing to inspect the marina's fishing boats and yachts. There are a variety of shops here with groceries, food, and assorted beverages.

22 Southern Hood Canal: Annas Bay

Annas Bay, the elbow of the Great Bend of Hood Canal, has the largest river estuary, the Skokomish River, in the area. Set against the spectacular backdrop of the immediately adjacent Olympic Mountains, this maze of winding channels and grassy banks abounds in birdlife and seals. At high tide a meandering route can be followed all the way across the estuary through these watery convolutions and miniature islets. Especially stunning are the fall colors of the wetland deciduous trees and shrubs in brilliant contrast against the mountains' greens.

Duration: Part day.

Rating: *Protected.*

Navigation Aids: SeaTrails WA 201; NOAA charts 18476 (1:40,000) or 18445 SC (1:80,000); Seattle tide table (add 10 minutes).

Planning Considerations: Best at high tide. Watch for windy conditions, which can create chop at the mouth of the river. Keep your distance from anglers.

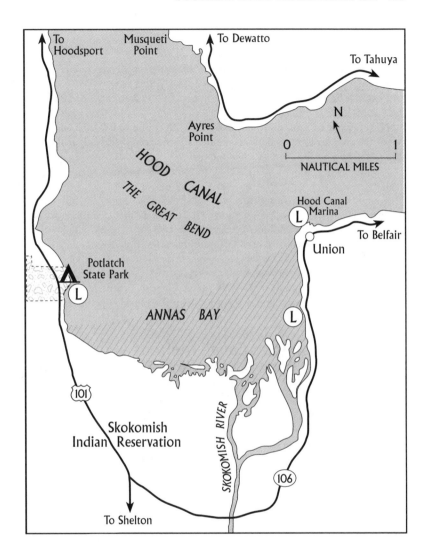

Getting There and Launching

Taking the Bremerton ferry, you can reach Union from Seattle in about one and a half hours. Launch from sites in or near the town of Union along State Route 106 or at Potlatch State Park on US Highway 101. The car-shuttle distance between these areas is about 5 miles.

Union: Launch from Hood Canal Marina, which offers secure parking, a full-service marina, and a slanting dock perfect for kayaks or SUPs. Union Paddle and Row Center operates the marina and offers kayak and SUP rentals and tours. For additional information: www.unionpaddleandrow.com.

An informal roadside pull-out along SR 106 about 1 mile south of Union gives the closest access to the eastern end of the estuary. In fishing season outhouses are placed along this stretch to assist anglers. Access to the water is down a steep embankment. Make sure to display your Discover Pass.

Potlatch State Park: Use the beach in the day-use area (a Cascadia Marine Trail site is also located here).

Note: Avoid launching on the Skokomish River due to log jams and heavy use of the river by local anglers. In the fall, the Skokomish tribe lines the river shore with salmon fishing nets.

Route

The one-way paddling distance across the estuary is about 2.5 miles. Add another mile if you start from Union. The tidelands in the estuary are the property of the Skokomish Indian Reservation. There may be many gill nets set across the river channels during the fall salmon runs.

Depending on the tide height, pick your route along the fringe of channels and islands defining the northern edge of the estuary. If the water level is fairly high you should be able to make it all the way across, except at the estuary's center where a causeway requires you to skirt to the outside open water.

23 Central Hood Canal: Quilcene and Dabob Bays, Dosewallips, Pleasant Harbor, Triton Cove, and Mike's Beach Resort

With the Olympic Mountain Range towering overhead, this part of Hood Canal is the meeting place of land and sea. When you can take your eyes off this gorgeous backdrop, there is plenty to look at up close: rich estuaries, lagoons, and a tideland that is renowned for its oysters. Be careful where you collect them; most tidelands in Hood Canal are private. Check Department of Fisheries regulations for the current season if you're interested in finding oysters. These trips will focus on the west side of Hood Canal along US Highway 101.

Duration: Full day or overnight.

Rating: *Protected* or *Moderate*. *Moderate* may include winds tunneled down the canal making sizeable wind waves.

Navigation Aids: SeaTrails WA 201; NOAA charts 18476 (1:40,000) or 18445 SC (1:80,000); Seattle tide table (add 5 to 15 minutes).

Planning Considerations: Best at high tide to enter the mudflats, estuaries, and lagoons. Check the forecast for wind, which can either be a benefit or a problem.

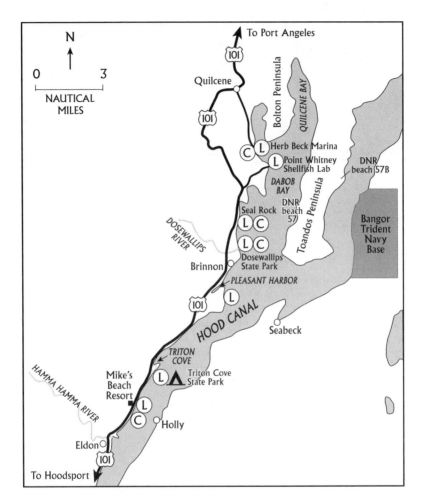

Getting There and Launching

Coming from the Hood Canal Bridge, on State Route 104, take Center Road south to Quilcene. If coming from the north end of the Olympic Peninsula, stay on US Highway 101 south of Discovery Bay. If coming from Olympia, take US 101 north, or from Kitsap Peninsula, take SR 106 east, then US 101 north.

On the west side, there are at least five alternative launch spots off US 101 between Quilcene and Pleasant Harbor.

Quilcene/Herb Beck Marina: This is the best launch for exploring upper Quilcene Bay. From Rogers Road take a left on Linger Longer Road. Follow it 1.5 miles to this small boat harbor. This is a full-facility marina with showers, restrooms, water, camping, and overnight parking. Check in

The narrow high-tide channels of Dosewallips State Park

with the marina office before parking long term. Launch at the sandy beach south of the marina. The facility is managed by the Port of Port Townsend, 360-385-0656.

Though roads lead directly to the shores of upper Dabob Bay, launching there to paddle this interesting area is not advised since both the tidelands and shores are private. Local owners are concerned about trespassing on the rich oyster beds. You can, however, paddle to public access beaches managed by the Department of Natural Resources (DNR). On the Toandos Peninsula across Dabob Bay from Quilcene, is DNR beach 57, and on the other side of the peninsula is beach 57B.

Point Whitney Shellfish Lab: Start here for access to Dabob Bay or for paddling south toward Dosewallips and Pleasant Harbor. From Quilcene follow US 101 south 8 miles to Bee Mill Road, which is marked for Point Whitney. Turn left and go 2.5 miles to the Washington Department of Fisheries Shellfish Lab at Point Whitney. The gravel beach next to the boat ramp is fine for launching in all but strong northerly winds when shore break may be quite large. Public restrooms are nearby.

Seal Rock Campground: One of the few Forest Service campgrounds on saltwater, Seal Rock has a nice gravel beach with pleasant views of Hood Canal and points east. There is camping, restrooms, and picnic tables. Launch on the north side of the beach by the small boat ramp. There's very little beach at high tide so pull your boat up high and secure it to a tree or similar. Seal Rock is 2 miles north of Brinnon.

Dosewallips State Park: Launch in the high-tide channels adjacent to the day-use area located south of the river. This is a full-facility park with camping, restrooms, parking, and easy access to the channels.

Pleasant Harbor: Use the Fish and Wildlife boat ramp on the south side of the harbor. About 2 miles south of Dosewallips State Park turn left off US 101 at Black Point Road about 0.25 mile north of Pleasant Harbor

Marina. Immediately take the left fork following the boat ramp sign to the lot below. A Fish and Wildlife or Discover Pass are required here. There is a restroom but no other facilities.

Triton Cove: South of Pleasant Harbor a few miles is Triton Cove State Park, a boat ramp and Cascadia Marine Trail site. The trail site is located on the south side of the park. A tall seawall directly above the beach leading to the site is difficult to access during high tides or heavy seas. A picnic table is placed just above the wall with the campsites farther up the embankment on a nice grassy field. Restrooms are about 300 yards up the hill by the main parking lot.

Mike's Beach Resort: Located just north of the beautiful Hamma Hamma River mouth and near North Hamma Hamma Road, Mike's Beach Resort provides a launch for the public for a small fee. The access is crucial for exploring this side of the canal where public access is limited. Cabins and tent camping are also available. For additional information: www.mikesbeachresort.com/.

Routes

There are several opportunities for both day and overnight trips along this stretch. Create your own trip connecting day-use areas or overnight campsites such as the Cascadia Marine Trail site at Triton Cove.

Quilcene Bay and Point Whitney: *Protected* to *Moderate*. Quilcene Bay and its estuaries are perfect for beginning paddlers or those seeking an idyllic, peaceful paddle. Paddling south from Point Whitney follows a natural tree-lined rugged shoreline with tiny pocket beaches. On a clear day water visibility is quite good, allowing you to see far down below your boat. North of Point Whitney takes you along oyster-strewn beaches with nice views of Bolton and Toandos peninsulas.

Doesewallips State Park: *Protected* to *Moderate*. The shallow winding grass-lined channels of Dosewallips State Park are a fun ride and great for novice paddlers. Only available on higher tides, the channels open into Hood Canal through tiny grass-topped islets. Check your tide tables closely to avoid being stranded in the tide flats. Small tide rips appear below the main Dosewallips river channel from opposing wind.

Pleasant Harbor: *Protected*. Pleasant Harbor is a picturesque cove and full-service marina surrounded by thick forests. Very protected with a narrow opening, the harbor is ideal for beginning paddlers or those seeking glassy conditions when Hood Canal may be windy. Kayak Brinnon rents kayaks and offers tours from the harbor. For additional information: www.kayakbrinnon.com/.

Farther south on US 101 near Eldon, large river deltas such as the Hamma Hamma fan out into Hood Canal. Hamma Hamma meant "stinky stinky" to native peoples representing the smell of rotting salmon after a run. The river mouth has lush grassy river channels with older homes lining its shores. Unfortunately, due to commercial oyster production nearby, deltas such as this one are off-limits to paddlers. A few miles south is Lilliwaup, another river mouth with an interesting community of colorful houses and watercraft along its shores.

24 Whidbey Island: Coupeville and Penn Cove

Founded in 1852, Coupeville is the oldest town on Whidbey Island, and part of Ebey's Landing National Historical Preserve. Coupeville's colorful, false-front buildings line the main street and extend to the gravel beach below. The Port of Coupeville Wharf reaches into Penn Cove offering paddlecraft tie-ups and kayaking rentals in summer. The museum inside the wharf has a full skeleton of a gray whale hanging from its ceiling. Penn Cove itself is mostly rural with medium-bank bluffs dotted with a few homes. Enjoy distant views of Mount Baker to the north. There is a Cascadia Marine Trail site in downtown Oak Harbor 4.2 miles to the north, otherwise there is no camping nearby that can be accessed by water.

Duration: Part day to full day.

Rating: *Protected* or *Moderate.*

Navigation Aids: SeaTrails WA 102; NOAA charts 18423, and 18471 (1:40,000 for Penn Cove).

Planning Considerations: A strong south wind can build rough swells as it sweeps up Saratoga Passage and into Penn Cove.

Getting There and Launching

Oak Harbor: From southbound State Route 20, continue going straight on to South Beeksma Drive when the highway turns right (west) in downtown Oak Harbor. If coming from Coupeville, once in Oak Harbor, take a right onto South Beeksma Drive when the highway turns right (north). The launch is in Windjammer City Park, which has parking, restrooms, and a Cascadia Marine Trail campsite.

Captain Thomas Coupeville Park: From SR 20, turn north onto North Main Street and go 0.5 mile, taking a right onto Northeast 9th Street. Drive 0.3 mile to Captain Thomas Coupeville Park on the left. There are restrooms, picnic tables, and parking. A ramp and float serve for launching boats in this day-use-only park.

Routes

Penn Cove: *Protected.* Penn Cove, only open to the larger water of Saratoga Passage at its east end, is well sheltered from most major blows. Starting from Captain Thomas Coupeville Park, you can explore the docks, wharfs, and overhanging buildings comprising Coupeville's waterfront. Coupeville is the oldest town on Whidbey Island and it, along with the surrounding shoreline of Penn Cove, is within the Ebey's Landing National Historical Reserve that stretches to the west side of Whidbey Island. You might want to secure your boat and visit the Whidbey Island Historical Society's Museum at the foot of the wharf. Try the Penn Cove mussels at Toby's Tavern, a classic spot in town.

From Coupeville you can paddle west past the historic Captain Whidbey Inn and visit the many floating pens growing the famous and delicious Penn Cove Mussel. Remember not to disturb or climb on the pens. Beyond this at the head of the cove, you can poke around Kennedy's and Grasser's Lagoons in search of waterfowl, raptors, deer, and other creatures that inhabit the shoreline. The one-way distance from the ramp to the lagoons is 2.6 miles.

Penn Cove to Oak Harbor: *Moderate.* The relatively direct paddling distance from Penn Cove to Oak Harbor consists of 4.2 miles. Keeping to

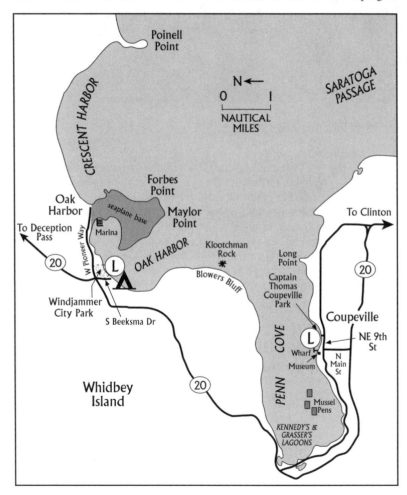

Looking north over Penn Cove from the historic town of Coupeville

the western shoreline, at 2 miles you pass by Klootchman Rock, a fair-sized erratic boulder left behind as the last glaciers melted, sitting beneath Blowers Bluff. On days when a south wind blows, the seas can build along this stretch, possibly breaking as they reach the shallow beaches. This trip can be done as a one way from either end, with an easy car shuttle of only 11 miles between the two city launches, or as a round trip. There are plenty of choices for food and drink at either end. The Cascadia Marine Trail site is on the Oak Harbor waterfront at the west end of the Windjammer City Beach Park west of the boat launch ramp. Bring ear plugs if you wish to stay overnight, the navy has a large air base nearby and it is not uncommon to hear jets screaming overhead. There is no camping on Penn Cove in Coupeville.

25 Whidbey Island: Keystone to Hastie Lake Boat Ramp

This trip passes by Fort Casey State Park, Ebey's Landing National Historical Reserve, and Fort Ebey State Park. See the historic lighthouse above Admiralty Head, the windswept grassy bluff and estuary of Ebey's Landing, and miles of vertical bluffs and empty beaches. With no areas of wind protection, swirling currents from the strait and Puget Sound colliding, and possible large surf at Patridge Point, the route is listed as *Exposed*.

Duration: Part day to overnight.

Rating: *Exposed.*

Navigation Aids: SeaTrails WA 102, 103, 104; NOAA charts 18441 (1:80,000); 18440 (1:150,000); 18471 (1:40,000); Port Townsend tide table.

Planning Considerations: This route can be glassy calm or heavy seas with strong current, rips, and swell. Large surf may be present off Fort Ebey State Park and near Hastie Lake Boat Ramp. Know surfers' etiquette before landing here when surfers are present in the water (see Resources). Watch the currents and be comfortable with rough-water paddling.

Getting There and Launching

Driftwood Park–Keystone/Coupeville Ferry Terminal: If coming from Port Townsend, take a right after leaving the ferry onto State Route 20, then another right into the day-use boat ramp parking area adjacent to the ferry dock. From Coupeville take South Main Street west past the high school toward Fort Casey State Park. Main will become South Engle Street, and after a few miles lead you to the Keystone-Coupeville ferry terminal. Just past the terminal (south), take a right into the public boat ramp lot. A Discover Pass is required to park. The lot has a boat ramp, restrooms, and picnic tables. Camping is available in Fort Casey State Park adjacent to the ferry. Some also park on the street across from the terminal. Stay clear of the ferry when paddling north of here. Farther south of here is Ledgewood Park, another day-use area with beach access. Both are Island County Parks, for additional information: www.islandcounty.net.

Ebey's Landing National Historical Reserve: From the Coupeville ferry terminal, take a left off the dock on South Engle Road. In about a mile, take a left on Hill Road, which will give you a bird's-eye view of the route. Hill Road will drop to the beach and end at the park. From Coupeville, take South Ebey Road or South Ebey Road off State Route 20. Follow it to the park. The lot here is small, so park on the water side of the street if necessary. The park has restrooms, picnic tables, and hiking. For additional information: www.nps .gov/ebla/index.htm.

Fort Ebey State Park: From SR 20 north of Coupeville, take West Libby Road west. Follow signs to Fort Ebey State Park. A Discover Pass is required in the park, or pay a fee at the booth. Follow signs to the beach. Parking is tight on busy days, but it is a short carry to the beach. There's a Cascadia Marine Trail site just below the beach parking lot, but the lot is day use only. Wind waves and swell from the Strait of Juan de Fuca can be quite large here. The beach is rocky with a few boulders. It is also a popular surfing spot for locals. Know surfers' etiquette before launching here when surfers are present (see Resources). There is camping on the south side of the park on the bluff, which has no water access.

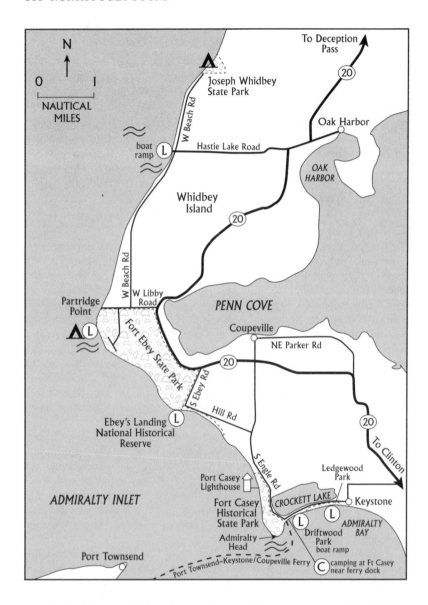

Hastie Lake Road Boat Ramp: From SR 20, turn west on Hastie Lake Road just south of Oak Harbor. Follow 2.5 miles to the road end. Access the park from Fort Ebey State Park by continuing west on Libby Road. Take a right on West Beach Road and follow it north for about 2 to 3 miles to Hastie Lake Road. The ramp is on your left. The boat ramp has a small lot and no facilities. Houses are on both sides; respect neighbors. If surfers are present, use surfers' etiquette and pass by on the outer water side.

Route

Choose your own route and launch location. This trip can be done in short segments or as one longer paddle. A Cascadia Marine Trail site is located above the beach launch at Fort Ebey State Park

Check wind and currents prior to departing. Currents can swirl around Admiralty Head creating challenging conditions if you're not comfortable with such water. If you're traveling near Fort Ebey and Hastie Lake, check swell conditions to avoid dealing with large breaking waves. A west or northwest

The tall bluffs of Whidbey Island above Admiralty Inlet as seen from Ebey's Landing

swell over 7 feet at Cape Flattery, or strong southwest, west, or northwest winds can make sizeable surf at those locations. This route can be glassy calm or quite the opposite.

When launching from the Coupeville ferry terminal, be cautious of a docked or moving ferry. Or time your launch for when the ferry isn't there. The beach on Admiralty Head below Fort Casey is strewn with driftwood. Look for interesting driftwood shelters here. Take a short hike up the bluff to explore the pre–World War I gun emplacements and pill boxes. The fort was part of the "Triangle of Fire" a three-fort system that included Fort Worden in Port Townsend and Fort Flagler on Marrowstone Head, both across Admiralty Inlet. The forts were designed to prevent invading fleets from entering Puget Sound.

The shoreline north of the ferry terminal rises to a bluff and stays steep until Ebey's Landing where it drops to the beach. The beach is rocky with some sand and is minimal during higher tides. Across Admiralty Inlet see views of Marrowstone Island, Port Townsend, and the Olympic Mountains.

Take a restroom break at Ebey's Landing and a short hike up the bluff trail for impressive views of Admiralty Inlet, the eastern entry to the Strait of Juan de Fuca, and the San Juan Islands to the far north. Along the bluff you may see some small prickly pear cactus, a sign of the arid climate for this area. Below see Perego's Lagoon, an expansive tidal lagoon, one of the few not destroyed by development in the region.

Continuing north, the bluffs rise again to tall vertical cliffs. The empty sand and gravel beach has few visitors thus giving you solitude. Bald eagles, hawks, and seagulls frequently fly over the bluffs, taking advantage of the pillow of air provided by the active beach below.

The bluff drops again at Fort Ebey State Park. Partridge Point is a rocky extension where waves often build, making this a popular surfing area for local residents. Go wide on the outside around the point if you're not skilled in dealing with breaking waves. Because good surf is hard to find inside of the coast, surfers are sensitive to those who can't surf safely or may hog waves. This spot in particular is known for its "localism." Sea kayaks are fast but can't turn well on waves, thus could be a hazard to others in the water.

Just around the point, look for a wooden-planked walkway leading up the hill. This is the path to the Cascadia Marine Trail. Restrooms are available to the left in the parking lot. The main hiking trail from the rest of the park comes down just above the site. If you're up for a hike, follow the trail to the right up the hill. A World War II observation bunker can be entered about five minutes from the beach. A larger gun emplacement from the same era is on top of the bluff about a quarter mile from Partridge Point.

Back in the water and moving north, the bluff will remain lower and homes will appear above. A little over 2 miles north is the Hastie Lake Road boat ramp, a good rest stop or launch. A Cascadia Marine Trail site is 3.2 miles north of Hastie Lake in Joseph Whidbey State Park. Bring ear plugs as flights from the naval base nearby can be noisy.

26 Skagit River Delta

The Skagit River Delta is a birder's paradise and more. A maze of marshland channels, river dwellers' shanties and floating houses, and even overgrown pre-World War II coast artillery emplacements are included in the rich estuary country within the Skagit Wildlife Area.

Duration: Part day to full day.

Rating: *Protected.*

Navigation Aids: SeaTrails WA 101; NOAA chart 18423 SC (1:80,000) or USGS 7.5 Minute Series (1:24,000) topographic map for the Utsalady Quadrangle; Seattle tide table (add about 20 minutes).

Planning Considerations: Midtide or higher, at least 4 feet above mean low water, is required for paddling outside the main Skagit River channel and outside Swinomish Channel. Both Skagit River and Swinomish Channel reverse their currents with the tide. This occurs for the channel at least one hour after the tide change for the river, but in practice the channel current is not easily predicted. Currents affect paddling efforts to and from all launch locations.

You may wish to avoid the heavy bird-hunting period from mid-September through December; contact the state Department of Wildlife for specifics. Each member of your group must have a Discover Pass in his or her possession to go ashore in the Skagit Wildlife Area. The owners at Blake's Skagit Resort and Marina told me many paddlers don't time the tides correctly and end up struggling to paddle back to the launch. Keep in mind river flows are stronger after heavy rain and during spring runoff from snowmelt. Take the ebb downriver and the flood upriver.

Getting There and Launching

Choose from launch sites along the Skagit River or in downtown La Conner. An approximately 10-mile car shuttle could be made between them.

Skagit River: From Interstate 5 take the La Conner–Conway exit and within a short distance branch right to Conway. Continue about 5 miles on Fir Island Road. For the lower river launch at Blake's Skagit Resort and Marina, turn left on Rawlins Road. Located approximately 1 mile above the delta area, Blake's is the lowest launch point on the North Fork of the Skagit River. The resort charges a launch fee, which also covers parking for the first day. For additional information: 360-445-6533.

A state Department of Wildlife launch site is located farther upriver. Turn right off Fir Island Road onto Moore Road about 0.35 mile beyond Rawlins

Road, just before the North Fork bridge, then take the first unsigned dirt road to the left 0.25 mile beyond at the S-curve. The Discover Pass is required to use this launch site. Follow the dike west and look for a sandy path through the trees to the river.

La Conner: To launch from La Conner, continue on Fir Island Road over the North Fork bridge. The road becomes Best Road. Take a left in 2.4 miles onto Chilberg Road and continue another 2.4 miles to La Conner. The La Conner public boat ramp is located below and just north of the Rainbow Bridge. After entering La Conner, turn left on Maple, then right on Caledonia Street, left on Third, and finally right on Sherman Street. The ramp is straight ahead at the waterfront. Parking in summer is difficult. Use the lot across the street or along the street beyond if space is available.

There's a Cascadia Marine Trail site in Pioneer Park in La Connor above the boat ramp.

Routes

Skagit River to Craft Island: *Protected.* The paddling distance is 3 to 5 miles each way. Time your start to ensure that you will have mid- to high tide in the delta once you get downriver. The distance to the shallow delta area from Blake's is about 1.5 miles, and about 3 miles from the upper river launch.

There is a downstream current from both river launch sites during the ebb and an upstream flow as far as the upper launch on larger flood tides (except during heavy river runoff), though this begins as much as an hour after low tide.

Heading downriver approximately 1 mile below Blake's, you reach a sharp bend to the right; just beyond are pastoral farm buildings and river dwellers' houses and shacks on the right bank. This is the tiny community of Fish Town. Just downstream on the left is the first side channel into the delta. Take this channel for Craft Island and keep bearing left. The distance is a little more than 1 mile after leaving the river.

Interesting rock formations are not uncommon along the rugged shores of Ika Island.

Craft Island is really a hill jutting up from an otherwise flat marsh and tideland west of the river as it nears the mouth. From the top you can see a sweeping panorama of the marshlands to the north and south and, at low tide, the vast gray tide flats to the west. This and other upland islands are a particularly sensitive habitat for raptors, including bald eagles and red-tailed hawks. If you go ashore, avoid approaching or disturbing these birds, particularly when the nesting sites are in use.

Timing for the Craft Island excursion is important, as the side channel to it is dry below midtide. If you have the time, you may wish to head downriver at early ebb, paddle to the island, and spend the last of the ebb and early flood lunching, exploring, or just enjoying the view.

If your tide timing is off for paddling to Craft Island, you can walk there after returning to the launch point. Drive to the end of Rawlins Road beyond Blake's. A rough trail about 0.75 mile is accessible on lower tides leading across the marsh meadows to the island.

A side trip along this route is to Ika Island, which is the large island to your west just beyond Craft Island. You can't land on Ika, but enjoy the interesting rock formations and craggy shoreline around its base.

La Conner to Goat Island to Skagit Delta: *Protected.* The paddling distance for the loop is 7 miles; additional side trips are possible.

Most of this loop can be paddled at tide heights of 3 feet or more. Avoiding a lower tide is not as critical here as for the Craft Island route. However, you will be scooping sand much of the way in a foot or less of water; getting out to wade and tow your boat may prove easier in spots. Spending the low-tide interval exploring Goat Island is worthwhile if you can afford the time.

From the public launch at La Conner, follow the channel south through the twisting narrows of Hole-in-the-Wall. Beyond, the channel opens to flats with intertidal islets and shallow waterways that invite exploration if the tide is in. To the south is a log storage area bounded by a stone jetty extending to Goat Island. The route later returns through a tiny gap in this jetty.

Goat Island has both the dense forest and the grassy meadows with madrona trees that are typical of the more arid San Juan Islands. On the northwest end is Fort Whitman, a component of the extensive coast artillery defenses for Puget Sound built at the turn of the century. There are mounts for three guns in the emplacements, with associated rooms and tunnels similar to those found at Fort Worden and Fort Casey state parks. Such defenses were obsolete by World War II, when aircraft became more effective than coast artillery against invading fleets.

To reach the emplacements, look for the old dock along the island's north shore. Behind it is a rocky, muddy beach and the start of a rough trail that climbs to the right. Follow this about 250 yards to the battery.

As with other islands in the Skagit Wildlife Area, this is a particularly sensitive habitat for resident raptors. The Department of Wildlife asks that you respect the privacy of these birds, particularly during spring nesting. As elsewhere within the Skagit Wildlife Area, no camping is allowed.

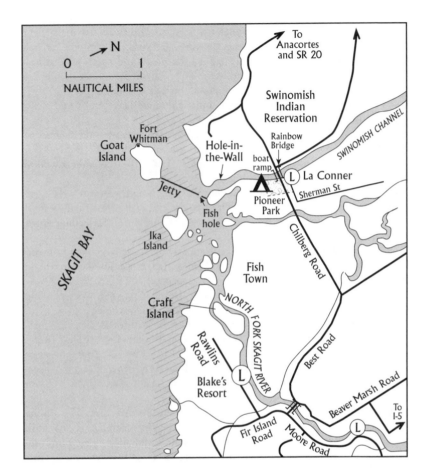

Paddling around the south side of Goat Island brings you into the shallowest part of this route, though enough water can be found in the shifting channels of the Skagit River on all but the lowest tides. On ebb tides and the first portion of floods, downstream currents will make moving up into the delta hard and slow work, with few eddies to assist your progress.

At this point, you could take time to explore the many sloughs off the Skagit River's channel and perhaps cut through the delta to Craft Island, about 2 miles to the east, if the tide is high enough.

The return to Swinomish Channel from the Skagit River is via the "fish hole" in the jetty, a small opening allowing migrating salmon that made a wrong turn into Swinomish Channel to get back to the river. Located about 200 yards from the eastern end of the jetty, this gap is not visible as you approach from upriver, but follow the jetty and you will find it. The hole is dry below midtide.

27 Hope and Skagit Islands

Though currents are swift in this area, the protection of nearby Fidalgo and Whidbey islands makes Hope and Skagit reasonable destinations when other places are a bit on the rough side. Ashore on these state park islands are grassy hillsides with flowers in season, forest trails, and plenty of sand and gravel beaches for sunbathing. However, Skagit Island and nearby Ala Spit both offer a Cascadia Marine Trail campsite as easily accessible, wonderful overnight destinations.

Duration: Part day to overnight.

Rating: *Moderate+.* Currents can produce turbulence in certain areas and rough seas when opposing southerly winds. Avoid strongest currents at the west end of Hope Island unless you have the skills to handle strong eddy lines and tide rips.

Navigation Aids: SeaTrails WA 101; NOAA charts 18423 SC, 18421 (both 1:80,000), or 18427 (1:25,000); Deception Pass current table.

Planning Considerations: Currents here are dependent on those in Deception Pass. The flood flows south. If possible, plan to catch the flood current going to the islands and the ebb for the return. Strong wind that opposes current can create sizeable waves.

Getting There and Launching

Deception Pass: Launch from the Cornet Bay area of Deception Pass State Park. Follow signs to Cornet Bay from State Route 20 about 1 mile south of the bridge and go about 1.25 miles to the launching ramp area. Use the gravel beach just below a timbered bulkhead in front of the parking area or, if the tide is high and covers the beach, use the launching ramp or floats. For overnight parking, use the lot across the road from the boat launch. A Discover Pass is required to park here.

Snee-oosh Beach: This gentle beach near La Conner is a pleasant alternative that avoids most of the current on the west side of the islands. Drive west from La Conner over the Swinomish Channel bridge on Pioneer Parkway for 0.6 mile to Snee-oosh Road; turn left and proceed another 1.9 miles. Bear left onto Chilberg Avenue for 0.3 mile and then make a U-turn onto the dirt access road to the beach. There are no amenities, but you can enjoy a beautiful view across to Hope and Skagit islands.

Route

From Cornet Bay to Hoypus Point, the state of the current dictates how far offshore to paddle—head out 100 feet or so to catch a ride on the flood current. If it is ebbing, there are eddies that make easy paddling along the

Goat and Ika islands from the Cascadia Marine Trail site on Ala Spit

tree-lined gravel beach to Hoypus Point, but you will have to fight the brunt of the current as you round the point. Watch for busy boat traffic here in summer. Likewise, there are some eddies south of the point toward Ala Spit that will help against an ebb.

You may wish to cross directly from Hoypus Point to Skagit Island, adjusting to offset the effects of the current as you go across. Its strength diminishes during the second half of this 1-mile crossing.

Skagit Island is rocky and steep along its north and western shores. There are gravel and shell beaches at the east and southeast ends. A trail circles the island, winding through fir and salal forest on the north side. The south side of the island is a series of rocky meadows interspersed with madronas, with a lot of nice spots for lunch in the sun. Expect the Cascadia Marine Trail campsite to be busy on weekends throughout the warmer seasons. Current can run swift between Skagit and Kiket Island to the east. At the time of writing this edition, landing on Kiket Island, an undeveloped state park, is prohibited.

Hope Island is far larger. Trails circle this island, but most visitors prefer hiking the beaches or paddling along shore to walking in the thick forest. Gravel beaches on the south side of Hope Island are the biggest attraction for day-use paddling, with chances for walking and secluded rest stops.

During large tidal exchanges, currents at both the east and west ends of Hope Island can be swift and dangerous for anyone not skilled in dealing with moving water. If you are unsure, avoid going around to the south side, or go back around via the east end where currents are a little weaker. Both ends can have sharp eddy lines and possible tide rips. Stay close inshore on the east end where you will probably need to cross only one eddy line, and then paddle in eddies the rest of the way around.

The west shore has a very strong eddy line that has capsized kayaks in the past. The current between Hope Island and Ala Spit, about 0.35 mile distant, may be as swift as you can paddle, requiring hard work to get across against an opposing flow without losing too much ground. The flow along the spit is slower, but still takes hard paddling upstream against a flood current to reach the eddies north of the spit.

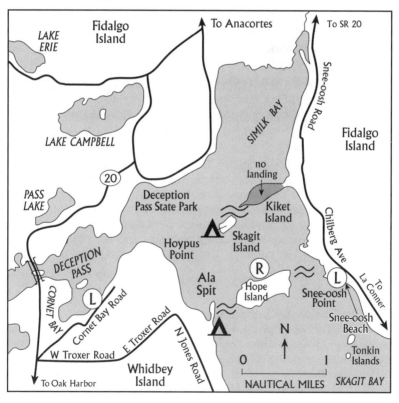

28 Deception Pass

Deception Pass offers outstanding beauty that can be explored safely on the fringes of the high-current area in the pass itself. You can also paddle through the pass when currents are weakest if a novice. Beginners should avoid the pass unless certain of correctly identifying the slack current time; there is plenty of easy paddling in areas of little current within view of Deception Pass' full magnificence.

Experienced paddlers eager to expand their skills can expend some adrenaline practicing in Washington's strongest currents—crossing eddy lines, developing bracing reflexes in swirls and turbulence, and maybe descending into a whirlpool! Currents mostly average 5 or 6 knots at their maximum, while the occasional strongest ones exceed 8 knots. Speeds rapidly decrease within 0.5 mile of both sides of the pass.

Routes in Deception Pass can be combined with those in the Hope and Skagit islands area to the east (see the Hope and Skagit islands chapter). The Cascadia Marine Trail campsite at Bowman Bay also affords the opportunity to make extended trips.

Duration: Part day to full day.

Rating: *Protected, Moderate+,* or *Exposed.* Heavy boat traffic, wind, or ocean swell in the pass may create rough conditions.

Navigation Aids: SeaTrails WA 101; NOAA charts 18427 (1:25,000) or 18423 SC (see 1:25,000 inset for Deception Pass); Deception Pass current tables.

Planning Considerations: Seek or avoid strong current periods depending on your skills and preferences, using the Deception Pass current table. Launch and take-out locations depend on current flows, described below. The flood current flows east through the pass. Avoid times of strong wind from the west, particularly during ebb currents, which can produce particularly nasty seas and tide rips. Watch for boating and jetboat traffic in both passes. A Discover Pass is required to park at all launches.

Getting There and Launching

There are three launch sites within Deception Pass State Park. Which you use depends on where you wish to paddle and the state of the current in the pass. Tactics for planning with currents are described under routes.

Bowman Bay: The launch is accessed from State Route 20 about 0.5 mile north of the Deception Pass Bridge. This is a good place for protected paddling

A triple kayak running the swift flood current in Canoe Pass

north of the pass or for one end of a shuttle trip of about 3 miles driving distance from Cornet Bay. Launch on the gravel beach in front of the parking lot.

West Beach: This is the easiest access to the pass from the west. Turn off SR 20 about 0.5 mile south of the bridge and follow signs to the West Beach parking lot. In windy weather or when a large swell is penetrating the Strait of Juan de Fuca, the sand and gravel West Beach can have substantial surf. If it is not to your liking, a 200-yard-long path leads from the parking lot to a protected launch on North Beach just behind West Point. West Beach is day use only, a Discover Pass is required for parking. Parking is tight on busy summer weekends. If conditions in the pass are rough, try paddling southeast of the lot in Cranberry Lake.

Cornet Bay: This launch serves paddling to the east of the pass. Follow signs to Cornet Bay from SR 20 about 1 mile south of the bridge and go about 1.25 miles to the boat ramp area. Use the gravel beach just below a timbered bulkhead in front of the parking area or, if the tide is high and covers the beach, use the launching ramp or floats.

Routes

Bowman Bay: *Protected.* Paddling anywhere within this bay, located between Rosario Head and Reservation Head, you will avoid dangers from currents, and waters should be relatively smooth. There is plenty of rocky shoreline to explore, plus opportunities for lolling on the beaches, exploring ashore at Sharpe Cove to the west or at the spit adjacent to Lottie Bay to the east. Enjoy rock gardening opportunities south of Reservation Head, which has a coastal feel with small sea caves, rock slots, and surge channels. Swell from the Strait of Juan de Fuca can push against the rocks here making for good coastal paddling practice.

Portaging across to Lottie Bay is easy, and Lottie Bay is rated *Protected* to its mouth, where currents can be strong. Avoid portaging during extreme low tides when the bay's thick mud can be a slog, especially if you're carrying a fully loaded boat.

West Area Exploration: *Moderate +.* Currents west of Lottie Bay are generally less than half the strength of those predicted for the pass, and probably are suitable for intermediate paddlers with some experience with currents. If there is any doubt about the abilities of members of your party to handle currents, avoid times when the currents in the pass are predicted to exceed 5 knots. Crossing the mouth of the pass from Bowman Bay to North Beach should be done cautiously during flood currents that could set you toward the stronger currents in the pass. This area can be extremely rough when swells from the Strait of Juan de Fuca oppose an ebb current flowing out of the pass. At such times or in windy weather, the eastern portion of the pass area (Cornet Bay) is a more prudent choice.

Plan to spend some time exploring the rocky shores between Reservation Head and Lottie Bay, where you will find a number of pocket beaches for secluded lunch stops. Ashore, this area is accessed by a trail from Bowman Bay. You can portage via a small rocky cove behind Lighthouse Point if the rip or currents are too strong on the point. There's a fun, small, surfable standing wave on the flood on the west side of Lighthouse Point directly below the navigational marker.

The park extends north to include part of Rosario Bay, as well as Northwest Island and Deception Island. Neither of the islands are developed and access is not easy. Gravel beaches on the north side of Deception Island offer fairly easy landings on lower tides, but it's a hard scramble to gain access to the island above.

Cornet Bay: *Protected.* Explore this bay as far north as Ben Ure Island (private) or east toward Hoypus Point, about 1 mile from the boat launch. Currents in Cornet Bay are weak and often flow the opposite direction as in the pass to form a long, tapering back eddy on ebbs along the shore toward Hoypus Point. At the latter, currents may be strong while accompanying rips make it unsuited for *Protected*-rated paddling. Likewise, the strong currents and eddies around Strawberry Island are appropriate only for experienced paddlers.

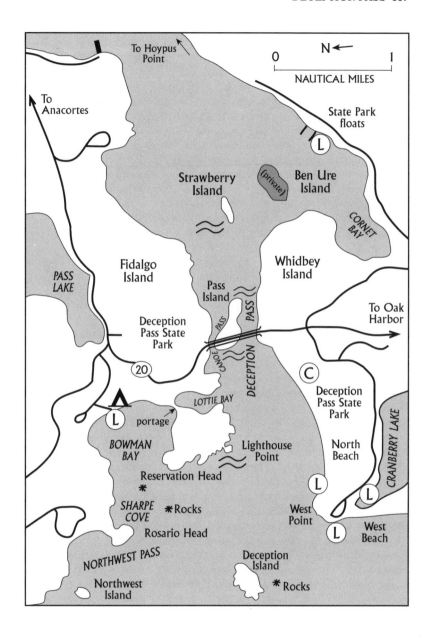

To Hoypus
Point

To
Anacortes

N ←

0   1

NAUTICAL MILES

State Park
floats

L

Strawberry
Island

(private)

Ben Ure
Island

CORNET
BAY

PASS
LAKE

Fidalgo
Island

Whidbey
Island

Pass
Island

To Oak
Harbor

Deception
Pass State
Park

CANOE PASS

PASS

DECEPTION

C

Deception
Pass State
Park

20

LOTTIE BAY

L   portage

BOWMAN
BAY

Lighthouse
Point

North
Beach

CRANBERRY LAKE

Reservation Head
*

L

L

SHARPE
COVE   *Rocks

West
Point

L

West
Beach

Rosario Head

NORTHWEST PASS

Deception
Island

Northwest
Island

*Rocks

Bowman Bay to Cornet Bay (or reverse) through Deception Pass: *Moderate +.* You can see it all in this 3-mile traverse through Deception Pass. Timing for at least near-slack in the pass is critical; you may want to arrange your travel to catch the last of the current going your way at the beginning or the new current at the end. Allow plenty of time to explore the coves west of the pass. Stops ashore near the pass are easy on the beaches at Gun Point and another small beach directly north across the channel. Pass Island has fair access ashore on rocks on the east end. Access at Strawberry Island is similar.

Boat traffic in the pass is a significant hazard, especially if the current forces boats to speed up or reduces their control. Canoe Pass, the smaller passage to the north of Pass Island, is the safer and more interesting way through when currents are weak, as little traffic goes this way. However, a bend in this channel reduces visibility for oncoming powerboats. If you paddle in Canoe Pass, move to the shore to let boating traffic go through. Boat wakes can get large here, so hold on to a rock or be prepared to brace.

Deception Pass Current Play: *Exposed.* Depending on the current strength and your skills, capsizing here is probable; a wet- or dry suit is essential. A helmet is a good idea too as well as neoprene gloves, due to the rocky barnacle-covered shoreline. You should be prepared to rescue yourself and members of your party if there is a capsize.

A number of sea kayak retailers and outfitters hold classes for intermediate-level paddlers in Deception Pass to give them practice in negotiating currents and bracing. They usually seek current strengths up to 7 knots.

Five knots offers eddy lines strong enough to capsize the kayaker who does not prepare for them, especially in narrower boats. Seven knots requires strong leaning and bracing in all boats when crossing eddy lines, and can create swirl zones and boils that may be intimidating to all but the most blasé white-water boater. On ebbs, whirlpools form downstream from Pass Island but do not last. On strong floods, more persistent whirlpools form on the edge of the main channel east of Pass Island. These are a thrill for those who care to chase them down and put one end of their boat or SUP into the vortex.

Canoe Pass is preferred to the main channel for eddy play, primarily because of the boat traffic going through the pass at all but the strongest current times. Wakes can make big waves as they meet eddy lines on either side of the channel. On ebbs Canoe Pass has eddies on both sides just west of the bridge, and ferrying back and forth from one to the other is easy. The flood is stronger than the ebb and creates a series of small eddies close to the island's steep rock face, and a long back eddy forms along the opposite shore. Hopping from one to the other is possible but requires more maneuverability than during ebbs. Watch out for sharp barnacles along both shores that can scrape your boat or board.

Surfable standing waves can develop during lower tides in Canoe Pass when the ebb current collides with incoming swell or a strong wind. Those experienced in such conditions can enjoy a great surfing experience far from the ocean.

29 Burrows Island

The paddling at Burrows Island is interesting and exhilarating with both sheer rock and lively currents. Ashore you will find an abandoned US Coast Guard light station perched on a cliff on the west side. Hike beyond the station to steep grassy shorelines or climb the hill above for a spectacular view of southern Rosario Strait.

There's a secluded Cascadia Marine Trail campsite on the east side of the island in a small cove with great tide pooling nearby.

Duration: Part day to overnight.

Rating: *Moderate* to *Exposed.* Currents usually exceed 2 knots and tide rips are likely. Wind and a westerly swell can make this area quite dangerous during times of strong current.

Navigation Aids: SeaTrails WA 001; NOAA charts 18423 SC or 18421 (both 1:80,000), or 18427 (1:25,000); Rosario Strait current tables with corrections for the Burrows Island–Fidalgo Head area.

Planning Considerations: Use the flood current to travel west in the channels on either the north or south side of Burrows Island and for rounding Fidalgo Head from the south. Flood currents here are generally stronger than the ebbs.

Getting There and Launching

Choices for launching are either Skyline Marina, the closest to Burrows Island, or Washington Park, which adds another mile or so of paddling around Fidalgo Head. These two launch points are about a 0.5-mile walk apart, so consider starting at Washington Park and taking out at Skyline Marina.

Skyline Marina: From Anacortes, follow signs for the San Juan Island ferry, about 4 miles west of town. From Commercial Avenue, take a left on 12th Street (State Route 20) which will become Oakes Avenue. Enjoy views on your right of Guemes and Cypress islands and Bellingham Channel. At the Anacortes ferry terminal continue going straight at the Y intersection. The road will become Sunset Avenue. Take a left on Skyline Avenue and follow signs into the marina. On the bottom of the hill, take a right on Cabana Lane. Go to the end and unload and park on the street or park in the pay lot by the water. Street parking is free, but the lot is $5 a day.

Washington Park: Following the same directions to Skyline Marina, continue straight past Skyline Avenue and go right at the Y intersection. Park in the "A" lot to carry your boat across the lawn to the gravel beach. Then move your car to the "B" lot to park. There is a daily parking fee.

Route

Moderate to *Exposed*. Most of the shoreline of Fidalgo Head, Burrows Island, and neighboring Allan Island is steep rock with grass and madronas growing above and sharp drop-offs that allow close-in paddling. Beaches are infrequent. All of Fidalgo Head west of Skyline Marina is in Washington Park; expect to see a lot of people along its shores. Public land on Burrows Island is restricted to the 40 acres and 1000 feet of shoreline in Burrows Island Light Station State Park on the island's west and southwest corner. Visitors ashore here are rare. There are no public lands or tidelands on Allan Island and the small island between the two to the east.

Expect to find strong eddy lines and nearby tide rips in the channels separating Burrows Island from Fidalgo Head and Allan Island. It is possible to ferry across these currents to reach the island, though you may have to work hard to maintain your position as you cross.

The only landing at the park on Burrows Island is on a gravel beach just north of the light station. The challenge here is scaling the steep rocks adjacent to the old supply-landing facility, which can be precarious in wet weather. Above are the equipment shed and residence building that have been boarded up since the station was automated. The lighthouse and a horn that operates in all weather are located at the point. The Cascadia Marine Trail campsite sits in Alice Bight on the east side of Burrows Island, and as it is bordered by private land, please be respectful. A staircase leads up to two sites, served by a vault

Kayak beached below the Cascadia Marine Trail campsite on Alice Bight of Burrows Island

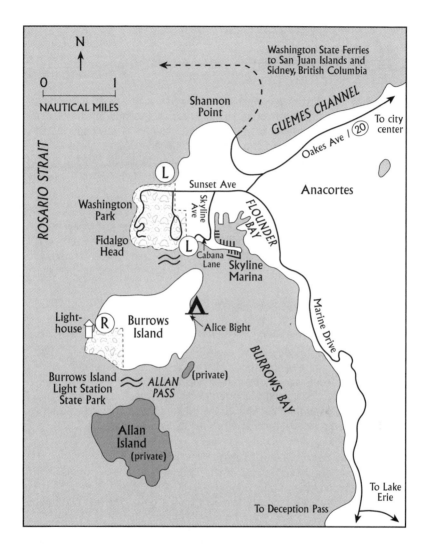

N

0   1
NAUTICAL MILES

ROSARIO STRAIT

Washington State Ferries
to San Juan Islands and
Sidney, British Columbia

Shannon
Point

GUEMES CHANNEL

Oakes Ave / (20)

To city
center

L

Sunset Ave

Anacortes

Washington
Park

Skyline
Ave

FLOUNDER BAY

Fidalgo
Head

L

Cabana
Lane

Skyline
Marina

Light-
house

R

Burrows
Island

Alice Bight

Marine Drive

Burrows Island
Light Station
State Park

ALLAN
PASS

(private)

BURROWS BAY

Allan
Island
(private)

To Lake
Erie

To Deception Pass

toilet farther above. The site is in a thick forest with a great view of the bay and
crescent-shaped sandy beach below.

To the south are wild and rugged grassy slopes above cliffs that drop to
the water, a chance for exploring where few others go. If you would like an
excellent vantage point, follow this shore a few hundred yards around to the
east and climb up the rocks and grassy slopes to the hilltop. To get there from
the light station, walk on the path behind the lighthouse into the trees, as the
shoreline here is not negotiable. Beyond, the trees and brush thin out as you
continue. Be wary of steep drop-offs to the cliffs below. This is no place for
small children.

30 Lummi Island

Though it has most of the amenities of the San Juan Islands, including a Cascadia Marine Trail campsite, Lummi Island, sufficiently off the beaten cruising path to be overlooked by many powerboaters, is very popular with sea kayakers. The southern end has all the ruggedness that makes alongshore paddling so interesting, and a campground to match. This trip could be extended to Clark Island, covered in a separate chapter, which has an alternative route via Lummi Island.

Duration: Overnight.

Rating: *Moderate* or *Exposed*. The *Moderate* route involves currents and some open-water paddling in a channel that can become very rough with southerly winds. The *Exposed* route involves more of the same with potential commitment to miles of paddling in rough conditions.

Navigation Aids: SeaTrails WA 005; NOAA charts 18423 SC, 18421 (both 1:80,000), or 18424 (1:40,000); Rosario Strait current tables or Canadian *Current Atlas.*

Planning Considerations: Moderate currents in Hale Passage affect paddling ease along these shores. Strong currents along Lummi Island's southwest shores can be hazardous against a contrary wind. Watch for the Lummi Island ferry from Gooseberry Point, which runs hourly. If you take the ferry to the island, only cash is accepted for a round-trip fee and is collected on the ferry during each run.

Getting There and Launching

Launch from Gooseberry Point in the Lummi Indian Reservation. From Interstate 5 take Exit 260 (Lummi Island–Slater Road) and turn west onto Slater Road. After almost 4 miles turn left onto Haxton Way. Follow Haxton Way for 6.5 miles to the Lummi Island ferry landing at Gooseberry Point. For overnight parking at Gooseberry Point look for signs for the right lane, which is for ferry traffic. Instead stay in the left lane and turn into the long-term parking across the road from the ferry terminal. For day-use parking, use the lot by the beach north of the dock and behind the store.

As an option you might paddle across Bellingham Bay. (See the Chuckanut Bay chapter.)

You may also want to launch from Lummi Island. Take the ferry across. Fees are collected in cash on the boat. Once on Lummi, take a left onto South Nugent Road. Then a left on Legoe Bay Road. After passing the beach

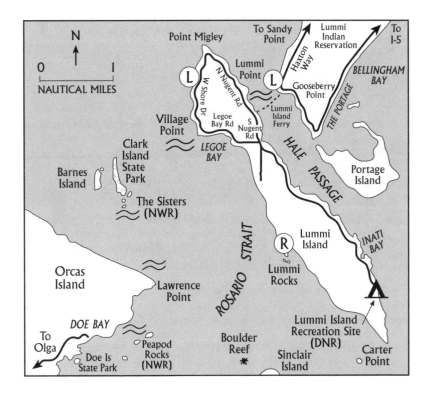

community of Legoe, the road will curve north to West Shore Drive. Follow this along the shoreline past Village Point. Start to look for an unmarked pull-out along the west or left side of the road. This is a public access area with a nice gravel beach. You've gone too far if you've passed the Willows Inn. Make sure to fuel up and buy all your supplies before reaching the island, which has limited resources.

Routes

Hale Passage Loop: *Moderate.* The total paddling distance is about 13 miles. This pleasant overnight trip follows Lummi Island's east shore south to a campsite at one of the more interesting DNR recreation sites. Return can be by the same route or, for a little variation and weather permitting, cross Hale Passage to Portage Island for the return to Gooseberry Point.

Although the crossing from Gooseberry Point to Lummi Point is only about 0.65 mile, swift currents of up to 2 knots can make paddling to the opposite shore tiring, and it can be dangerous in winds opposing the current. Some have experienced six- to eight-foot swells and currents exceeding 4 knots here in these conditions. Flood currents run at 350 degrees true and during extremes

Reef net fishermen in Legoe Bay on Lummi Island

may reach 2.8 knots. Ebb currents run southeast 145 degrees and may reach or exceed 1.8 knots. A 100- to 300-yard-wide shoal extends from Lummi Point approximately 3.6 miles north across Hale Passage to Sandy Point. The shoal can create rough conditions when the wind opposes the current.

Time this crossing for near the slack and then catch the ebb down Lummi Island's shore if possible. Though the alongshore currents are not terribly swift, they are persistent with few eddies to assist, and can be tiring against a contrary tide.

Northern Lummi Island is a mixture of farms and residences. A café, grocery store, and library are near the ferry landing. There is little wild shoreline on the northeastern side as it's heavily developed with beach homes. Along Hale Passage homes become sparser as you come abreast of Portage Island on the opposite shore. The number of homes gradually diminishes as the shoreline steepens and then disappear altogether just north of Inati Bay, where there is also a large gravel pit. Round one more point of land and after this you will find that Lummi Island is wild to the south.

Inati Bay is a fine spot for a stretch onshore, though it is likely boats will be moored there during the cruising season. The Bellingham Yacht Club leases the head of the bay for a private boaters' shore stop. The woods behind are well worth a walk inland, and there is an old road that eventually leads to the main road from the north.

The Lummi Island DNR recreation site is less than 1 mile south of Inati Bay and is nestled among rocky shores that gradually become steeper as you travel south. This DNR site, which also carries Cascadia Marine Trail status, is a particularly interesting one as it is fitted into the rocky benches of a steep hillside. Steps and switchbacking trails connect two tiny coves to upland campsites that make use of every level spot. The result is a remote-feeling campsite especially attractive to kayakers because it provides poor moorage for other boats with no protection against southerly blows. The campsites are more secluded than those at similar recreation areas, making this a nice resting place even if others are present. As with other DNR sites there is no water service, but picnic tables and vault toilets are provided. In the summer months this site has become increasingly busy due to its easy access from the mainland. Practice minimum impact camping for this site. The Whatcom Area Kayak Enthusiasts club (WAKE) maintains the site.

At this point the Hale Passage loop route turns back to the north. You can opt to cross to Portage Island for the return if currents will be against you. They will probably be slower along the shallow eastern shore of Hale Passage. Portage Island, part of the Lummi Indian Reservation, is quite wild with beaches fronting on woods and meadows beyond. Landings are prohibited for nontribal members without permission. The island is connected to the mainland by a spit that dries at midtide.

Lummi Island Circumnavigation: *Exposed.* The total paddling distance is approximately 19 miles. The portion from Gooseberry Point south along Hale Passage is described above in the Hale Passage Loop route. The description continues south from Lummi Island Recreation Site.

Venturing south toward Carter Point and around to the southwest side of Lummi Island takes you into a world of unforgiving rocky shorelines and steep, narrow beaches backed by talus slopes. There are few opportunities for anything but an uncomfortable emergency bivouac should the weather turn against you. After rounding the point, the shore is a continuous scree slope punctuated by cliffs that rise abruptly to the ridgeline. It gradually ascends toward 1600-foot Lummi Peak as you move north. Viti Rocks, a San Juan Islands National Wildlife Refuge can be seen offshore to the west.

There are few haul-outs until you are opposite Lummi Rocks where the country gradually flattens. Lummi Rocks, owned by the Bureau of Land Management and leased to Western Washington University for research and education, is a nice spot for a lunch stop and a stroll over its grassy knolls. There are no facilities here and camping is not recommended.

Pastoral and residential developments appear gradually as you move north from Lummi Rocks, though most are kept at bay from the shore by bluffs until you start approaching Village Point.

Just south of Village Point, the eclectic beach community of Legoe is home to the Lummi reef net fishing fleet. In salmon season, dozens of barges anchored to offshore reefs use ladder-like structures to spot schools of sockeye as they swim by. This has been a Lummi people tradition for centuries—a few modern tools have been added but the basic concept remains the same. Current can run swiftly around Village Point.

Rounding Point Migley the shore is low, mostly sandy beach with residential housing. If a stiff north wind is blowing, crashing surf can easily build.

As you return to your start at Gooseberry Point, the same considerations for current hold in Hale Passage as at the trip's beginning. Try to cross at near slack and time your return with an ebb to make for easy southward paddling.

31 Chuckanut Bay

The rocks around Chuckanut Bay make this Bellingham-area trip an interesting exploration. Convoluted hollows and the delicate saltwater-eroded Chuckanut sandstone formations, fossilized remnants of ancient palm trunks, and even a long-gone artist's sculpture on a seaside rock reward the curious paddler.

Duration: Part day to full day.

Rating: *Protected* or *Moderate.* The longer *Moderate* route is exposed to southerly seas. Rocky shores could make landings difficult if the weather takes a bad turn.

Navigation Aids: SeaTrails WA 005; NOAA charts 18424 (1:40,000) or 18423 SC; Port Townsend tide table (add about 45 minutes) for launch at Chuckanut Park.

Planning Considerations: Plan for higher tide levels or an incoming tide for paddling south of Wildcat Cove and in Chuckanut Bay. The southern portion of Chuckanut can dry out up to 1 mile from shore on lower tides.

Getting There and Launching

All five launch points are accessible from State Route 11, also called Chuckanut Drive.

Boulevard Park: This extensive waterfront park has been the location for local paddling races. It has extensive parking, restrooms, picnic tables, and even a coffee shop. Enter the water on the north side. From Bellingham, take North State Street, which becomes Boulevard Street. Just past Adams Avenue where Boulevard Street becomes 11th Street, take a right into the park.

Harris Street: The Harris Street boat ramp is in Fairhaven, really part of south Bellingham. Take Harris Street west from SR 11 0.25 mile and turn right just before Fairhaven Boatworks. Keep right, outside the chain-link fence, to the boat ramp. Kayaks are available for rental next door. Parking is limited during busy weekends.

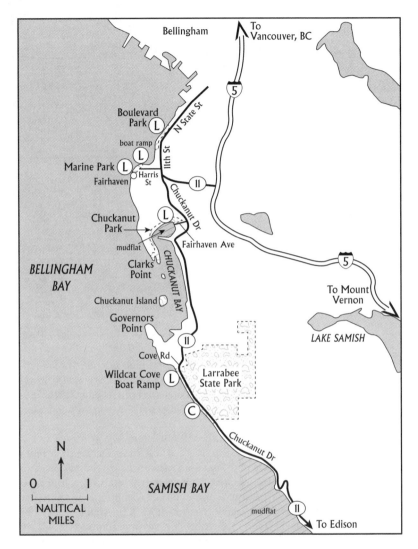

Marine Park: This tidy little park with picnic tables and restrooms is at the end of Harris Street just past the Alaska Marine Highway ferry terminal and a boatyard. There is ample parking, yet it often fills on summer days. Launch, best at mid- or low tides, on the sand and gravel beach. If you plan an overnight, pull your car back out onto the street or park in the paved lot across from the ferry terminal.

Chuckanut Park: The park is located in a cove in the northern part of Chuckanut Bay and provides the only access for the *Protected* route in the bay.

Paddlers enjoying the sea-sculpted sandstone shorelines at Larrabee State Park

However, this cove dries to extensive mudflats, so high-tide use is required. Follow SR 11 1.5 miles south from Fairhaven to Fairhaven Avenue (formerly 21st Street). In 0.4 mile the road dead-ends at the water's edge. Parking is limited with only two spots. There are no facilities at this park, which is day-use only.

Wildcat Cove: About 1 mile south of Chuckanut Bay, Wildcat Cove is part of Larrabee State Park. Follow SR 11 south from Fairhaven 5 miles to Cove Road. Follow it downhill, turn left after crossing the railway, and go straight into the boat launch area. Launch on the gravel beach next to the boat ramp. Overnight parking is not allowed. Camping is an option at Larrabee State Park, which is a mile farther down Chuckanut Drive. For safety, there is a PFD (lifejacket) loan kiosk for paddlers and boaters. Heavy seaweed builds on the shore in late summer creating a mess in removing boats from the water.

Routes

Chuckanut Bay: *Protected.* Make loops as long or as short as you like. Stay within the shallow cove at Chuckanut Park or paddle up to 4 miles around the entire bay. With the exception of the park and Chuckanut Island, all shorelines are private with some Burlington Northern right-of-way. There are fine rocks to view within the cove before paddling under the railroad bridge to the larger bay. Clarks Point has a very attractive inner bay with four fossilized palm-tree trunks in the rocks. They are easily examined from your boat. Across Chuckanut Bay east of Clarks Point is a rocky outcrop and some small beaches along the railroad. This area is known as Teddy Bear Cove; Bellingham area residents use it as a nude sunbathing and swimming area.

Chuckanut Island is owned by The Nature Conservancy, which allows stops ashore but no camping or fires. There are no facilities on the island, and they ask that you stay on the trail that rings the island. At high tide a small beach on the southwest side is the best landing with a steep scramble to the island above. On lower tides beaches on the north and southeast are uncovered. The latter landing is surrounded by interesting rocks but lacks access to the upper island.

Fairhaven to Wildcat Cove: *Moderate:* This 5-mile trip is best done with a 6-mile car shuttle between the Harris Street or Marine Park launch and Wildcat Cove. It can be shortened 1 mile with a high-tide launch at Chuckanut Park. The Fairhaven end can begin with a tour of shipyards and the southern terminus of the Alaska Marine Highway.

To the south the railroad parallels the shore with two miniature coves behind it. They can be reached under low bridges. The second provides an exciting sluice under the bridge at midtide. Beyond, watch for a rock just above high tide that a sculptor rendered many years ago. Add as much of Chuckanut Bay as you like to the route (see *Protected* route above for features). Governors Point defines the south end of Chuckanut Bay. South of here the eroded rocks take on a delicate lacy quality.

Wildcat Cove South: *Protected* to *Moderate.* Paddling south from Wildcat Cove you'll see more interesting rock formations, craggy steep forested cliffs rising far above the water, and a few tiny pocket beaches. In summer, college kids can be seen jumping off the large boulders that line the shore. Sightings of otter and harbor seals are common. There is no water access from the main section of Larrabee State Park or farther south until you reach Edison. Follow this route for as long as you like but beware of the extensive mudflats that develop in lower tides. Pass Taylor Shellfish Farms toward the southern section and notice the mini lighthouse in front of the facility. The steep mountainous coastline below Chuckanut Drive continues to Colony Creek where it begins to flatten into Samish Bay.

32 Hood Head

Shine Tidelands State Park, north of the Hood Canal Bridge, features an interesting bay, lagoon, and a gravel spit, all preserved in this undeveloped state park. All this, plus easy access make this a nice afternoon's destination or easy overnight trip using the Cascadia Marine Trail site on Hood Head. Ducks, herons, and other waterfowl are plentiful in the lagoon during the winter months. The alongshore paddling and largely protected waters constitute a suitable trip for new kayakers. Paddling at Hood Head could be combined with other paddling routes in the area, such as Port Gamble and Mats Mats Bay trip (see the Mats Mats Bay chapter).

Duration: Part day or overnight.

Rating: *Protected* or *Moderate.*

Navigation Aids: SeaTrails WA 105; NOAA chart 18477 (1:25,000) or 18445 SC (1:80,000); Port Townsend tide table.

Planning Considerations: Midtide or higher required to explore the inner lagoon. Respect private property signs by staying off the spit near homes. Watch for wind waves off Hood Head.

Driftwood dragon on Point Hannon of Hood Head

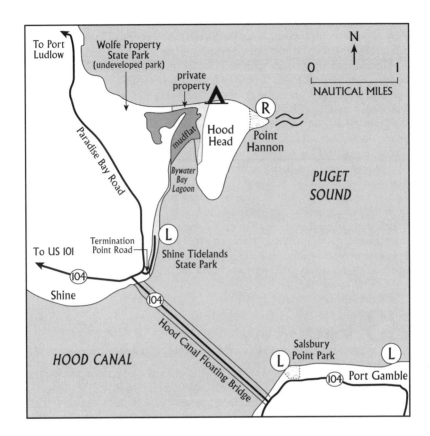

Getting There and Launching

Shine Tidelands State Park: Access is simple, just turn down Termination Point Road immediately north of the west end of the Hood Canal Bridge. Follow it north (left) where it dead-ends at the Shine Tidelands State Park. Launch on the gravel beach. This is a day-use-only park with a toilet and picnic table. A Discover Pass is required to park here.

Alternative launches include Port Gamble, Salsbury Point Park, Twin Spits on Foulweather Bluff, Port Ludlow, Shine, and Mats Mats Bay.

Routes

Bywater Bay Round Trip: *Protected*. Launching from Shine Tidelands State Park, the paddling distance is about 4 miles. Follow the beach north to the entrance just short of the spit connecting Hood Head to the mainland. You may encounter some current at the entrance to the bay, but probably not enough to cause any problems. At higher tides you can paddle southwest to grassy flats bordering alder forest that make a good spot for a picnic stop, some bird-watching, and exploration. This inner lagoon area is called the Wolfe

Property State Park, which is undeveloped. The lagoon dries during lower tides. Stay off the spit where private property signs are posted.

Hood Head Circumnavigation: *Protected* to *Moderate.* Add 2 miles to the lagoon round trip. Rounding Hood Head, enjoy the large driftwood dragon sculpture on Point Hannon, part of the Wolfe Property. Measuring nearly 30 feet long, the dragon is worth a peek. Wind waves can create surf south of the point. Make sure you secure your boat high on the beach if you plan on going ashore. Rounding the north side of the point, the Cascadia Marine Trail site is located halfway between the point and where the lagoon spit begins. The campsite has a vault toilet, two tent sites, and great views north toward Marrowstone and Whidbey islands.

You might also get as close as you ever will to a passing Trident submarine from the Bangor base to the south of the bridge. Stay a considerable distance from the sub if you do see one. You will be able to paddle across the spit only on the highest tides; otherwise a short carry is needed above midtide. The mud-flats are extensive south of the spit on the lowest tides. Some of the tidelands south of Point Hannon are privately owned and are marked accordingly.

33 Mats Mats Bay

This quiet little bay north of Port Ludlow is just right for paddling practice or touring anchored yachts. The bay has a pastoral feel to it, with residences generally low key and set back from the shore. A narrow, tree-lined entrance leads out to interesting offshore rocks, popular with divers, less than 0.5 mile away. You can extend this trip by paddling to or from Port Ludlow about 3 miles away.

Duration: Part day.

Rating: *Protected.*

Navigation Aids: SeaTrails 105; NOAA chart 18445 SC (1:80,000, see 1:40,000 inset).

Planning Considerations: The steep rocky shoreline outside the bay's entrance can create rough conditions during high tides due to refracted waves and few places to land. Aside from the boat ramp, there are no public shorelines along this route.

Getting There and Launching

From State Route 104, turn north on Paradise Bay Road just west of the Hood Canal Bridge. Follow this 6 miles, passing Port Ludlow, to the intersection with Oak Bay Road. Turn right and go another 2 miles and turn right on Verner Road. Go 0.5 mile to the launching ramp on Mats Mats Bay. The launch has

The protected waters of Mats Mats Bay

a restroom, picnic table, a big parking lot, an antiquated boat ramp, and a floating dock. Put in on the beach to the right of the dock.

Route

The bay and entrance, plenty to see on their own, make a 2-mile loop if you follow the shore passing moored recreational boats, commercial fishing boats, and beach homes. The entrance to the bay narrows to less than 100 yards with range markers to guide larger craft through. There are a few homes on the northern shore.

Paddle out to Klas and Colvos rocks if the weather isn't too windy, as these are great to explore on calm days. The rocks can be covered in harbor seals so keep a distance of 100 yards. On a trip there once, a dozen seals entered the water as I paddled by and followed me discreetly for a half mile. Enjoy views to the north of Marrowstone Island and to the south of Foulweather Point and Hood Canal. Colvos Rock, the largest of the offshore rocks in the area, is a poor place to get out of your boat—it's about 50 feet across, barren, and too

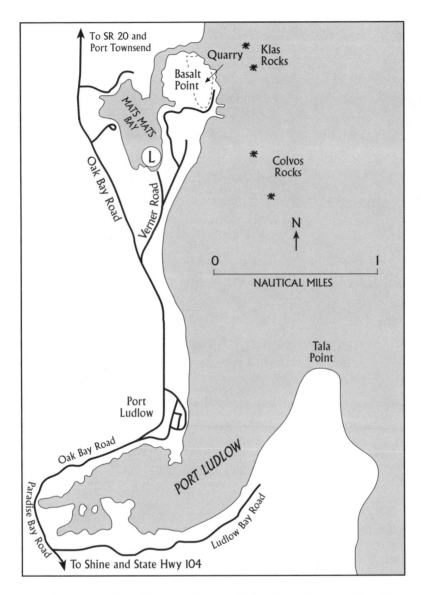

steep for easy landings. The round trip to Colvos Rock from the Mats Mats Bay boat launch is 3 miles. You might also paddle south toward Port Ludlow.

A quarry and gravel operation occupies the real estate for almost a mile south of the bay entrance. Though there are a few beaches unaffected by the work behind, do not go ashore.

34 Indian Island

Located less than two hours from Seattle, Indian and Marrowstone islands are a quick getaway with scenery and paddling opportunities rivaling those of the San Juan Islands to the north. Somewhat off the beaten path, the islands provide solitude with miles of seemingly untouched beaches, tidal estuaries, protected coves, and a rural landscape. The southern section of Indian Island is known for its sandy beaches, interesting geological features, and madronas that overhang the shore. Swift currents run below the bridge connecting the island to the mainland, giving paddlers a free ride. The rest of the island is home to the Naval Undersea Warfare Engineering Station, which is off-limits to the public. The naval base won a conservation award for management of its wildlands, and there's little visual evidence of any base at all. There are three Cascadia Marine Trail sites on the island.

Duration: Full day or overnight.

Rating: *Protected* or *Moderate. Moderate* route involves some fast-water paddling and possible tide rips for a short distance.

Navigation Aids: SeaTrails WA 103, 105; NOAA charts 18423 SC (1:80,000), 18471 (1:40,000), or 18464 (1:20,000); Port Townsend tide table and Deception Pass current table with corrections for Port Townsend Canal.

Planning Considerations: Coordinating your launch time with high tide will dramatically reduce the carrying distance at the Marrowstone Island–Indian Island causeway and will aid in catching favorable currents. At low tide the portage is at least 300 yards of tide flats; high tide reduces it to as little as 75 feet. Also plan for favorable current in Port Townsend Canal. Make sure to stay 200 yards off the Naval Base on Indian Island.

Getting There and Launching

From the Seattle ferries, follow signs to the Hood Canal Bridge. As soon as you cross the bridge, take your first right to Paradise Bay Road. Follow north to Port Ludlow, then take the a right onto Oak Bay Road (State Route 116). You'll pass Mats Mats Bay (chapter 33) and continue north. In a few miles, you'll see signs to Fort Flagler—Marrowstone and Indian Islands. Take a right on Flagler Road.

From Port Hadlock, take Oak Bay Road (SR 116) south until you see the Fort Flagler—Marrowstone and Indian Island signs. Take a left onto Flagler Road.

Oak Bay County Park: The first possible launch is from Portage Way just before the turn to Indian and Marrowstone islands. Oak Bay County Park provides access to the southern end of the islands and Port Townsend Canal, and is a Cascadia Marine Trail site. It has one site, is $15 per night, and has toilets and water. No fires allowed. Fort Flagler is 7.8 miles away, and Port Hadlock is 1.6 miles away. Watch for boating traffic, fast current, and rips in the canal.

Port Hadlock Marina: This launch is on Oak Bay Road (SR 116) just before the turn off to Indian and Marrowstone islands if you're headed south. It's one block south of Port Hadlock town center. Take a left on Lower Hadlock Road and follow to the marina. Park on the dirt lot north of the Ajax Café by the estuary. No facilities are provided. Launch at the beach to the right of the marina dock. This puts you on the north side of the Port Townsend Canal.

Portage Beach: Take Flagler Road off Oak Bay (SR 116) and follow over the canal bridge. As soon as you cross the bridge, take an immediate right into the lot at Portage Beach. Watch for speedy traffic along Flagler Road. There's a Cascadia Marine Trail site for four sites in the bushes on the south side of the lot, but they are only accessible from the water. The boat carry is down a grassy 100-yard hill. A portable toilet is provided but no fires are allowed. The park, which is managed by Jefferson County, has extensive sandy beaches to the south and a great view and access to the canal. Twenty-five yards past the bridge to the north is the end of the public access, and where the Naval property begins. Keep 200 yards off the shore beyond this point.

Indian Island County Park: Drive approximately 0.75 mile beyond the Indian Island bridge. Ample parking is available with launching on sand or gravel beaches, which are dry for a considerable distance at low tide. Plan your launch or take-out for higher tides. This also happens to be a popular clamming spot if you are so inclined.

Marrowstone Island–Indian Island Causeway: Follow Flagler Road to the south end of Indian Island and park on the right off the road just before the isthmus that connects both islands. Enjoy views north to Port Townsend and south toward Mats Mats Bay. Watch for fast drivers here as they come off the hill on Marrowstone Island. In previous editions of this book it was recommended to run the current through the causeway culvert below the road. Since the last printing, barnacles and other debris have filled the bottom third of each tunnel making it impossible for a safe run through. This is a portage over the roadway at high tide. Low tide means a 300-yard slog through tide flats on both sides.

Mystery Bay State Park on Marrowstone Island: Use Mystery Bay State Park to access the water by Nordland. The park area has ample parking, toilets, a picnic table, and easy access to a sand and gravel beach as well as a boat ramp. Take Flagler Road north up Marrowstone Island and turn left just past Nordland and the oyster farm. A Discover Pass is required for parking here.

Fort Flagler State Park: Take Flagler Road to the north end of Marrowstone Island and into Fort Flagler State Park. You have three options to launch here.

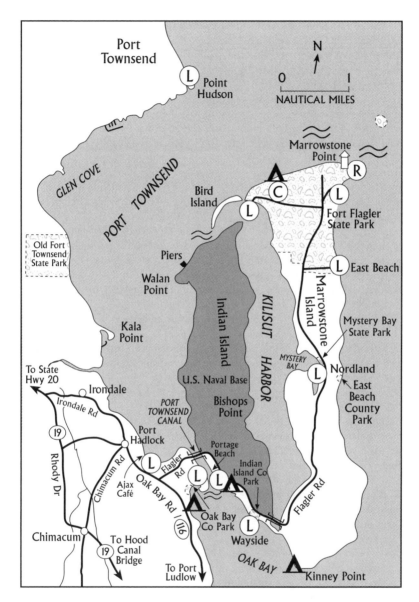

For Kilisut Harbor, take a left inside the park following signs to the camping area. Launch from the boat ramp and park nearby. A Discover Pass is required for day and overnight parking. There's a lot of camping here plus a Cascadia Marine Trail site (water access only) on the east side of the campground. A small store, toilets, and other amenities make this a full-service launch.

The second launch from Fort Flagler is on the east side of the park. As you enter the park, take a right on Wansboro Road and follow it to the beach. There's room for a few parking spots, and the sandy beach is a short distance away. The wharf that used to be at this location has been recently removed. There are no facilities.

You can also launch from Marrowstone Point south of the lighthouse. As you enter the park, continue on Flagler Road past the buildings and parade ground and follow signs to the lighthouse. After you go down the hill on the one lane road to the beach, park on your right. Restrooms and picnic tables are provided.

Routes

Indian Island Circumnavigation: *Moderate.* The total paddling distance is 11 miles. Launch from any of the sites listed above—Portage Beach, Indian Island County Park, Oak Bay County Park, or Port Hadlock.

Indian Island is an interesting blend of attractive "forbidden fruit," a restricted government property, surrounded by accessible public lands. Most of the island is occupied by the Naval Undersea Warfare Engineering Station, which stores ships' ammunition, reportedly nonnuclear. There are piers and buildings along the northwestern shore, but the remainder of the shoreline is remarkably pristine. The navy employs a wildlife biologist to manage the island's habitat, and the station won national honors in a Department of Defense conservation award for its management.

However, landings within the station boundaries are strictly prohibited to 200 yards. Nonetheless, cruising along the station's shorelines is a pleasant interlude with a largely undisturbed environment. Plus, there are plenty of places on non-navy property to stretch your legs. Look for river otter along the rocky shores.

The southern end of Indian Island, on both sides, has interesting sandstone formations with embedded nodules of harder rock that have eroded into studded surfaces, some forming tiny bridges like handles. Look for these south of Bishops Point on the Kilisut Harbor side and just north of the Port Townsend Canal on the west side.

If you are launching from the southern end of Indian Island, Mystery Bay State Park on Marrowstone Island is the first chance for a shore stop, about 2 miles north of the causeway. There are toilets, picnic facilities, and the quaint Nordland Store nearby in Nordland. Mystery Bay is lined with recreational boats, beach homes, and has a coastal New England feel.

Following the west shore of Indian Island south out of Kilisut Harbor involves an hour or so of paddling along shores with no opportunities to get out. A good plan is to take a stretch break at Fort Flagler beforehand. It has a wonderful beach over a mile in length. Besides a Cascadia Marine Trail site, Fort Flagler has picnic facilities, bathrooms with running water, and a concession stand that sells snacks during the summer months. The six Cascadia Marine Trail sites are secluded in the woods just east of the main campground.

The western edge of the harbor is a low sand spit covered with grass and connected to the park at low tide. Called Bird Island locally, its southern end

Port Townsend Canal from Portage Beach and the Cascadia Marine Trail campsite on Indian Island

is a popular place for large groups of seals to haul out. Paddling out through the channel you may find yourself surrounded by fifty or more of them. On the flood, enjoy a light tide rip through a break in the spit.

Be sure to honor the navy's requirement that you stay 600 feet from their docks at Walan Point and at Crane Point one mile to the south. Also remember that you must stay at least 200 yards from any naval vessel. Just beyond Crane Point is an inviting park facility, but it's for naval personnel only.

You could make a 1.5-mile detour west to Port Hadlock before entering Port Townsend Canal. There is a private marina, a very popular shoreside café called the Ajax Café, and the town's center a few blocks up from the water. The Northwest School for Wooden Boat Building has a branch in Port Hadlock across from the Ajax Café. Lodging is available in the historic cabins by the café. You can also launch from the beach by the café.

The navy's property line on Indian Island turns inland at the midpoint of a shell beach just north of the narrows of Port Townsend Canal. Immediately south are excellent stops ashore in the beginning of the county's parklands. Also south of the beach is the old Indian–Marrowstone ferry landing.

Port Townsend Canal has currents of up to 3 knots. Shore eddies form, except between the jetties at the southern end, where you have no choice but to fight the current if it is against you. Otherwise, if the water level is high enough, you can opt to paddle behind the jetty on the Indian Island side. Fairly large rips can form in the channel at the downstream end of the narrows, which may be dangerous for paddlers inexperienced with rough water.

Adjoining the southern end of the canal are Oak Bay County Park on the west side and Indian Island County Park on the east side. The sand and gravel tide flats are productive clamming areas. Both parks have outhouses, picnic tables, and fresh water. Oak Bay County Park is also the location of a Cascadia Marine Trail group area with two tent sites in summer and one from October 31 to May 1. Beware, during higher tides the sites may flood.

From the south entrance of Port Townsend Canal, it is but a brief paddle back to your start at the Marrowstone Island–Indian Island causeway.

A paddle-in-only Cascadia Marine Trail campsite is located at Kinney Point, on the south end of Marrowstone Island. Kinney Point has two tent sites and a vault toilet; no fires are allowed.

Fort Flagler State Park and Kilisut Harbor: *Protected.* Choose your own paddling distance. This area is popular for short trips in the warmer protected waters. It is also a good place for new paddlers to work on their skills. Be careful of the entrance channel to Kilisut Harbor, which can run at more than 1 knot.

35 Marrowstone Island

Originally named "Marrow-Stone Point" in 1792 by explorer George Vancouver, Marrowstone Island later gained popularity between 1920 to the 1940s for production of premium turkeys. On the north end of Marrowstone is Fort Flagler, a coastal defense fort constructed in 1898 to keep invaders from attacking Puget Sound. Now a 784-acre state park, Fort Flagler provides hiking trails, beach access, building rentals for educational groups, and fortifications to explore. The rest of the island is comprised of beautiful rural farms, an oyster farm, and vacation homes. Located a little over an hour from Seattle, the island is easy to access for a quick escape.

Duration: Full day or overnight.

Rating: *Protected, Moderate,* or *Exposed.* The *Protected* route includes mellow Kilisut Harbor and Scow Bay; the *Moderate* route involves some fast-water paddling and possible tide rips for a short distance. The *Exposed* route includes Marrowstone Point for its fast current, tide rips, and surf from shipping traffic.

Navigation Aids: SeaTrails WA 103, 105; NOAA charts 18423 SC (1:80,000), 18471 (1:40,000), or 18464 (1:20,000); Port Townsend tide table and Deception Pass current table with corrections for Port Townsend Canal.

Planning Considerations: Plan your travel for the currents and for wind on the east side. Shipping traffic and high wind can produce large surf on Marrowstone Point and along the eastern side of the island.

Getting There and Launching

Use the Indian Island directions above (chapter 34). If you prefer, launch at Oak Bay or Port Hadlock instead of driving to the island. Also consider Portage Beach, Indian Island County Park, or the islands' causeway for launching from Indian Island.

After crossing the Port Townsend Canal bridge, follow Flagler Road down Indian Island and across the narrow isthmus connecting both islands. Curve north (left) on Flagler Road driving past rural farms heading north up Marrowstone Island. Visit the Nordland Store to get supplies and a taste of the easygoing island community. Across the street are kayak rentals for Mystery Bay, a quiet bay with an oyster production business, fishing boats, and eclectic beach homes. North of Nordland about 300 yards is Mystery Bay State Park, which provides a protected launch for Kilisut Harbor.

Fort Flagler State Park: Continue north on Flagler Road to Fort Flagler State Park. Either launch from the campground boat ramp, at Marrowstone Point south of the lighthouse, or via the east side of the park from Wansboro Road. See directions on the Indian Island trip. Display your Discover Pass when parking.

East Beach: To launch from the east side of the island, go past Nordland about a quarter mile and take a right on East Beach Road. This will take you to the beach in about a mile. This is a day-use facility with picnic tables and a sandy beach.

Marrowstone Point from Fort Flagler State Park, Marrowstone Island

Route

The circumnavigation of the island is 15 miles. Launch from any of the sites listed and work with the currents and wind for your preferable direction. There is a Cascadia Marine Trail site on the northwest corner of Fort Flagler State Park, and on the south side of the island on Kinney Point. Optional marine trail sites are on Indian Island south of the bridge at Portage Beach and across the channel at Oak Bay County Park.

Starting from the south end of Indian Island head southeast past several estuaries with sloughs that empty to mudflats at low tides. As you near Marrowstone, the shore begins to rise to a medium bluff with a few homes above. On the very south side of the island look for a seasonal stream, which is the location for Kinney Point, a Cascadia Marine Trail site. The trail leads you to a kayak storage rack. Kinney Point has a vault toilet, two sites, and is best reached on higher tides to avoid a long carry. Campfires aren't allowed nor is sleeping on the beach. Rounding the point and heading north along Puget Sound, Lip Lip Point is about three-quarters of a mile past Kinney Point. Known for its rocky shores, this is a great place for tide pooling. A few miles past Lip Lip is East Beach, a county park and launch. Few facilities are available. For the next several miles high bluffs rise above the beach, providing solitude with empty beaches, even on the hottest summer days.

As you near the lighthouse on Marrowstone Point, a wide sandy crescent beach is a sign of entering Fort Flagler State Park. A low sandy point juts out into the Sound below the bluffs giving the lighthouse an extended view into Admiralty Inlet. Fishing and beachcombing are popular near the point. Give anglers extra space when passing by. There are no facilities aside from a restroom and picnic table. An eddy occurs on the south side of the point on flood tides, and on ebbs expect a strong pull to the point. Give the point a wide berth in heavy wind, which can produce chop near shore. Keep your eye on passing ships as they can produce a sizeable surf wave on the north side.

A noisy tide rip north of the point can be heard from the bluffs above. Keep your distance if you're not comfortable with rough water—but for those who are, it's a fun source of standing waves.

On the north side of Marrowstone Point where the bluff rises again above the beach, a concrete bunker can be seen hanging from the cliff. This is Battery Lee, a searchlight battery whose dark tunnels we enjoyed while playing hooky at a music camp there in the 1970s. Above Battery Lee are several larger coastal defense fortifications once equipped with twelve-inch guns designed to fire a shell 15 miles into Admiralty Inlet. Dark tunnels and slit window pill boxes make for an interesting side trip. There's a rough trail in the woods below Battery Lee that leads up the hill. Above the bluffs is a commanding view of Port Townsend, Whidbey Island, and Mount Rainer far to the south.

High bluffs continue along Marrowstone Head all the way to the state park campground a few miles west. Here the flood current splits in half as it hits shore sending some to the east and the rest to the west. Occasional chunks of concrete can be found on the beach, remnants of the fort above, eroding away.

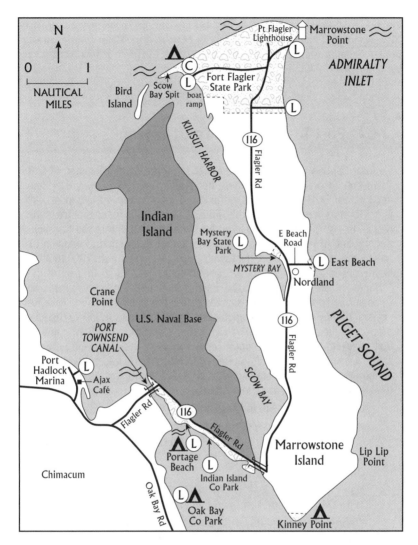

The beach is mostly gravel, with some sand and larger rocks. The state park has full facilities including a small store.

Birders will enjoy Scow Bay Spit, which extends east into Kilisut Harbor from Fort Flagler. On a flood, shoot the current through the gap in the spit and head south to the mostly bucolic Kilisut Harbor. At this point, choose whether to turn south to Kilisut Harbor, or continue west to go around Indian Island. (See chapter 34.)

Alternative day trips for Marrowstone Island: Launch from East Beach and paddle to Marrowstone Point; launch from Indian Island or Oak Bay on a low tide to enjoy the tide pooling at Lip Lip Point on the southeast corner of Marrowstone. If you like to surf, launch at Marrowstone Point and time southbound shipping traffic for surf on the east side of the point below Battery Lee. Bring a helmet if you do, the beach here is rocky.

36 Port Townsend to Point Wilson

Explorer Captain George Vancouver noted that the current location of Port Townsend, located on the northern tip of Quimper Peninsula, had a "fine deep harbor." Like many towns in the Puget Sound area, "PT," as locals call it, got its start in the 1850s. By the 1880s, it was the hub for commerce in the region. In 1887, Tacoma was picked for the northwest link to the transcontinental line of the Union Pacific railroad. Commerce began to wane in PT and by the 1893 depression, the town's population went from 7000 to 2000 nearly overnight. In 1898, the US government chose PT to be part of the "Triangle of Fire," a ring of coastal defense forts aimed at keeping invading ships at bay. Fort Worden's guns aimed across the Strait of Juan de Fuca for years until they were considered obsolete by the airplane. In the 1970s, PT's property values were cheap, which attracted artists of all kinds who in turn built a strong creative community. Today Fort Worden's "Centrum" organization uses the former fort's grounds to bring world class cultural events to the area, including a fiddling festival, a jazz and blues festival, a much renowned film festival, and other events.

Duration: Part day to full day.

Rating: *Protected* or *Moderate.* Confined waters in some conditions and slightly moderate in others make this a good place for new kayakers. The paddling is easy and scenic with few likely challenges.

Navigation Aids: SeaTrails WA 103; NOAA chart 18465 (1:80,000) or 18471 (1:40,000); Port Townsend tide table (subtract 30 minutes).

Planning Considerations: Wind from the south or northwest can affect this route. Ship wakes may break on the shore inside Point Wilson.

Getting There and Launching

Port Townsend Boat Haven: Entering Port Townsend on State Route 20 (also Sims Way), drive to the bottom of the big hill toward downtown. At the bottom, take a right at Port Townsend Brewing onto Haines Place. Follow this through the shipyard to the water. You'll see a small shorefront parking strip with beach access. Parking is day use. Watch for bicycles on the biking trail along the waterfront. At low tides the carry to beach can be about 100 yards. For additional information: www.portofpt.com/boat_haven.htm.

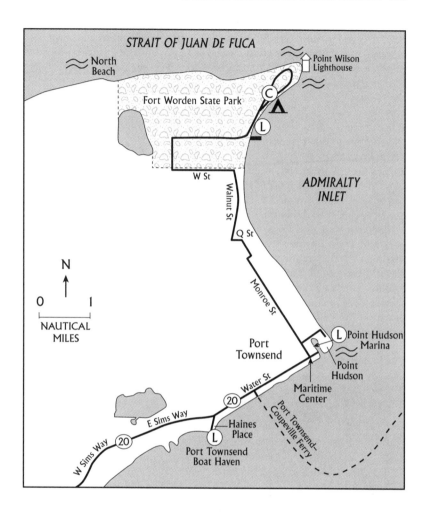

Point Hudson Marina: Located on the southeast corner of downtown by a full-service marina, this is a great launch for paddling near the city center and to access destinations such as Fort Flagler or Point Wilson. The launch has plenty of parking, restrooms, laundry, showers, and camping. Restaurants and other services are a short walk from the marina. Watch for breaking waves on the point where the launch beach rounds the corner toward the waterfront, (east). For additional information: www.portofpt.com/point_hudson.htm.

Fort Worden State Park: From downtown Port Townsend, take Water Street through the city center. Just before Point Hudson Marina or Maritime Center, take a left on Monroe Street. Follow Monroe north and swerve onto Jackson Street. Jackson will go up the hill and curve left into Q Street. Take a right on Walnut Street and follow this as it curves left into W Street. Look for signs to enter Fort Worden State Park. Once in the park, follow signs to the beach. As you go down the hill to the beach, park by the wharf and small boat marina. A boat ramp goes to the water in a very protected launch protected on three sides by the wharf. A Cascadia Marine Trail site is located in the main camping area below the bluff.

Route

If launching from the shipyard, be cautious of the ferry terminal. Give ferries a wide berth and don't cross in front of a moving boat.

Enjoy views of downtown historic Port Townsend and its grand Victorian architecture. A town with deep roots in boat building, you may see various types of wooden boats moored or sailing nearby. On a sunny day, the Cascades can be seen to the east and the steep sandstone bluffs of Marrowstone Island and Fort Flagler to the south.

Paddling west past Point Hudson, the bluffs of the residential neighborhoods of Port Townsend begin to rise majestically above Admiralty Inlet. Madrona trees stretch out over the embankment with sight of a few homes above. About a mile from downtown, the bluffs lower to the border of Fort Worden State Park. From the water you can see the old fort's orderly Officer's Quarters above you. The beach below is sandy and crescent shaped. A sandy beach on the south side of the Quartermaster's Wharf is a good rest stop. A restroom is located across the street and in summer a small café offers basic

The historic Port Townsend waterfront

snacks. Beyond the wharf, the sandy beach curves toward Point Wilson and its historic lighthouse built in 1915. Prominently placed on the tip of the point, the lighthouse can be seen for miles even without its blinking light. On busy summer days, anglers can be seen lined up around the point—give them plenty of room. Ship wakes wrap around the point and into the bay providing surfable waves. Land anywhere along here to take a stroll to the lighthouse or to explore the pre–World War I gun emplacements on the point. On the forested bluff above the beach, several rows of concrete gun emplacements provide a commanding view of the Strait of Juan de Fuca and Admiralty Inlet.

The waters off Point Wilson can get very rough from wind and ocean swell. Don't venture around the point unless you have strong experience in rough water and surf. A noticeable tide rip occurs northwest of the point—fun surfable standing waves for some, a hazard to others. There have been several kayakers rescued off the point in recent years. Currents can pull unsuspecting paddlers into the frigid fast moving waters of Admiralty Inlet. Experienced paddlers might want to venture around the point toward North Beach on the eastern border of the park. The beach in between is of gravel and boulders. Watch for breaking waves at North Beach. Current can run a few knots along this stretch. Plan your trip with the current to avoid a long slog back to your launch.

37 Sequim Bay–Protection Island–Diamond Point Loop

Three-quarters of the seabirds in Puget Sound nest on Protection Island, including about 17,000 pairs of rhinoceros auklets, glaucous-winged gulls, pelagic cormorants, tufted puffins, pigeon guillemots, double-crested cormorants, and black oystercatchers. The island is also a pupping and hauling area for about 600 harbor seals. Explorer George Vancouver named the island noting how it protected the entry to Discovery Bay. With a colorful history, the government owned and sold it in the 1860s. It was a farm for awhile, then in the 1940s an out-of-control beach fire burned the entire island. The island almost became a 1100-unit housing development in 1968 until environmentalists stopped construction. In 1988, the island became a National Wildlife Refuge partially managed by the US and Washington State Fish and Wildlife Service. There is no public access on the island to protect wildlife, and paddlers must stay 200 yards offshore of the island. The last time I was there, I could hear the island birds 1 mile away from Diamond Point and a whale breaching in the distance.

Duration: Part day to full day.

Rating: *Protected* or *Exposed.* Confined waters and alongshore routes make this a good place for new kayakers. The paddling is easy and scenic with few likely challenges.

Navigation Aids: SeaTrails WA 103; NOAA chart 18465 (1:80,000) or 18471 (1:40,000); Port Townsend tide table (subtract 30 minutes).

Planning Considerations: A rising tide is best for exploring the lagoon behind Gibson Spit in Sequim Bay. The crossing to Protection Island can be met with current, strong wind, and chop. Stay 200 yards offshore from Protection Island; landing is not permitted.

Getting There and Launching

Sequim–John Wayne Marina: The launch, on land that was donated to the county by John Wayne, is off US Highway 101 about 2 miles east of Sequim. Turn right on White Feather Way (if going west) and follow signs about half a mile to the marina. Use the ramp on the west side for launching. The marina is full service and has a café.

Sequim Bay State Park: The park lies on both sides of US 101 about 4.75 miles east of Sequim. Turn east off the highway, toward the water, and follow the road downhill through the campground to the boat launch. A Discover Pass is required for parking.

Marlyn Nelson County Park: The park is reached by turning north from US 101 onto Brown Road about 0.5 mile west of Sequim. Follow it 1 mile to Port Williams Road, turn right and go about 2.5 miles to the park. Launch from the gravel beach. There are no facilities at this launch area.

Diamond Point Launch: From US 101 near Gardiner, turn off (north) at Diamond Point Road. Follow the road all the way to the public access beach launch. Located between two houses, unload your gear then park in the small lot on the west side of the road across from the estuary. There are no facilities.

Routes

Sequim Bay: *Protected.* Beginning at either Sequim Bay State Park or John Wayne Marina, paddle north along the beach. Shores between these points and the bay's entrance are wooded with occasional homes above the gravel beaches. About 1 mile north of the marina are Battelle Institute's laboratories. They are located just inside the dredged entrance that skirts Kiapot Point at the end of Travis Spit. The spit is a long sand and gravel obstruction that extends from the east shore nearly to the bay's western side. Just north is a smaller one, Gibson Spit, running perpendicular to Travis Spit from the north. It further constricts the entrance. At the laboratories, you can either cut across to explore the north side of the spit or continue along the shore to the lagoon and Gibson Spit. This is a narrow, dredged channel, so stay close to shore to assure that larger boats will have the room they need.

The two spits have public tidelands: on the north side of Travis Spit and the east side of Gibson Spit. The areas above the mean high-tide line on both spits are the property of Battelle Institute. Their scientists do research there from time to time and they ask that you not trespass.

The lagoon is a fine place to ride in on a rising tide starting about midtide. The bird-viewing is good with a pastoral backdrop of farmlands. At high tide you should be able to follow the tidal channels for a mile or so. The tidelands

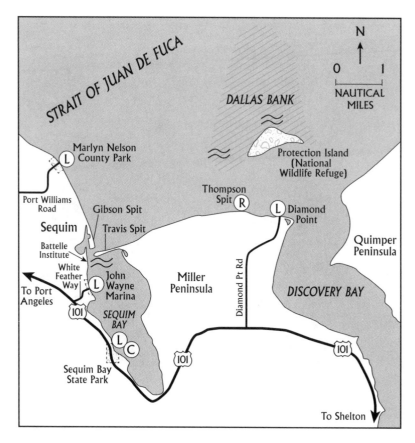

in the lagoon west of Gibson Spit are also research areas, as is the drying shoal called Middle Ground south of Travis Spit. Stay in your boat except on the public tidelands. Though shellfish are plentiful in Sequim Bay, they cannot be harvested because of contamination.

The route from Gibson Spit to Marlyn Nelson Park follows the gravel beach north. Bluffs begin at the foot of the spit less than 1 mile south of the park. The park's present site was once Port Williams, where steamers called with freight and passenger service for the community of Sequim.

To access Protection Island from here, paddle alongside the undeveloped shore of Miller Peninsula, and if winds are low, begin your crossing to the island. The closer you get, you'll hear more and more sounds of birds.

From Diamond Point: *Protected* or *Moderate.* Launch on the public put-in between houses. Head west along the shore past the houses. Note: The beach access road seen after launching is a private road locked by the local community. Following the shore, you'll soon reach DNR beach #410, also called Thompson Spit. This 2710-foot-long public beach is a great rest stop. An abandoned building can be explored alongside driftwood and the tidal

The southwest corner of Protection Island, a National Wildlife Refuge

estuary behind the beach. From here, either continue past the spit to explore the empty, untouched beaches of Miller Peninsula possibly entering Sequim Bay (see the Sequim Bay route information), or if the conditions are right, start your crossing to Protection Island.

Circumnavigation of Protection Island: *Moderate* or *Exposed*. The crossing is exposed to swell and wind, which can make this paddle difficult for those not familiar with rough-water paddling. Staying 200 yards off the shore of the island, start by going around the spit that points northwest. You may see seals off the spit ducking below the water and a few brave ones following your progress. The island immediately rises to a sheer cliff facing north. The cliffs stay high until the far northeastern shore of the island. Watch for tide rips and surf caused by wind or ship wakes along the western edge, also called Dallas Bank. It's very shallow here and for some distance offshore. The east end has a long spit with an artificial harbor that opens on the east south side.

Alternative Route: *Moderate* or *Exposed*. Start from Sequim Bay, paddle through the spit to paddle halfway down Miller Peninsula. Cross to Protection Island and paddle from west to east on its northern side, then cross over to Thompson Spit on Miller Peninsula. Then work your way back along the peninsula's beaches back to Sequim Bay.

38 Dungeness Spit

This 5-mile-long spit is a National Wildlife Refuge set aside for waterfowl and shorebirds. As many as 10,000 birds winter in the refuge, particularly the black brant. Sandpipers and other shorebirds scour its beaches for food. Shallow Dungeness Bay, south of the spit, harbors clams and oysters as well as the crab that takes its name. Captain George Vancouver visited the spit in 1792. Built in 1857, the Dungeness Lighthouse was the first light station in the inland waters of the region. Originally it was 100 feet tall but was later shortened due to structural issues. The S'Klallam people lived along the Dungeness River for thousands of years. In 1872 they were forced by European-American homesteaders to live for one difficult year on the spit, then later forced to live on a reservation elsewhere. In 1868 the Tsimshiam people were camping on the spit after coming back from harvesting hops in the Puyallup Valley. The S'Klallam people attacked them, killing everyone except one woman who took refuge in the lighthouse. The lighthouse is now managed by the New Dungeness Lighthouse Association, who rents the building out to volunteer lightkeepers.

> **Duration:** Part day to full day. No camping is allowed along these shorelines. Landing is only permitted at the lighthouse by reservation only.
>
> **Rating:** *Protected* or *Moderate*, depending on route. The *Moderate* route may involve exposure to rough seas, beach surf, and tide rips.
>
> **Navigation Aids:** SeaTrails WA 103, 301; NOAA chart 18471 (1:40,000); Port Townsend tide table (subtract about 45 minutes).
>
> **Planning Considerations:** Best on higher tides. Tide flats south of the spit and in the lagoon are extensive at low tide. A loop around the spit is not possible due to restrictions on crossing the spit. Only landing is permitted at the lighthouse and requires a free reservation by calling this number: 360-457-8451. Winds can be strong on the spit due to lack of cover. Prevailing winds in summer are from the northwest and from the south to southeast in winter. Fog is common from August to September. Keep a distance from harbor seals hauled out on shore. Dungeness Kayaking offers kayak tours to the spit. For additional information: www.dungenesskayaking.com.

Getting There and Launching

Cline Spit County Park: From US Highway 101 in Sequim, turn north on Sequim Avenue and go 6 miles. This becomes Sequim–Dungeness Way and later Marine Drive. After 6 miles the spit comes into view on the right. Turn down a side road that drops sharply over the bluff to Cline Spit County Park and launch from the gravel beach north of the parking area. The ramp has restrooms, garbage cans, and plenty of parking. For additional information: Clallam County Parks, 360-417-2291.

Dungeness Boat Launch on Oyster House Road: This boat ramp is located a half mile east of Cline Spit (see above) off Marine Drive. It has extensive parking, full restrooms, garbage cans, and a covered bird viewing platform.

An alternative route is to take Kitchen–Dick Road off US 101, west of Sequim. After 3.6 miles, take a right on Lotzgesell Road. After a winding 2.4 miles, take a left on Clark Road and follow to Marine Drive. Take a right on Marine Drive and go 0.6 mile to the Oyster House road access, and you will see a sign leading to the boat ramp on your left.

There is no camping on the spit. The closest is the Dungeness Recreation Area, a Clallam County park not far away. To get there, continue driving west on Marine Drive beyond the turnoff to Cline Spit County Park, which then turns left becoming Cays Road. Turn right on the Lotzgesell Road and follow it to the park entrance.

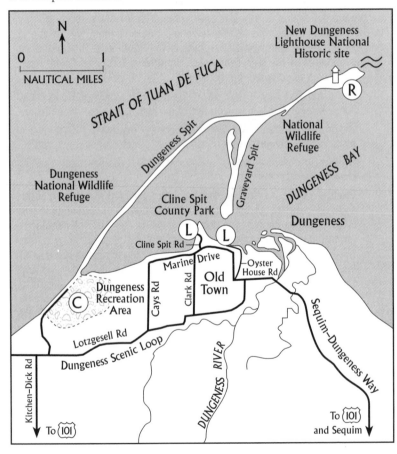

The Dungeness Lighthouse

You can only land on the spit at the Dungeness Lighthouse—and only between the yellow poles. Landing requires a free reservation: 360-457-8451. There is a $100 fine for landing elsewhere on the spit.

Routes

Cline Spit to Dungeness Lighthouse: *Protected.* A loop trip is not possible since portaging across the spit at the lagoon is not allowed. Always keep outside the "Area Closed" signs. In windy weather you may prefer to stick to the lagoon north and east of Cline Spit, which affords sheltered paddling yet easy viewing of the shoreline south of the spit. The south side of the spit usually is calm except in southerly winds. The waters on either side of Graveyard Spit are closed from October 1 to May 14; call ahead to confirm these dates.

The manned lighthouse at the end of the spit is open to the public for daily tours. The climb up the tower's spiral staircase is worthwhile in its own right; the view along the spit is even better.

Outer Spit: *Moderate.* In calm weather, consider paddling around the end of the spit into the Strait of Juan de Fuca proper. The feasibility of this depends on the sea conditions. If too big, retreat to the south side of the spit. Currents passing over the bar at the end of the spit and interacting with the eddies behind it can produce tide rips on both the flood and ebb. You may be able to avoid them by cutting across close to shore unless seas are rough. Ebb current and Dungeness River flow can pull you into the strait—pay attention to your position and avoid paddling here if you're unfamiliar with paddling in current.

Paddling the northern side of Dungeness Spit allows a close-up look at this wild, driftwood-strewn beach, staying as close in as the surf or, where enforced, a 100-yard buffer allows. Keep an eye offshore for wakes from the constant stream of ships passing in and out of the Strait of Juan de Fuca, as these will break farther out. Give beached harbor seals a wide berth as they're protected by the Marine Mammal Protection Act.

39 Port Angeles Harbor and Ediz Hook

In 2003, a construction project on Ediz Hook to build a state dry dock unearthed *Tse-whit-zen* (pronounced *ch-WHEET-son*), the largest Native American village ever found in the Puget Sound region. Much like Dungeness Spit, Ediz Hook was once a natural sand spit shaped by wind and waves. Since the early 1900s it has been built on, thus ending its natural life but also providing a solid foundation for a pulp mill, US Coast Guard station, bike trail, and protection for Port Angeles Harbor. A town supported by logging, a working harbor, and tourism, Port Angeles sits below the backdrop of the Olympic Mountains, and views across the Strait of Juan de Fuca of Victoria, British Columbia, and Mount Baker to the east. Also a hub of outdoor recreation, "PA" as it's known locally has good hiking, white-water kayaking, surfing, and, some say, the best sea kayaking on the West Coast.

Duration: Part day.

Rating: *Protected* to *Moderate.*

Navigation Aids: SeaTrails WA 301; NOAA chart 18468 (1:10,000); 18465 (1:80,000); Port Angeles tide table. Race Rocks current table (adjusted for Angeles Point) or the Canadian *Current Atlas.*

Planning Considerations: Strong westerly winds can produce large wind waves in the harbor. Also watch for busy shipping traffic making sure to give right-of-way to the Victoria ferry. On the ebb, a tide rip can occur off Ediz Hook. Avoid paddling to the exterior of the hook in heavy seas.

Getting There and Launching

Hollywood Beach: Coming from the east, take US Highway 101 into Port Angeles. Also called East Front Street, take a right on North Lincoln Street and go one block. Take a right into the Hollywood Beach parking lot. This launch includes restrooms, garbage cans, drinking water, and restaurants nearby. Launch at the beach to the north of the lot.

Ediz Hook: Coming from the east, take US 101 into Port Angeles. Also called East Front Street, continue to the downtown area following signs for the truck route. Passing the waterfront, the road will become Marine Drive. Stay on Marine Drive past the marina and onward to Ediz Hook. Three miles from

Tribal Journeys canoes on Hollywood Beach in Port Angeles

town, the road will curve past a pulp mill then leads on to the hook. There are two public access waterfront parks inside of the hook that are great for launching. Both are supported by the local paddling club, Olympic Peninsula Paddlers. Facilities include restrooms, parking, and picnic tables. The larger of the two, Ediz Hook Boat Launch has a boat ramp.

Route
Protected to *Moderate*. If launching from Hollywood Beach, consider a paddle east along the Discovery Trail shoreline below the bluff. The extended dock a quarter of a mile from the launch was once the Rayonier Mill site, one of the largest logging mills in the region. Farther east, the bluffs rise high above the beach, dropping for a waterfront housing community, then rising again all the way to Dungeness Spit nearly 11 miles away. For an extended trip toward Dungeness, check out the man-made "Chinaman's Cave" (the Lake Farm Tunnel) two miles east of Port Angeles. The cave is man-made, and there are several stories surrounding its origin dating to the 1800s. Three miles east of Port Angeles is Green Point, which on the right swell can produce large surf. The shore is littered with rocks and boulders—paddle wide around it if breaking to avoid getting caught by a wave.

Large ships dock in the harbor west of Hollywood Beach. Incoming international shipping traffic must check in with customs in Port Angeles before continuing to their destinations. Be cautious of the Black Ball Ferry *Coho*, which docks a few hundred yards west of Hollywood Beach and goes to Victoria, British Columbia, twice a day. Paddling to the west end of the bay brings you past a logging mill with logs stacked high being prepped for shipping overseas. Port Angeles Boat Haven is home to the local fishing fleet and many live-aboard yachts and a few odd boats. The Tse-whit-zen village site is located where the Hook meets the shore but is off-limits to the public at the time of writing. Ediz Hook is 1.7 miles from the launch. Watch boating traffic if you paddle to the hook.

There are three launches on Ediz Hook. Ediz Hook Boat Launch is the closest to the mill on the inside. The second launch is halfway to the US Coast Guard Station, and the last on the strait side is near the station entry. All three have spectacular views of the Olympic Mountains. Paddle any length of the spit, into the harbor, or poke around the hook for a glimpse of the Strait of Juan de Fuca. A rip can occur near the red buoy off the hook when the ebb current collides with a westerly wind. Stay clear of paddling on the outside of the hook on large swell and wind days. There is no beach on the outside and waves can pound the shore. Also remember to give boaters the right-of-way, paddle 100 yards offshore of the coast guard station.

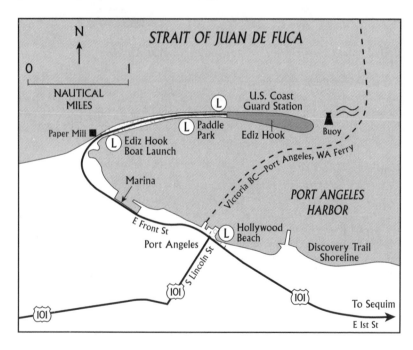

40 Freshwater Bay to the Elwha River

In 2011, the largest dam-removal project in North America began to remove the Elwha River's two dams. Aside from preventing the upstream travel of the river's once 100-pound salmon, the dams also prevented a natural flow of silt into the strait. In time beaches west of Port Angeles began to erode, leaving rock- and boulder-strewn shorelines, and residents scrambling to protect their homes from eroding away. The S'Klallam people have a rich history here as do the Makah tribe farther west, who often raided the S'Klallam for slaves. The Lower Elwha River tribe, based on the east side of the river, now fish and launch their canoes from the river. Local angler's trails can be followed upriver for miles below the eroding bluffs. Driftwood shelters from beachcombers can be found near the mouth of the river, which sometimes last through several winters. Wildlife is abundant at the mouth.

Duration: Part day to full day.

Rating: *Exposed.* Surf and strong currents are likely. Surf may prevent landings and force you to turn around. Only go on small swell (three-foot) or no swell and wind days.

Navigation Aids: NOAA chart 18465 (1:80,000); Race Rocks current tables (adjusted for Angeles Point) or the Canadian *Current Atlas.* Check swell direction, size, and wind predictions from various surf forecast websites.

Planning Considerations: For experienced paddlers only, the Elwha River current can produce a rip pulling paddlers into the strait. Medium to large swell or high wind can build very large breaking waves off the river mouth. This is a popular surfing spot for those seeking steep, fast waves that break in shallow boulder-strewn water. The surfers here are known for their attitude, so best to stay clear, or go when there is no swell or when there's no one there. Learn surfers' etiquette if you choose to surf here. Sea kayakers shouldn't surf here if they don't have strong rough-water and surfing skills.

Getting There and Launching

Freshwater Bay: Drive on State Route 112 west from its junction with US Highway 101 just a few miles west of Port Angeles. After 5 miles, turn right on Freshwater Bay Road and follow it for 3 miles to Freshwater Bay County Park. The launch is on a gravel beach to the left of the boat ramp. Yield to anglers launching boats—this launch can be very busy in summer. This day-use park has vault toilets, a picnic table, but no other services. Freshwater Bay is very protected and is a great place to go when other areas are too rough.

A kayaker surfs a rapid on the Elwha River just above the river mouth.

Port Angeles to the Elwha: Launch from one of the three access points from Ediz Hook (see chapter 39). Round the hook and paddle west 9.4 miles to Angeles Point. This is an *Exposed* route affected by wind and swell. Run a shuttle to Freshwater Bay's boat ramp for a total of 12.7 miles.

Route

Freshwater Bay to the Elwha River and Angeles Point: *Exposed.* In 2011, two dams along the Elwha River that were built in the early twentieth century began to be demolished to restore the river's once great salmon runs. By November 2011, the dams were reduced enough for the river to once again flow freely. The process to restore the river will take years, but scientists think the sediment built up behind the dams will flow to the mouth of the river and rebuild the beaches that have been eroding at a rapid rate. Note that the dam-removal process will alter the river mouth, possibly making some of the information here outdated over time. For additional information about the Elwha River restoration, visit the website for Olympic National Park: www.nps.gov/olym/index.htm.

This trip offers the experienced paddlers a variety of tricky conditions to test their skills, such as river current, surf, strong tidal currents, and a long-distance day paddle. Angeles Point is 3.36 miles east of the Freshwater Bay boat ramp. Paddle through thick kelp beds or along the bay's rugged shore below eroding clay bluffs. Few travel this way so expect solitude and great wildlife viewing. In 1.4 miles, to the east of the boat ramp, Colville Creek enters the bay. Surf sometimes breaks here. Be cautious as it's rocky and shallow, but in calm seas is a good rest area.

After 3 miles, the tall bluffs drop to a sandy and gravel beach. Beach homes will appear all the way to the west side of Angeles Point. The beach here is steep, which can be difficult for landing if waves are breaking. As you near the point, determine if waves are breaking near the shore. If so, stay at least 50 yards offshore as waves here break in shallow water off the shore. The Elwha River pours into the Strait of Juan de Fuca just around the corner on the western edge of Angeles Point. As you round the point, watch for river current that may pull you out into the strait. If you get stuck in the current—much like a rip in the ocean—paddle parallel to the shore.

Only experienced paddlers should paddle here. In strong westerly swell and wind conditions, large surf up to ten feet can pound the rocky shore around the river mouth and farther east around the point. This is a popular surfing break for advanced surfers. Stay clear of surfers or practice surfers' etiquette should you decide to participate. Generally sea kayakers shouldn't surf near shorter watercraft due to being unable to make quick turns to avoid a collision.

On small (three-foot) or no swell days, you can enter the mouth of the river and paddle upstream. Use the middle of the channels, which are the deepest when entering; the edges are rocky and shallow. Keep watch for swells

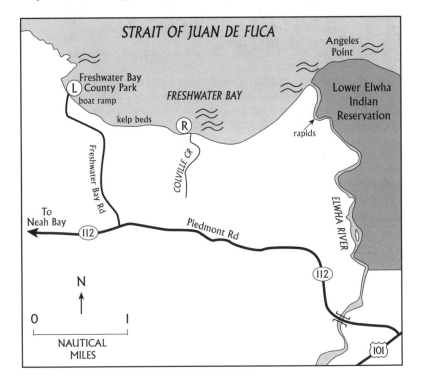

developing north of the mouth and if needed surf one in or ride in between swells. Avoid going up the mouth if the waves are big and beyond your skill level. Waves here can jack up quite large with little warning.

Three hundred yards above the mouth of the river, where it narrows, the river splits into two channels. The right channel has an area of unpassable Class II rapids with small surfable standing waves. Stay off the river shore on the east side as it is private property belonging to the Lower Elwha–Klallam tribe. You can, however, land on the rocky west shore 10–25 yards just inside the mouth. Avoid landing in this area 50-plus yards back as salmon use it for spawning. If wave action is low, land on the western beach facing Freshwater Bay. The beach is a good rest stop, but no camping or fires are allowed.

Floating downriver back to the mouth and out to the strait, paddle east but remember to stay off the shore as it is tribal land. On calm days the strait can be glassy with a few kelp beds. Current can also push you around the point. Soon the shore will rise to bluffs with views of the mill in Port Angeles 3.8 miles to the east. Above the forested bluff, there is an overgrown World War II observatory bunker with a fine view of the strait. The rocky beaches below are shallow at high tides and can produce significantly large surf. Approach with caution when landing.

41 Freshwater Bay to the Salt Creek Recreational Area

Here is a taste of Washington's outer coast just a few miles west of Port Angeles. Swells penetrating the Strait of Juan de Fuca are still large enough to make challenging surf on the area's beaches and pack enough power to bore a double sea arch along this route. Depending on the swell size, landings are possible on many tiny gravel beaches along the way that are inaccessible from the cliffs above. Preservation of the uplands as the Department of Natural Resources' Striped Peak Recreation Area makes this one of the wildest stretches along the Strait of Juan de Fuca coast close to Port Angeles. The routes include short day trips, full day trip, or even an overnight.

Duration: Part day to overnight. (Add time for car shuttle or double the route distance for a paddled return.)

Rating: *Protected, Moderate,* or *Exposed.* Surf and strong currents are likely. Surf may prevent landings along the route and commit you to paddling in the current while possibly exposed to the effects of wind and opposing current for the full distance between Crescent and Freshwater bays.

Navigation Aids: SeaTrails WA 301; NOAA chart 18465 (1:80,000); Race Rocks current table (adjusted for Angeles Point) or the Canadian *Current Atlas.*

Planning Considerations: Travel with the current direction or at times of little current as forecasted in the current tables or the *Current Atlas*. Alongshore currents can exceed 2 knots. Breaking swells may prevent using inshore eddies to work upstream. A large swell may produce large surf at Crescent Bay and may also prevent landings along the way. Avoid when weather conditions include strong east or west winds for the Strait of Juan de Fuca. If paddling to Crescent Beach, learn surf etiquette to prevent collisions with other surfers. You may consider taking a local sea kayak tour of this route to familiarize yourself with it prior to doing it on your own.

Getting There and Launching

This route can be accessed from either Freshwater Bay to the east or Salt Creek Recreational Area to the west. Camping is available at Salt Creek Recreational Area and Crescent Beach and RV Park. An easy 9-mile vehicle shuttle can be made between the two parks.

Freshwater Bay: Drive on State Route 112 west from its junction with US Highway 101 just a few miles west of Port Angeles. After 5 miles turn right on Freshwater Bay Road and follow it 3 miles to Freshwater Bay County Park. Launching is on a gravel beach to the left of the launching ramp. Yield to anglers launching boats—this launch can be very busy in summer. This day-use park has vault toilets, a picnic table, but no other services. Freshwater Bay is very protected and is a great place to go when other areas are too rough.

Salt Creek Recreational Area: Continue another 3 miles beyond the turn-off to Freshwater Bay on State Route 112 to Camp Hayden Road. Turn right and go 3 miles to Salt Creek Recreational Area. Continue straight into the park for camping or curve left to the day-use launch. The launch has a restroom and small parking lot that can be filled on sunny weekends. During low tides, the carry to the beach can be 300 yards. During medium to high tides you can paddle or take the current of Salt Creek to the beach. The south (right) side of the creek is private property and is strictly enforced.

Salt Creek provides a large number of campsites, many of which are sited spectacularly at the edge of sea cliffs with panoramic views of the strait, and offers access to extensive tide pools at Tongue Point. This area has unique coast defense artillery installations that are well worth a visit. These were built during World War II rather than prior to the First World War, as in the case of others farther inland. You can see Crescent Beach and the seastack from the viewpoint via the large drive through the gun emplacement. Take the first left in the park to access this route. For additional information: 360-928-3441; www.clallam.net/Parks/SaltCreek.html.

Crescent Beach and RV Park: Use the same directions above to access Salt Creek Recreational Area. As you reach the day-use launch, continue driving past and down the road paralleling the beach. In about one-eigth of a mile, turn left into the Crescent Beach and RV Park. You have to register to enter the park. Pay $6 for day use of the beach and use of the facility's showers, restroom, parking, and laundry room. Tent camping is $37 per night but a seasonal pass of twenty visits is $60. The RV Park owns all the beach west of Salt Creek adjacent to the recreational area and extending to the other side of the bay, Agate Point, and beyond. For additional information: 1-866-690-3344; www.olypen.com/crescent/.

Routes

Freshwater Bay: *Protected* or *Moderate.* Freshwater Bay by the boat ramp is very protected and is great for paddlers of all skill levels. The beach is mostly sandy and surrounded by rocky tide pools on its west (left) side. Even at high tide, the water here is quite shallow 100 yards or so offshore. Allow boaters right-of-way on the boat ramp and below where they have to use a paddle in the shallow water to get to shore. Paddle near the shore, exploring the rocks and thick forested tree line above. Northeast winds can affect the bay. This route is popular with local sea kayaking tour companies. Beginner paddlers shouldn't go beyond Observatory Point on the northwest corner of the bay.

Paddling east in Freshwater Bay, explore the bay's thick kelp beds, empty, rugged beaches, and below tall wooded bluffs. East of the boat ramp is an erratic boulder left by an ice age glacier. While mostly calm, the bay can have large waves generated from wind and swell. Strong flood currents and wind can create a bay-wide gyro or eddy that can confuse paddlers unaware of the situation. In this case a straight line isn't the most efficient way to your destination. Use shore currents to paddle back to the boat ramp.

Paddling West to Salt Creek Recreational Area: *Exposed.* The *Exposed* rating is merited by the swells, wind, and current. They can make landings along this 4-mile route difficult and can commit you to reaching one end or the other if the weather takes a turn for the worse.

Planning with the current is more important here than along other routes where it is possible to use eddies to travel against contrary flows. Unless the swells are very small, surge and shore break prevent using the eddies inside the kelp. This can commit you to traveling along the outside of the beds where the current is strong.

Round Observatory Point with care. A large rock pillar called Bachelor Rock is connected to the point at lower tides. Surf and wind waves can break on the rock. Only go between if you know you can make it. The inside section just below the point has a lower depression allowing for a crossing if you don't mind an occasional scrape or two on your hull. West of the point, a pocket beach with vertical walls reaching up nearly 50 feet opens up thus giving you a taste of the terrain for the next 3.5 miles. Don't go ashore in this first beach as it is private property. West of here, the shore is part of DNR beach 419—thus public access.

Magnificent sheer rock cliffs topped with cedar, fir, and madronas tower above the many pocket beaches in this section. The rocks extending from Freshwater Bay to Tongue Point are part of the Crescent Terrane and are tertiary volcanic

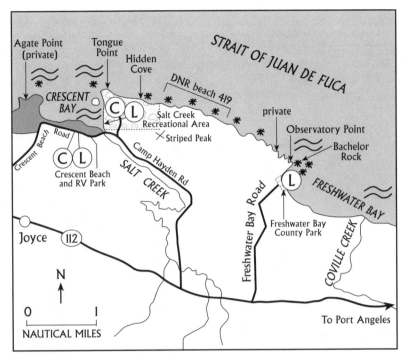

and sedimentary rocks that are roughly 52.9 million years old. A local geologist friend described these as *tholeiitic basaltic* and *tuffaceous* rocks.

Swell and wind waves pound the shoreline and fill the surge channels creating challenging paddling conditions. Paddlers who enjoy "rock gardening" come here to play in the surge as it draws in and out of rock slots, sea caves, and rocks just under the waterline. Local sea kayak guides keep their inexperienced paddlers far on the outside of the action to safely view from a distance. Extensive kelp beds border this entire coastline.

The route is great for wildlife with abundant sea life ranging from birds, harbor seals, the occasional orca, to huge schools of smelt threading through the undersea forests of kelp. Starfish, anemones, and, in summer, jellyfish can be found under you. In calm conditions and lower tides, take a rest stop or lunch break in one of the many pocket beaches. One of the most interesting landing spots is at the midpoint of the route near a double arch best reached from a beach just to the east. Near the end of this stretch, a rocky point which juts out to the northwest hides a protected beach called "Secret Beach" that can be hiked to via Salt Creek Recreational Area. A waterfall is in the trees above the beach near the trail. West of here the shoreline cliffs drop in elevation and flatten in features as you near Tongue Point.

If the conditions are flat and the tide is high, you can paddle over Tongue Point below the cliff. If the tide is low, go around the point. Sometimes on an

Low tide at Crescent Beach in Salt Creek Recreational Area

incoming tide, a scissor wave (two waves colliding from two directions) rips down from the point to the cliff and can throw a kayak in the air a few feet, sometimes capsizing it. A few friends enjoy this feature and go there specifically for the effect. Others should go around the point. If there's large surf and breakers off the point, go wide around it or even determine if you need to turn around. There are several rocks just below the waterline on both sides of the point—navigate carefully. SUP paddlers should watch for the thick kelp beds on the west side of the point.

Tongue Point is a marine sanctuary and is also one of the best tide pooling spots in the state. Don't take any sea life from this area. There are two stairways leading to the beach east of the point. If the wave action is light you can use these to finish your paddle or take a break.

On the west side of Tongue Point begins Crescent Beach. The park's iconic seastack lies below the cliffs just inside the point. Another stairway leads down from the park onto this side of the point. This access is too steep and narrow for hauling out gear. When entering Crescent Beach—if there's no wave action, paddle to shore on either side of the island and land on the east (left) side of the creek if facing the beach. If the tide is low, paddle around the right side of the island to land, as shallow reefs lie between the island and the cliff. Make sure you don't land on the west (or right) side of the creek. This is private property and unfortunately is strictly enforced. The landowners regularly patrol the beach and will threaten criminal trespassing if you land or choose to argue with them. Private property here includes the beach below the low-tide line, which is uncommon for this region. Many surfers have stood here in chest deep water only later to find the property owners waiting for them in the public parking lot ready to deliver a lecture, take their vehicle license number down, and deliver a printed flyer detailing the trespassing issue. The signage for their beach is very poor, thus many have been caught here without knowing. One friend, who was new to the area, was perplexed when he found himself going to court. If you pay the RV Park $6 a day or $60 a year, you can use the beach without worry.

If there is wave action and surfers in the water, give them a lot of space when going through the surf break to land. If the waves are too big for your skill level, determine if landing here is the right choice. In the past decade, the popularity of this beach for surfing has increased considerably. Unskilled sea kayakers have gained a reputation for dropping in on surfers and creating a stir. For the surfers (includes all types) a seventeen-foot sea kayak barreling out of control on a wave toward them is frightening, thus a need to take precautions. Learn about surfers' etiquette (surf kayakers also use this) prior to padding in any popular surfing area.

If the surf is up and you can find a spot far from others, this is a great beach to practice your wave riding skills. The beach is sandy and the waves generally are well formed on a good day. Wave size varies widely from flat calm days to winter surf up to fifteen-foot close-outs. Surf on the strait is inconsistent compared to the open ocean beaches thus good planning is required to get waves. If you're going there to surf, look for a medium tide from four to six feet, a west or northwest swell under twelve seconds, and little wind. Less than four-foot tide level, the waves will close-out. Onshore wind (wind going toward shore) creates close-out conditions or "mushy" waves, which is fine for kayakers but less preferred by board surfers. Watch for the rip on the west or outside edge of the seastack on an ebb, especially after a big rain—a few boaters have been sucked out into the strait from it.

42 Cypress Island

The wild ruggedness of Cypress Island, along with the chance for a hike to catch the panoramic views from Eagle Cliff, and the two seasonal, public camping areas with Cascadia Marine Trail sites around the island contribute to its popularity with kayakers. Cypress Island has an added bonus, unique in the San Juan Islands: ferry trips are not required. The DNR owns about four-fifths of the island and manages it primarily for recreation. Plan one to two nights out to the island's two campsites or circumnavigate the entire island.

Duration: Full day to overnight.

Rating: *Moderate.*

Navigation Aids: SeaTrails WA 001, 005; NOAA charts 18423 SC or 18421 (both 1:80,000), 18430 (1:25,000); Rosario Strait current tables (with corrections for Bellingham Channel, Strawberry Island, Guemes Channel, or Shannon Point, depending on your location) or the Canadian *Current Atlas.*

Planning Considerations: Camping is closed from Labor Day to Memorial Day for both Cypress Head and Pelican Beach, but day use is still permitted. The toilet is open for use during this period. The trail to Eagle Cliff is normally closed from January to mid-July because of peregrine falcon breeding activities. Strong currents can create very dangerous localized conditions off Cypress Head in Bellingham Channel; avoid big tides or aim for slack current in this area. Currents strongly affect traveling speeds on all sides of the island—use flood current for going north and ebb current for the return.

Getting There and Launching

There are three launches from Anacortes: the ferry dock for Guemes Island, downtown Anacortes inside Cap Sante, and Washington Park.

Anacortes Ferry Dock (to Guemes Island): From Commercial Avenue, take a left on 6th Street, which will take you to the dock. Unload your boat from the day-use park on the west side of the dock, which allows for four-hour parking. For overnight parking, use the seventy-two-hour lot one block east on 6th Street and K Avenue. There is a short paved pathway on the north side of the lot that takes you directly to the ferry dock. When launching, watch for ferry and recreational boating traffic in the channel.

Dusk at Cypress Head, a Cascadia Marine Trail campsite

Anacortes: Use Seafarer's Memorial Park just south of the marina. Parking here is day use only. Check with nearby marinas for overnight parking. Call the harbor office for additional information: 360-293-0694. To get to Seafarer's Park, turn east from Commercial Avenue onto 15th Street to Q Avenue, then east again on Seafarer's Way along the south edge of the marina. There is an easy carry to the gravel beach and restrooms.

Washington Park: From Anacortes, follow signs for the San Juan Island ferry, about 4 miles west of town. From Commercial Avenue, take a left on 12th Street (State Route 20) which will become Oakes Avenue. Enjoy views on your right of Guemes and Cypress islands and Bellingham Channel. At the Anacortes ferry terminal continue going straight at the Y intersection. The road will become Sunset Avenue. Follow Sunset Avenue to Washington Park.

Overnight parking is allowed in lot "B" for up to fourteen days. To get closest to the beach, drive down to the day-use parking lot "A" to unload, then carry your boat across the lawn to the gravel beach. Move your car to the overnight "B" lot. There is a daily parking fee. For additional information: 360-661-3611. Be cautious of the boat ramp activity on busy weekends. The park is owned by the city of Anacortes and does have regular car camping elsewhere in the park.

Route

Circumnavigation: A complete circumnavigation of Cypress Island is approximately 15 miles. Use the Canadian *Current Atlas* to visualize and plan your trip around the currents in Bellingham and Guemes channels and in Rosario Strait. The stage of the tide affects which launch point is more practical for starting out at that time.

Camping is closed on Strawberry Island off the southwest corner of Cypress. There are no facilities on the island. Due to overuse, Cypress Head and Pelican Beach are only open for camping from Memorial Day to Labor Day. All three areas are open for day use.

Watch for recreational boating traffic when crossing Guemes Channel. Fast moving current can move the boats closer to you than expected. Boat wakes can also get quite large when opposing strong current.

The easiest launch in Anacortes is on the west side of the Guemes Island ferry dock. Launch on slack, the end of the ebb current, or early in the flood current and cross over to Guemes Island. Follow the Guemes shore west, then north, and finally ferry or cross over to Cypress Island.

The launch point in downtown Anacortes is at Seafarer's Memorial Park. Time it so you get the tail end of the ebb, or during slack in Guemes Channel then let the flood take you north up Bellingham Channel. Round Cape Sante and cross the 0.5-mile-wide Guemes Channel, usually possible on most tide stages, and then work west along Guemes Island and up its western shore. Wait until the current slacks before crossing Bellingham Channel to Cypress Island.

The Guemes Island and Seafarer's Park options are safer and more versatile for starts at different tide stages than the Washington Park put-in near Fidalgo Head. On flood currents, Washington Park may be an easier launch point as the current flowing northward can be ridden into Bellingham Channel. Be watchful of outgoing and incoming ferry traffic at the terminal just east of the park.

Currents sweep strongly around this body of land, and the crossing from here to Cypress Island is more than 2 miles. As the ebb current sets southwest, reaching Cypress Island from the Fidalgo Head/Shannon Point area on even average tides can be almost impossible. There is a good possibility of being swept out into Rosario Strait in the process. This situation would be very rough with a southerly wind.

Midway up Bellingham Channel and 4.6 miles from Washington Park is Cypress Head. This protuberance creates back eddies, strong eddy lines, and associated rips that can be very dangerous, particularly on large ebbs. If you approach while the current is flowing, hug the shoreline. The back eddy extends 100 feet off Cypress Head and the safest route is right along the shore inside the kelp.

Cypress Head is a DNR recreation site with Cascadia Marine Trail designation. Campsites are in the woods on the head and at the neck connecting it to the main island—a great place to watch the action in a big ebb exchange. Hear porpoises pass and the sound of the current running on big exchanges.

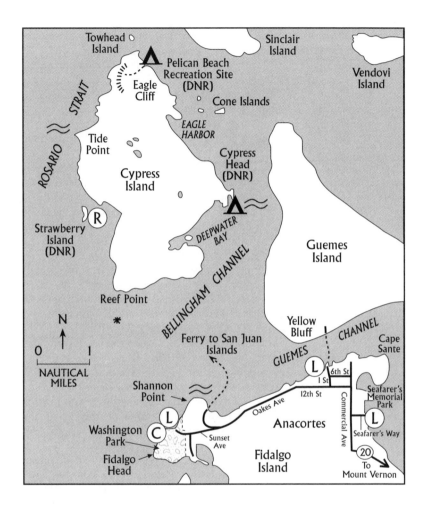

Enjoy views to the north of the undeveloped Cone and Sinclair islands with Lummi Island in the distance to the northeast. The swift currents off Cypress Head may be beneficial to those seeking to practice their skills in moving water.

Landings are at the rock and gravel beaches on both the north and south sides of the neck. The three campsites on the west end of the neck are the most convenient from the beaches, but the more distant sites in the woods offer better weather protection. There are vault toilets, but water is not available. Use minimum impact camping techniques.

About 2.5 miles north of Cypress Head is Pelican Beach, another DNR area designated with Cascadia Marine Trail status. This area was originally developed with help from the Pelican Fleet: owners of a type of beachable cruising sailboat often found hauled up on this fine pebble beach. One of the nicest features here is Eagle Cliff, a spectacular 840-foot overlook of the entire Rosario Strait area, and very popular with campers who climb up for the sunsets. The trail is a little more than 1 mile long. The climb is easy except for the last few hundred yards. The open-meadowed uplands around Eagle Cliff invite independent exploration with an alternative loop to another overlook. The trail to Eagle Cliff is closed, however, from February through mid-July because of falcon nesting there. There are other walks that are accessible from the campground such as to Duck Lake or to Eagle Harbor.

At the beach there are five to ten camping spaces. Though more can be accommodated, the narrow beach strip quickly becomes very crowded on sunny weekends, typically with kayakers. Behind is a covered picnic shelter and vault toilets. Water is not available. Camping is not allowed on the beach beyond the campsite limits, and fires must be built only in the firepits.

The currents along the Rosario Strait side of Cypress Island are strong enough to merit planning around them, though there are enough eddies in this irregular shoreline to work against them for most of the distance. Topography is at its most impressive here; Eagle Cliff and other precipices are far above.

Strawberry Island is yet another DNR recreation area but it is only open for day use and has no facilities. Access is via a small beach at the south end that is gravel at high tide but rocky at low water. As elsewhere along Rosario Strait, be wary of huge breaking wakes from passing tankers when you beach your boat. A trail continues north up the island to an overlook.

If Fidalgo Head is your destination from Reef Point at Cypress Island's southern end, formulate tactics for crossing. Keep the powerful offshore currents in mind. On a flood tide, crossing to the Washington Park area can be exhausting, even impossible. Ebbs, however, make this easy barring any strong southerly winds and with some course correction to counteract westerly drift. Watch for boating and ferry traffic, which can be heavy on weekends.

If you are bound for Guemes Channel, use a slack or early flood current to cross to Yellow Bluff on Guemes Island. Then get a lift from the flood up Guemes Channel to the ferry landing. In calm weather the crossing to Guemes Channel can be made directly and quickly from Reef Point with the right timing. You use the last of the ebb to cross toward Washington Park and position yourself to catch the southerly portion of the new flood current that will sweep into Guemes Channel rather than north up Bellingham Channel.

Anacortes to Cypress Head and Pelican Beach. Paddling to Cypress Head or Pelican Beach provides a great way to experience Cypress without a longer trip. These are accessible as a long day trip, but many favor the idyllic camping sites especially on Cypress Head with it's craggy madrona-lined cliffs and wide-angle view of Bellingham Channel. Large groups and kayak clubs tend to converge on the spacious site at Pelican Beach. Cypress Head is about 4.5 miles to Washington Park. Add 2.5 miles from Cypress Head to reach Pelican Beach.

43 James Island

Rugged James Island State Park has plenty of trails and enough secluded coves to keep you busy for more than an overnight stay. Camping includes a Cascadia Marine Trail site along with general public camping facilities. For variety coming and going, there are two ways to get there from Lopez Island. And if you feel up to it, you can make the exposed Rosario Strait crossing from Fidalgo Head to James Island and avoid San Juan Island ferry hassles. This trip could be combined with one to Obstruction Pass (see the Obstruction Pass chapter) and Doe Bay or perhaps with a circumnavigation of Blakely Island.

Duration: Overnight.

Rating: *Moderate* or *Exposed*. The *Moderate* route involves some currents and possible tide rips. The *Exposed* route requires a 3-mile open-water crossing with currents, tide rips, and shipping traffic.

Navigation Aids: SeaTrails WA 001, 002; NOAA Charts 18423 SC, 18421 (both 1:80,000), or 18430 (1:25,000); Rosario Strait current tables with corrections for Thatcher Pass.

Planning Considerations: Currents affect ease of travel and safety on both routes. See specifics about each. Raccoons are a problem on the island. Make sure you secure your gear and food.

Getting There and Launching

Two approaches begin from Lopez Island, while a third originates from Washington Park on Fidalgo Head in Anacortes.

Washington Park: From Anacortes, follow signs for the San Juan Island ferry, about 4 miles west of town. From Commercial Avenue, take a left on 12th Street (State Route 20) which will become Oakes Avenue. Enjoy views on your right of Guemes and Cypress islands and Bellingham Channel. At the Anacortes ferry terminal continue going straight at the Y intersection. The road will become Sunset Avenue and you'll soon enter the park. Park in the "A" lot to carry your boat across the lawn to the gravel beach. Then move your car to the "B" lot to park. There is a daily parking fee.

Lopez Island–Spencer Spit State Park: Starting from Lopez Island requires driving a car aboard the ferry, as there is no public access to the beach at the Lopez Island ferry terminal for foot passengers with kayaks. Drive south from the ferry landing on Ferry Road a little more than 1 mile to Port Stanley Road, which is across the highway from Odlin County Park (which has a Cascadia Marine Trail site). Turn left and follow this road for approximately 3 miles as it winds past Shoal and Swifts bays. Turn left onto Baker View Road and follow this road another mile to the state park entrance.

Overlooking a salt marsh during busy summer months at Spencer Spit State Park

Within Spencer Spit State Park, after passing the registration booth, follow the main road to a gated gravel road. Take this narrow road that drops steeply down to a small lot just south of the lagoon. There is a 50-yard carry to the beach. After unloading boats and gear, move cars back up to the parking. A Discover Pass is required. There are no garbage or recycling receptacles at this park—you must pack out what you pack in. The main park is not open in the winter but you can still access the Cascadia Marine site from the water. Outdoor Adventure Center operates kayaking tours from the spit in the summer. For additional information: www.outdooradventurecenter .com/50247/Lopez-Island.html.

Lopez Island–Hunter Bay Boat Ramp: From the ferry, take Ferry Road south to Center Road. Follow to the south side of the island and take a left on Mud Bay Road. In about a mile, take another left on Islandale Road. Follow for a curvy 1.5 miles through a thickly forested residential area. The road will lead you to the boat ramp. There's parking and a pit toilet but may be busy in fishing season with boaters.

Routes

Spencer Spit to James Island: *Moderate.* One-way paddling distance via Thatcher Pass is 4 miles or 7 miles via Lopez Pass around the south end of Decatur Island.

Currents west of Blakely Island are weak and the waterway there is fairly well protected from wind-driven seas. However, East Sound, to the north and almost bisecting Orcas Island, can develop very strong, intensified northerly winds that may extend south as far as this route on warm, fair-weather afternoons. Currents in Thatcher Pass rarely exceed 1 knot and it can usually be paddled safely in any stage of the tide. However, currents are strong enough to be worth coordinating with the flow direction. The flood current flows west through Thatcher Pass.

The longer alternative route, looping south around Decatur Island, offers narrow inter-island passageways to thread through and views of this quiet and

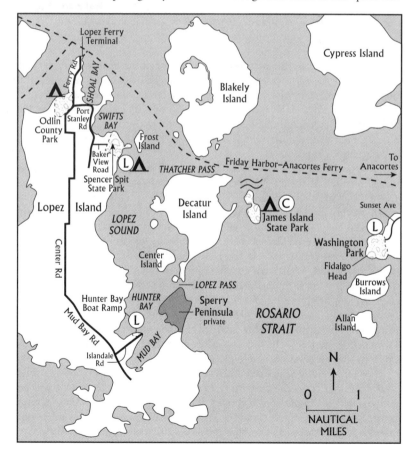

pastoral island. As with Blakely Island to the north, there is no public ferry service to Decatur. Places to go ashore here include a small, undeveloped island state park just north of the spit east of Lopez Pass and extensive publicly owned tidelands bounded above by private property. These tidelands include the shores of Center Island, which has some gravel pocket beaches. Another public tideland covers over 2 miles of sand and gravel beach, with one intermediate strip of private tideland, on the east side of Decatur between Lopez Pass and Decatur Head. The shore break here can be quite large when a southerly wind is blowing.

James Island has three camping areas with multiple sites at each, including one with Cascadia Marine Trail status. There is a network of trails over the island's steep, rocky hills and a secluded beach on the south shore. Its drawback is the rapacious raccoon population that lurks in wait for all visitors. Campsites are accessible from either the eastern or western coves. Water is available on the island in the main campground. The central area between the coves is the most popular with boaters, and it has a small picnic shelter. However, wind can howl across this isthmus from either direction. At the east side campsites, the southern side of the cove offers more protection.

The secluded Cascadia Marine Trail site between the main west beach and east beach is the most popular with kayakers. The trees that surround the site also make it the best protected in bad weather. Beyond the outhouse, a trail leads across the island to the eastern cove. The island is known for "commando" raccoons who will do anything to get into your food and gear. Kayak guides have reported tying zippers together and wrapping gear in two tarps bound by rope.

Fidalgo Head to James Island: *Exposed.* The one-way distance is 3.5 miles, 3 miles of which are open Rosario Strait waters. Currents in this area of the strait can exceed 2.5 knots and are usually strongest on the southern flowing ebb. Hence, southerly winds can make this an extremely dangerous body of water on a falling tide, while tanker and tug-and-barge traffic add to the hazard. Crossings should be made only in auspicious conditions; otherwise use the ferry. Be especially careful in the area north of James Island where dangerous rips can form when the westward-flowing ebb from Thatcher Pass and the southward current in the strait meet an opposing wind. One kayak fatality here was apparently due to this situation. NOAA chart 18423 SC provides the following warning for Rosario Strait, presumably applying to Thatcher, Lopez, Peavine, and Obstruction passes: "On the ebb tide, southerly winds cause dangerous tide rips off the entrance to the passes."

If conditions and your skills are appropriate for the Rosario crossing, time your start relative to the currents. Since your drift from the current will be considerable in all but very small tides, start the crossing about thirty minutes before slack so the currents will be minimal and will cancel each other out before and after the slack. Currents are particularly swift off Fidalgo Head.

44 Obstruction Pass

Convoluted shores and steep hillsides of madrona and rocky meadows make Obstruction Pass prime San Juan Islands paddling country. Currents in its passageways are strong enough for some exciting rides and require a measure of caution. Alternative launch points around this area make a variety of trips possible from short local paddles to one-night or longer adventures. By adding another day to the itinerary, you could combine it with the Cypress Island route to the east or the James Island route to the south (see the Cypress Island and James Island chapters). It is a Cascadia Marine Trail site.

Duration: Part day to overnight.

Rating: *Moderate.* Area has currents with associated tide rips and eddy lines, though the areas of swiftest flow can be avoided.

Navigation Aids: SeaTrails WA 001, 002, 004; NOAA Charts 18423 SC, 18421 (both 1:80,000), or 18430 (1:25,000); Rosario Strait current tables with corrections for Obstruction Pass.

Planning Considerations: See the Fidalgo Head to James Island route in the James Island chapter for safety considerations in the passes leading to Rosario Strait and including Obstruction Pass. Obstruction Pass Recreation Site has no launching access.

Getting There and Launching

Launch from Lopez Island at Spencer Spit (see the James Island chapter for details) or from two alternative places on Orcas Island.

Obstruction Pass: The closest launch site is the Obstruction Pass boat ramp 0.7 mile to the west. This site is approximately 20 miles from the Orcas Island ferry dock by road. After leaving the ferry, follow the road to Eastsound and then to Olga. Approximately 0.25 mile before Olga turn left where signs point to Obstruction Pass and Doe Bay. After another 0.25 mile there is a fork in the road; go right for Obstruction Pass. Left leads to Doe Bay. Use this ramp only for day-trip paddling as there is no overnight parking for the general public here. There are limited parking spots, both day use and seventy-two-hour, but this is a very busy place. Next to the boat ramp is the Lieber Haven Resort, a resort and marina that offers kayak and other boat rentals and has most of the amenities you might need. For additional information: www.lieberhavenresort.com/.

Doe Bay Village Resort: This is the other Orcas Island alternative. See the Clark Island chapter for details about launching and other services offered at Doe Bay.

Routes

Spencer Spit to Obstruction Pass: *Moderate.* The one-way distance is 4.5 miles. After crossing from Spencer Spit and Frost Island, this route follows the rocky shores of Blakely Island. The uplands of this large island are privately owned, but most of its tidelands are public. To avoid conflicts with residents, do not land in the coves along the western shore or near homes elsewhere. There are a number of fine, secluded gravel beaches along its predominantly wild shores. Stay below the high-tide line.

Blakely Island Marina at the west end of Peavine Pass has the only groceries on this route. The store operates on limited hours during the off-season. Land on the beach to the left of the fuel float.

Obstruction Pass Recreation Site, included within the Cascadia Marine Trail, provides camping and a chance for some walking on the extensive trail system. Located in a cove about 0.5 mile west of the pass, it is also accessible from the road via a 0.5-mile-long trail. Above the pebble beach are primitive campsites and vault toilets but no water.

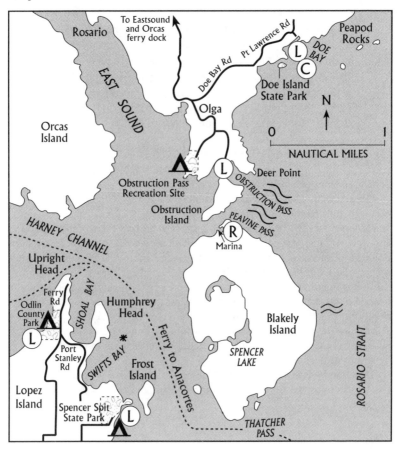

A view of Obstruction Pass and Island from the Leiber Haven Resort dock

Unless you are confident of your boat-handling skills for fast currents, use Obstruction Pass instead of Peavine Pass for travel to and from Rosario Strait. Currents in Obstruction Pass average about 1 knot; they average over 2 knots on the ebb in Peavine Pass. Both flow east on the flood toward Rosario Strait. Interestingly, this is opposite from the flow in Thatcher Pass, which is westerly on the flood.

Doe Bay to Obstruction Pass: *Moderate.* The one-way distance is 3.8 miles. This and the previously described route from Spencer Spit could be combined into a longer 8-mile overnight trip. However, traveling into the San Juans by ferry the day before would probably be required to leave enough time for paddling.

Doe Island is a six-acre state park located about 1 mile south of Doe Bay. It has a float during the summer season and mixed rock and gravel beaches on the northwest and southeast sides. There are five campsites; the best is in a hollow on the north end of the island. No water is provided.

The Orcas Island shoreline is private between Doe Bay and Deer Point. However, most of the tidelands are public with occasional gravel pocket beaches along the predominantly rock coast. You should be able to find beaches away from nearby homes.

Blakely Island Circumnavigation: *Moderate.* The distance starting from Spencer Spit is about 12 miles, 8 miles of which are from Obstruction Pass to Spencer Spit via the east side of Blakely Island. A leisurely two-night trip could be made by a second stop at James Island.

The eastern leg of the circumnavigation is significantly more exposed: fewer places to go ashore, strong currents, probable tide rips, and exposure to wind waves from either north or south. Tidelands are public along the entire east shore of Blakely Island and steep, rocky slopes above limit the residential use of this side. But they also limit the number of pocket beaches you will find. There may also be shore break on these beaches; be especially watchful for breaking tanker wakes. A powerful eddy line and associated tide rips may form during strong ebb currents in Rosario Strait at the easternmost point of Blakely Island. The current here is reported to turn to the flood an hour later than at Strawberry Island to the east. See the discussion of potentially dangerous conditions off Thatcher Pass and Peavine Pass for the Fidalgo Head route in the James Island chapter.

45 Lopez Island: Fisherman Bay

Located in Lopez Village, the island's main business center, Fisherman Bay is a protected lagoon surrounded by shops, homes, an active marina, and a few open spaces. The bay opens to San Juan Channel with marvelous views of Shaw Island to the north and San Juan Island to the west. Locals are known for the "Lopez Wave" making the island one of the most friendly in the region.

Duration: Part day.

Rating: *Protected.* **Navigation Aids:** SeaTrails WA 002; NOAA 18434, 18400, Check currents for San Juan Channel.

Planning Considerations: Watch for fast moving current and boat traffic at the mouth of the bay. Plan for higher tides to explore the bay's south end. If you're paddling into the bay from other islands, Lopez Village has lodging and full facilities for resupplying your trip.

Entrance to Fisherman Bay on Lopez Island

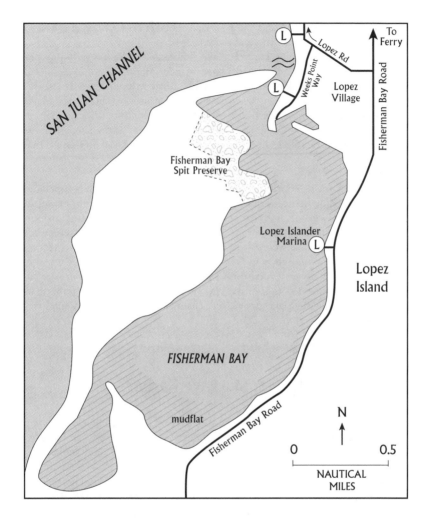

Getting There and Launching

From the ferry, take Ferry Road south for 2 miles. At the T intersection, continue to the right to Fisherman Bay Road. Follow it until you see signs for Lopez Village and take a right on Lopez Road, which takes you into town.

Weeks Point Way Launch: As you pass shops in Lopez Village, take a left onto Weeks Point Way. Follow for a few hundred feet past houses and take a right into the empty public access lot. There are about four spaces for cars here. Used by locals as a handheld boat launch, this access brings you right to the mouth of the bay. Watch for fast current on larger tidal exchanges. Respect homeowners on both sides of the access area.

Lopez Road Launch: As you near the west end of town after Weeks Point Way, turn left into the parking lot by the shops just above the water. There are steps leading to the beach and a few parking spots. If Lopez Road curves up a slight hill to the right, you've gone to far.

Lopez Islander Marina Launch: Take Fisherman Bay Road south of Lopez Village about a quarter mile to the Lopez Islander Marina. This is a protected launch deep inside the bay adjacent to a full facility marina. There is a fee to launch and park. Check with the marina office for information, Lopez Island Sea Kayak has a shop across the street offering tours, instruction, and both kayak and SUP rentals. Camping is available behind the kayak shop. For the kayak shop call: 360-468-2847. For Lopez Islander Marina, call 360-468-3383.

Route

The bay is a known hazard to boaters with its narrow and shallow opening. Paddlers will enjoy the thrill of riding up to 3 knots of current into or out of the bay during larger tidal exchanges. During slack or periods of less current, the channel provides idyllic views of Lopez Village, and beachfront residences along Weeks Point. The west side of the channel is a large sand spit protecting the bay from wind and chop in San Juan Channel. Choose your own route. Paddle inside the bay past recreational boats and the Lopez Islander Marina. Toward the southwest corner of the bay, another sand spit nearly connects to the other side providing another narrow channel to explore. At low tides this part of the bay dries to mudflats.

46 Lopez Island: Mackaye Harbor

With an annual rainfall of 22 inches, Lopez Island is located in the banana belt of Washington. Mackaye Harbor on the island's southwest side has an arid landscape in summer with golden meadows, warm water, and calm bays. It's an idyllic place for paddlers of all levels. Boaters mostly avoid the harbor and its bays due to shallow depths and numerous exposed and hidden rocks. Offshore, Long, Charles, and Iceberg islands are part of the San Juan Islands National Wildlife Refuge, but are off-limits for landing. Advanced paddlers can use the bay for a launch to enter current-laden Cattle Pass, cross to San Juan Island or to the rock garden south of Iceberg Point.

Duration: Part day.

Rating: *Protected.* Addition Iceberg Point is *Moderate* to *Exposed.*

Navigation Aids: SeaTrails WA 002; NOAA 18434, 18400. Check currents for San Juan Channel.

Planning Considerations: Novice paddlers should stay in the inner sections of Outer Bay, Barlow Bay, and Mackaye Harbor. Stay 200 yards off shore from the various San Juan Islands National Wildlife Refuge islands at the entry to both Mackaye Harbor and Outer Bay.

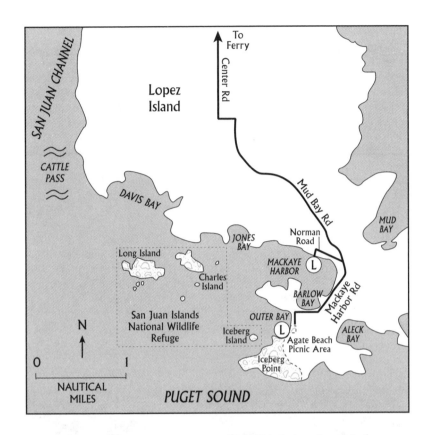

Lopez
Island

To
Ferry

Center Rd

CATTLE
PASS

DAVIS BAY

Mud Bay Rd

MUD
BAY

JONES
BAY

Norman
Road

Long Island

MACKAYE
HARBOR

Charles
Island

BARLOW
BAY

Mackaye Harbor Rd

San Juan Islands
National Wildlife
Refuge

OUTER BAY

ALECK
BAY

N

Iceberg
Island

Agate Beach
Picnic Area

0   1

Iceberg
Point

NAUTICAL
MILES

PUGET SOUND

*Long Island and the San Juan National Wildlife Refuge from Mackaye
Harbor on Lopez Island*

Getting There and Launching

Norman Road Boat Ramp: From the Lopez ferry dock, take Ferry Road south about a mile and curve left onto Center Road. Follow Center Road for several miles and eventually take a left on Lopez Sound Road, and immediately take a right on Mud Bay Road. Take a right on Mackaye Harbor Road, then in a short distance, take a right on Norman Road, which will take you to the boat ramp. There is an outhouse but no other facilities at the ramp. This is the only launch on the harbor for longer trip parking.

Agate Beach Picnic Area: From Mackaye Harbor Road, continue south to the bay. You'll pass a few beach homes, a B&B, then Barlow Bay, and eventually curve into Outer Bay. After passing a few homes, look for Agate Beach Picnic Area on your left. There is a small day-use lot. Launch across the street below the stairs.

Routes

Mackaye Harbor: *Protected.* Mackaye Harbor offers several options for day trips. Launching at Norman Road provides you access to wide sandy beaches to the east, and rocky shorelines covered with sea life on the north side. Johns Point on the southwest corner of the bay has great pocket beaches. Barlow Bay shows evidence of a busier time when Mackaye Harbor was the home to the Lopez Island fishing fleet. The docks on the bay are privately owned. Tucked in the southeast corner of Mackaye Harbor, Barlow Bay is very protected from winds.

Paddler on the north side of Shaw Island

The beach at Outer Bay is sandy and crescent shaped. Look for otters playing just off the beach. Enjoy views of the windswept barren islands offshore some of which are part of the wildlife refuge such as Round Rock, Secar Rock, and Hall Island.

Iceberg Point: *Moderate* to *Exposed*. Experienced paddlers may enjoy playing in the rocks and pocket beaches south of Otter Bay around Iceberg Point. Swell from the strait and wind can create conditions here similar to that of the outer coast.

47 Shaw Island: Circumnavigation

Located in the heart of the San Juan Islands, the waters around Shaw Island usually have the highest concentration of kayakers in the area during summer. Mild currents and alongshore paddling with few crossings make some routes here popular for less-experienced paddlers, particularly those trying kayak camping for the first time. Route options include an easy day, a short overnight, and a longer circumnavigation of Shaw Island with stops at neighboring parks and Cascadia Marine Trail sites. The circumnavigation can easily include Jones Island (see the Jones Island chapter).

Duration: Full day to multiple nights.

Rating: *Protected* or *Moderate*. A one-day protected route can be made from Odlin County Park to Indian Cove and back. The *Moderate* circumnavigation route involves currents and some open water that may become quite rough, particularly when current and wind directions oppose each other.

Navigation Aids: SeaTrails WA 002, 003, 004; NOAA charts 18423 SC or 18421 (both 1:80,000), and 18434 (1:25,000); San Juan Channel current table or the Canadian *Current Atlas* are helpful for the circumnavigation route; Port Townsend tide tables (add about 30 minutes) are handy if Indian Cove is included as a launch point or stop.

Planning Considerations: For kayakers wheeling their watercraft aboard the ferry, convenient water access is now limited to Friday Harbor. Access at the Shaw Island ferry isn't possible, and at Orcas Island it is not always certain. Timing with currents will greatly affect your speed and travel effort on the circumnavigation route. It is a fairly complex task in this area made easiest by the *Current Atlas*. Plan a high-tide arrival or departure at Indian Cove to avoid walking the mudflats. Campsites at Indian Cove and Jones Island are usually all spoken for on summer weekends. Fortunately, there are now Cascadia Marine Trail sites at these locations, yet it is still strongly suggested you arrive early.

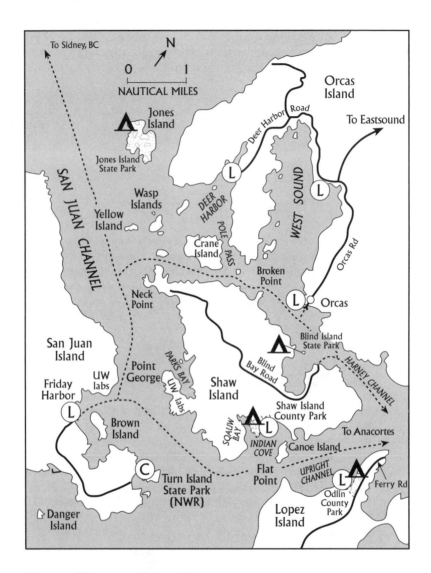

Getting There and Launching

The route described starts from Odlin County Park on Lopez Island. Drive a little more than 1 mile south on Ferry Road from the Lopez ferry terminal to Odlin County Park. There is easy access to the sandy beach. The campground includes Cascadia Marine Trail sites. Cars may be parked for a daily fee paid to the caretaker at the residence near the entrance.

As an option, the circumnavigation route can also start and end at the ferry stop at Friday Harbor or from Deer Harbor and West Sound on Orcas. See the Jones Island chapter for a description of these launch sites.

Route

The total distance of the Shaw Island circumnavigation is approximately 14 miles, beginning at Odlin County Park and proceeding counterclockwise. Add 2 miles for a side trip to Turn Island and 3 miles for Jones Island. Add 2 miles if you launch at Deer Harbor. Five places to camp are distributed around and on Shaw Island—Odlin County Park, Blind Island, Jones Island, Turn Island, and Indian Cove—allowing you to partition the trip into two or three fairly equal-length paddling days.

The distance across Upright Channel from Odlin County Park to Indian Cove is about 1.9 miles. The most interesting route follows the Lopez shore south from Odlin County Park to Flat Point, then heads across the 0.25-mile-wide narrows to Canoe Island and finally Indian Cove.

A little more than 1 mile south of Odlin County Park is the Upright Channel State Park, which is day use only. The park has toilets but no water. This 700-foot-long gravel beach with forested uplands is located just east of the residences near Flat Point.

Watch carefully for boat traffic before crossing from the spit at Flat Point to Canoe Island, particularly the ferries going to and from Friday Harbor. Currents in Upright Channel generally are weak but may have some force locally here. The flood flows north. Though Canoe Island beaches are public below mean high tide, the uplands are not, and owners who operate a youth camp specializing in French language and culture strongly discourage visitors.

Shaw Island County Park, encompassing western Indian Cove and part of the peninsula that separates it from Squaw Bay, has opportunities for camping with Cascadia Marine Trail sites, picnicking, or more secluded stops ashore. Because the foreshore in Indian Cove dries for a considerable distance becoming a muddy tide flat, plan around low tides for arrival and departure if possible.

Campsites are located along a road that starts near a low bank to the east and climbs as the bank increases to a bluff to the west. There are steps at intervals along the beach to the campsites, with the most easterly ones more readily accessible from the water. The designated Cascadia Marine Trail site and campsite #9 are reserved for paddlers. Sharing a site with others is a definite possibility during peak summer weekends. Water, vault toilets, and a cooking shelter are provided.

To make this a one-day trip of a *Protected* rating, you can return the same way you paddled or make a loop by following the Shaw Island shore north along Upright Channel. Then, opposite Odlin County Park, make the direct 1-mile crossing back to your start.

The Shaw Island shore north of Indian Cove is rocky and for the most part wild, continuing east into Harney Channel. Currents in Harney Channel are stronger than in Upright Channel, but still pose few problems for travel. The flood current here flows west.

Blind Island State Park, with a designated Cascadia Marine Trail site, is about 0.5 mile west of the Shaw Island landing and 3.5 miles from the County Park. Facilities on this three-acre island include a composting toilet and picnic tables, fire pits, but no water. There are two general sites and one Cascadia Marine Trail group site for four tents. Landings can be made on rocky beaches at the southwest end or at the southeast corner of the island. Trees on the island are few, but include cherry, apple, and filbert from an old homestead. The only wind protection is chest-high brush that shields some of the sites. Because it is small, Blind Island can become crowded with only a few parties camped there.

For the route west from Blind Island to Neck Point, including a possible side trip to Jones Island via Yellow and the Wasp islands, see the Jones Island chapter. Jones Island is 5.5 miles from Blind Island.

The small islets north and south of Neck Point are very popular with seals. It is not uncommon to see two dozen or so hauled out on the islands. Both islets are part of the San Juan Islands National Wildlife Refuge, so do not approach closer than 200 yards.

Rounding Neck Point and heading southeast along Shaw Island's west-facing shore, the San Juan Channel current can be quite strong, especially at the points that protrude into the waterway. There are eddy systems alongshore for much of the way with extensive eddies in the vicinity of Parks Bay. Though most of the northern portion of this shore is developed with summer residences, there are some points of interest. Beginning at Point George is a 1000-plus-acre biological preserve, owned by the University of Washington, that extends south and west almost to Squaw Bay. Managed by the University of Washington Friday Harbor Laboratories, this preserve is off-limits to all public use in the uplands and tidelands. Nonetheless, as you paddle by you can still enjoy the forests and meadows.

Turn Island State Park, located a little over 1 mile south of Shaw Island across San Juan Channel, is a side-trip opportunity for camping or a respite along this otherwise no-access portion of the circumnavigation. Located 3.1 miles from Shaw County Park it would also make a good first night destination for an afternoon start from Friday Harbor.

Be careful making the crossing of San Juan Channel to and from Turn Island. Currents are strong enough to require significant course adjustment to offset your drift, and steep seas can develop when the current opposes winds from either north or south. Watch for ferries and other heavy boat traffic associated with nearby Friday Harbor.

Turn Island is a unit of the San Juan Islands National Wildlife Refuge. A portion of the west end is leased to the Washington State Parks and Recreation Commission. Camping is allowed only in this park area. There are composting toilets, but no water is available. A rough trail circles the island. Keep in mind that public use of this refuge island is provisional on compatibility with wildlife. Avoid any nesting sites.

Rounding the southernmost point of Shaw Island you come upon Squaw Bay. The tips of both points forming the bay are private land, but two pocket beaches on the west side of the bay make more secluded landing spots. There is, however, a spur road down the rocky slopes providing land access to the beaches.

Head east to Indian Cove. From here it is usually an easy, protected paddle across Upright Channel back to your starting point at Odlin County Park.

48 Clark Island

Because moorings here are somewhat exposed, Clark Island gets fewer overnight boaters than other state park islands in the northern San Juans. The island includes paths winding through madrona bordering its shores, a gravel beach on one side and sand on the other, plus extensive tide pools to explore. Its location allows radically different approach routes. The southern route from Doe Bay on Orcas Island is the shorter, though it requires a ferry ride from the mainland. The launch point at Doe Bay Resort offers opportunities to camp, rent a cabin, or just take a soak in their hot tubs on the way home. The northern route originates in the Lummi Indian Reservation between Bellingham and Ferndale. Few kayakers think to use this northeastern approach to the San Juans; it has significant advantages.

Duration: Full day to overnight.

Rating: *Exposed.* Both routes require 1.5- to 2-mile crossings through a strong current with possible shipping traffic on the northern route. Tide rips are likely along either route.

Navigation Aids: SeaTrails WA 004, 005; NOAA charts 18423 SC or 18421 (both 1:80,000), or 18430 (1:25,000); Rosario Strait current tables with local corrections or the Canadian *Current Atlas.*

Planning Considerations: For the southern route aim for times of least current in the area between the north shore of Orcas Island and Clark Island. Pay heed to the behavior of the eddies in this area and accompanying hazards described below. For the approach from Gooseberry Point around Lummi Island plan for times of minimal current in Rosario Strait. Also try to avoid current flow conflicting with the likely wind direction. Currents in this area have no precise secondary reference station in the NOAA current tables. The station 1.5 miles north of Clark Island is closest. The Canadian *Current Atlas* is most useful for gauging the timing and strength of the currents on this crossing.

Getting There and Launching

Doe Bay Resort: From the Orcas Island ferry landing follow Orcas Road north to Eastsound. Veer right onto Main Street and follow through town. Main will become Crescent Beach Drive. Take a right onto Olga Road and follow it approximately 6 miles to Olga. Take a left on Point Lawrence Road

Isolated Clark Island and Barnes Island in the distance

to Doe Bay Resort. A popular retreat for people with an inclination toward natural foods and living, Doe Bay's cabins, saunas, and hot tubs are busy year round. An area for tent camping is nearby. There is also a café and a natural-foods general store. The management asks a nominal fee to camp and launch there. A soak in the hot tubs is an additional fee.

Gooseberry Point: See the Lummi Island chapter for directions to the Gooseberry Point launch. For Bellingham or Vancouver, British Columbia, residents, this northern approach is the most convenient access to the northern San Juans as well as Sucia, Maria, and Patos islands. Seattle-area dwellers wishing to access this area will find it takes less time to drive to Gooseberry Point than to ferry to Orcas Island. During busy summer weekends, the time saved may amount to a half-day or more due to San Juan Islands ferry traffic backups.

Village Point: This launch is along the road on Lummi Island, 0.6 mile north of the point off West Shore Drive. Look for two pull-outs and a trail going about 50 yards to a gravel beach. The beach is also 0.6 mile south of the Willow Inn.

Routes

Doe Bay to Clark Island: *Exposed.* The distance from Doe Bay to Clark Island is about 4 miles. Though the shoreline of Orcas north from Doe Bay makes pretty paddling, consider a detour 0.5 mile offshore to the Peapod Rocks when weather permits and currents are favorable. This San Juan Islands National Wildlife Refuge unit has abundant birdlife, seals, and sometimes sea lions. Remember no landings are permitted, and keep a distance of 200 yards from these and other refuge rocks.

Lawrence Point is DNR land and, though open to camping, is not a particularly good place for it. There are no facilities. The grassy point does make a pleasant lunch stop or a place to watch the swirling currents to wait for favorable ones. Access is via two narrow pebble beaches on the south side of the point.

The 1.5-mile crossing to Clark Island from Lawrence Point can expose you to hazards created by strong currents. Both flood and ebb tides produce large eddies around Lawrence Point, and powerful rips may occur at the boundaries with the main current streams. The Canadian *Current Atlas* gives the best picture of the complex flows in this area. Note that strong east-flowing currents

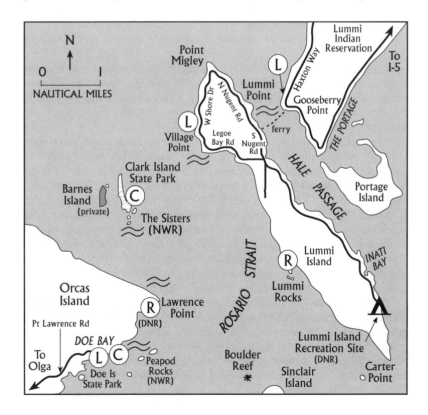

move along the shore of Orcas Island on large flood exchanges in this area, the opposite of what might be expected, and flow the same way on large ebbs too! The current can produce strong tide rips as it passes over a shoal not shown on chart 18423 SC, just east of a line between Lawrence Point and Clark Island. Hence, time your crossing to the Lawrence Point area to arrive at slack time. Also avoid this area on ebbs if southerly winds are likely. Because there are eddies near the point, a close-in route is usually safest if you must pass by while the current is running.

Gooseberry Point to Clark Island: *Exposed.* The paddling distance is approximately 7 miles each way around the north end of Lummi Island. The south end makes a much longer but interesting alternative, adding about 13 miles to the trip with a possible overnight stop at Lummi Island Recreation Site (see the Lummi Island chapter for details).

For the northern route, begin with the 1-mile crossing of Hale Passage. Realize the currents can be as strong as several knots. A flood current is advantageous for reaching the north end of the island; you can gradually work across while the moving water carries you north. The Lummi Island shore is mostly residential until you round Point Migley. From there it dwindles as bluffs prevent development along the water and conceal it from view. Strong wind opposing currents can make this section a treacherous paddle.

The 2-mile Clark Island crossing from Village Point is exposed to the Strait of Georgia to the north and Rosario Strait to the south. Swift currents with possible tide rips and busy shipping in Rosario Strait, particularly tankers en route to Ferndale's Cherry Point terminal, make this segment of the route challenging. Launch north of Village Point along West Shore Drive via a public beach accessed from the road. Look for cars or a pull-out along the road.

Currents move very swiftly around both ends of Clark Island and nearby privately owned Barnes Island. Watch out for tide rips. The Sisters Islands to the southeast of Clark Island are units of the San Juan Islands National Wildlife Refuge. Landings are prohibited; keep 200 yards distance to avoid disturbing the residents.

Paths circle the low bluffs around the southern end of Clark Island with open madrona woods onshore and extensive tide pools and flats exposing themselves at low tide. There are no trails to the brushy north end, but rounding the cliffs and offshore rocks makes a nice paddling excursion. There is a sand beach on the island's west side and a gravel one on the east. The west beach sites are for picnicking; camping is allowed on sites most easily reached from the eastside.

Eight campsites are spaced out along the east beach and are low enough that a loaded kayak can be dragged over the smooth gravel right into camp. No water is available on the island. The beach sites are vulnerable to bad weather; two sites in the woods at the narrowest point of the island are best at those times. Camping by individual parties is first-come, first-served for all sites but one, which can be reserved for groups by calling Washington State Parks at 360-376-2073.

49 Point Doughty on Orcas Island

Accessible only from the water, this little DNR Recreation Site at Orcas Island's northwest tip has attractive madrona and fir woods, tide pools, and spectacular cliffs complete with a small sea cave or two on the north side. The Cascadia Marine Trail's campsite has views facing south and west. (See chapter 50 for the map.)

Duration: Part day to overnight.

Rating: *Moderate.* A north wind can create rough conditions and surf along the Orcas north shore. Current and tide rips are likely off the point.

Navigation Aids: SeaTrails WA 004; NOAA charts 18423 SC or 18421 (both 1:80,000), 18431 (1:25,000); Canadian *Current Atlas*.

Planning Considerations: Aim for times of least current to avoid tide rips while rounding Point Doughty. Give the point a wide berth in rough seas.

Getting There and Launching

From the Orcas Island ferry dock, drive north to Eastsound. At Eastsound, drive north on North Beach Road.

North Beach Road End: Launch from the gravel beach at the end of North Beach Road. Parking is free and allowed along the road but is restricted to five cars. Do not expect to find space on summer weekends as it is an extremely popular launch. Respect the private homes on both sides of the launch. You can park in the lot for three days.

Outer Island Expeditions located just west of the North Beach launch offers a water taxi to carry you and your boat to the islands. They also offer tours and related services. For additional information: www.outerislandx.com; 360-376-3711.

Route

The round-trip distance from North Beach to Point Doughty is about 4.2 miles. Follow the beach west past occasional homes and small resorts. A mile short of the point the shore begins to rise, and sheer cliffs line the remaining distance. Rocks and shoals are extensive off the point, and together with swift currents produce significant tide rips. A close inshore route around the point may avoid them if the seas are smooth enough to allow it. Those with rock gardening experience may enjoy shooting the gap between the rocks on the point.

An unprotected moorage and largely rock beach limit visits by other boaters, though the point is popular with scuba divers. Access is via a small beach on the south side of the point. At midtide or above, landings are on pebbles and

A Cascadia Marine Trail site, Point Doughty is known for its sheer cliffs and fabulous views.

gravel; low tide approaches are rocky and may be hard on the boat if there is a southerly sea running.

There is one campsite with Cascadia Marine Trail designation, the other is open to all boaters on a first-come-use basis. Included are vault toilets, picnic tables, and garbage cans, but water is not available. One campsite has good views to the south and west, but poor weather protection. The other is tucked into the trees and is a good all-weather camp, but without views. Trails lead east from the campsites along the south bluffs and eventually to the YMCA's Camp Orkila, 1 mile to the east, though there is no public access by land.

50 Patos, Sucia, and Matia Islands

This chain of state park and wildlife refuge islands is famed for its intricate geology as well as its potentially treacherous waters. Separated by miles of sea from other islands in the San Juan group to the south, and open to the expanse of the Strait of Georgia, they are relatively isolated and very beautiful.

Duration: Overnight to multiple nights.

Rating: *Exposed.* Though this area is sometimes millpond smooth, it is also well known for producing strong but erratic currents and big seas that develop from northerly winds on fair afternoons. This is no place for inexperienced paddlers!

Navigation Aids: SeaTrails WA 004; NOAA charts 18423 SC or 18421 (both 1:80,000), or 18431 (1:25,000); Rosario Strait current tables or the Canadian *Current Atlas.*

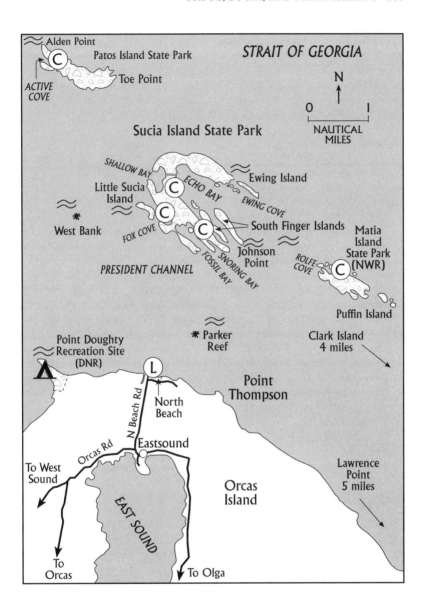

Planning Considerations: All routes to these islands put paddlers at the mercy of the weather and strong currents during long crossings. Definitely consult forecasts and be prepared to lay over in the islands during bad weather. Currents are strong throughout the area but not reliably predictable (see the discussion in the North Beach to Sucia Island route).

Getting There and Launching

From the Orcas Island ferry dock, drive north to Eastsound. At Eastsound, drive north on North Beach Road. Outer Island Expeditions, located just west of the North Beach launch, offers a water taxi to carry you and your boat to the islands. They also offer tours and related services. For additional information: www.outerislandx.com; 360-376-3711.

Routes

A weekend trip from North Beach to Sucia Island (about a 4.2-mile round trip), with an optional excursion to Matia (add another 2-plus miles one way) is one of the most popular kayak outings in the San Juan Islands. Including Patos Island in the agenda adds another 5 miles or more to the total distance and usually merits another overnight on that island.

North Beach to Sucia Island: *Exposed.* The round-trip distance is about 5 miles, depending on your destination on Sucia Island. The crossing from North Beach to the nearest point on Sucia Island is 2 miles. The greatest hazard en route is Parker Reef. It consists of two separate shoals located less than halfway across. The area around the reefs can develop dangerous rips in strong currents, sometimes exceeding 2 knots, which are made worse by contrary winds. As a warning, a kayaking fatality has occurred here. Looks can be deceiving. The crossing can appear glassy and inviting, yet can change rather quickly.

Generally, the west-flowing ebb current is considered the most dangerous. The Canadian *Current Atlas* shows the flood currents coming around the east and west sides of Orcas Island, meeting and weakening in this area. Timing of these currents is somewhat unreliable. There have been reports of slacks varying greatly from their predicted times and current even flowing reverse of what was predicted.

Nonetheless, this route attracts large numbers of paddlers during the summer months, including novices. As the record shows, more than a few first-time kayakers have had bad experiences between Sucia and Orcas, with some lucky to escape with their lives. To that point this route deserves an *Exposed* rating; the potential for risk remains very high and must be considered into the planning of this trip.

Sucia Island is the hub of cruising in the northern San Juan Islands for yachts and kayaks alike. You are least likely to find solitude in the summer on Sucia Island, but other attractions make up for it. This island complex, in actuality at least six separate islands, can absorb a day's exploring by kayak and another day by foot along the extensive trail system. Little Sucia Island is an eagle preserve. No camping or fires are allowed. The bizarre formations of water-dissolved rock are unsurpassed; seals abound on and around them.

The majority of visitors to Sucia Island are found in Fossil and Echo bays where there are extensive campsites with drinking water available in summer months and solar composting toilets. The low banks and mixed shell and gravel beaches make attractive camping for kayakers in Fossil Bay or in adjoining Fox Cove. Echo Bay and Shallow Bay just across the island to the west have similar camps with drinking water nearby at the picnic shelters in northern Shallow

One of many of Sucia Island's interesting geological features

Bay. There is a 125-foot portage from Echo to Shallow bay at the back side of each bay to avoid a long paddle around to each.

Fossil Bay and Echo Bay complexes are the best campsites for the off-season, more so since driftwood for fires piles up in Echo Bay during the winter. Kayakers visiting Sucia Island during the summer generally prefer Ewing Cove or Snoring Bay for the relative isolation from other boaters and campers that these areas afford. You can land but not camp at Ewing Cove. Elsewhere on the island camp only at sites designated with a fire ring and/or a picnic table. Camping outside these areas is prohibited. Watch for rips off Johnson Point.

Campsites are often full to capacity at Sucia on busy summer weekends. As a San Juan marine park, a special reservation service is provided for group camping only through Washington State Parks. This is best done well in advance by calling 360-376-2073. Otherwise, all camping is on a first-come, first-served basis.

North Beach or Sucia Island to Matia Island: *Exposed.* The crossing from Orcas to Matia Island is slightly longer, about 2.5 miles, and may involve strong currents, though the problems of the shallows at Parker Reef are easier to avoid.

Located a little more than 1 mile from Sucia Island, Matia Island is hard-pressed to maintain its wild quality in the face of nearby boating activity. Matia Island is owned entirely by the federal government as a national wildlife refuge for bald eagles and pelagic cormorants. Yet five acres at Rolfe Cove are formally leased to the Washington State Parks and Recreation Commission, which also manages the rest of the island for the US Fish and Wildlife Service.

Camping is confined to Rolfe Cove. Rolfe is a very protected cove with steep walls on two sides. No open fires are allowed. It affords well-protected sites above the gravel beach and low bluffs. A composting toilet is nearby, but no water is provided on the island (water can be found on Sucia in summer). Nearby Eagle Cove is outside the state park lease area and closed to camping.

Exploring ashore should be confined to a trail loop that runs down the center of the island and returns on the south side.

Around Matia Island are numerous coves best visited by boat to comply with refuge objectives of least on-shore disturbance. On the south side is the "hermit's cove" where remnants of a solitary island dweller's structures dating to the 1920s can still be seen. At the southeast corner are coves with pebble beaches. Refuge managers ask that you avoid the cove at the east end of the island facing Puffin Island because of the eagles that nest there. Keep at least 200 yards distance from Puffin Island to avoid disturbing that refuge as well.

North Beach or Sucia Island to Patos Island: *Exposed.* Patos Island can be reached from North Beach by following the Orcas shore west to Point Doughty, then crossing slightly over 4 miles of open water. Strong currents and tide rips are possible along this route. The safer but longer alternative is to head for Sucia Island first, then cut across to Patos Island at the time of slack water. Both routes are safer and far easier on the flood current. Watch for rips in the area of West Bank marked by an extensive kelp bed.

Patos Island is one of the wildest islands in the northern chain. A small portion of the island on the west side is managed by Washington State and the remainder is managed by the Bureau of Land Management's Wenatchee office. Four acres at Alden Point include a Coast Guard light station, which was established in 1893. All recreational use is confined to the west end of the island at Active Cove. There's also a 1.5-mile loop trail. Facilities include seven campsites, one picnic site, two pit and one vault toilet. There is no water or garbage service. Campers must register at the bulletin board near the beach.

Patos Island does merit a circumnavigation, taking care to avoid disturbing the eagles and other wildlife along the way. On the south shore are bluffs and low cliffs with the interestingly eroded sandstone conglomerate rocks that characterize this island chain. The east end has two coves with pebble beaches and long rock reefs. They are revealed at low tide a long distance from shore, giving Toe Point its name. These beaches characterize the majority of the northern shoreline.

Great Rectangle Route: *Exposed.* The paddling distance is about 25 miles. This string of Patos, Sucia, and Matia islands can be integrated into a large box route including Clark Island (see the Clark Island chapter) with the fourth side formed by the entire north shore of Orcas Island. Camping is at the three islands described above, Clark Island, and Point Doughty on northwestern Orcas Island (see the Point Doughty chapter). Plan on two or, better yet, at least three nights for this trip.

Getting from Matia Island to Clark Island involves a 4-mile crossing with active currents between Clark and Orcas islands, making both crossings precarious in unfavorable conditions. (The Clark Island chapter includes a description of currents between Clark and Orcas islands.) In unsettled weather it's safer to cut this area out of the rectangle.

The north shore of Orcas Island forms the return leg of the rectangle route. Though this 6-mile-long linear shoreline between Lawrence Point and North

Beach appears unexciting on the chart, it is gratifying to follow. However, there are few spots for an emergency camp, so do your best to plan for fair weather during this leg of the journey. Most of the shore is very steep with either wooded scree slopes or cliffs rising right from sea level. There are occasional narrow gravel beaches at the base, but rarely anywhere to go above.

The coast is wild—look for otter and hauled-out seals—and has a few surprise bits of history. At one point there is an old limestone kiln fitted into the steep slope so unobtrusively that most other boaters probably miss it. Farther on is an extensive, overgrown quarry long since covered by a vigorous young fir forest. Near the tiny extension of Moran State Park that reaches the sea is a rarity for the San Juan Islands—a waterfall spilling into the sea at high tide. Houses finally appear during the final third of the way to North Beach.

51 Jones Island

Sandy beaches, trails that meander through madrona groves and meadows, and a resident deer herd that mingles with campers make Jones Island one of the most popular San Juan Island destinations for kayakers. Other boaters enjoy it too, so much so that campsites are often scarce on summer weekends. This area can also be combined with a circumnavigation of Shaw Island (see the Shaw Island chapter) and a paddle through the Wasp Islands.

Duration: Full day or overnight.

Rating: *Moderate.* The trip involves a 0.5-mile open-water crossing in currents up to 2 knots.

Navigation Aids: SeaTrails WA 002, 003, 004; NOAA charts 18423 SC or 18421 (both 1:80,000), and 18434 (1:25,000); San Juan Channel current table or the Canadian *Current Atlas* in particular are useful for route timing with favorable flows.

Planning Considerations: Arrive early to secure a campsite on summer weekends. Coordinate with currents in Wasp Passage, Pole Pass, and, if Friday Harbor is a trip terminus, San Juan Channel. Raccoons on Jones can be a problem.

Note: For kayakers wheeling their watercraft aboard the ferry, convenient water access is now limited to Friday Harbor. Launching near the ferry dock at Shaw Island is no longer possible, and at Orcas Island questionable. However, three routes are still described using these landings as starting points in the hopes that they or nearby alternatives will be made available through the efforts of organizations such as WWTA. Including these routes also allows the kayaker the option to integrate them into the Shaw circumnavigation described in chapter 47 or as segments into trips of their own design.

Getting There and Launching

Take the San Juan Islands ferry to either Orcas Island or San Juan Island, depending on the launch site to be used.

West Sound on Orcas Island: From the ferry, take Orcas Road north. Take a left on Deer Harbor Road and follow it for about a mile to West Sound. After the marina but just before the T intersection at Crow Valley Road, there's a pull-out on the north side of the road where kayakers park. Launch across the street at the public docks. There are no facilities, but there are restaurants nearby.

Deer Harbor on Orcas Island: Continue past West Sound on Deer Harbor Road (see directions above) a few more miles to Deer Harbor. This launch site provides the closest access to Jones Island. Driving to Deer Harbor to launch reduces the one-way paddling distance to Jones Island to about 2 miles. Water access is at Deer Harbor Marina and Resort. They charge a fee to launch and to park, which you can pay at the store. All the basic amenities are there, including restrooms with showers, water, a boat cleaning hose, a small store for essential provisions, public telephone, along with sea kayak rentals. Call the marina for additional information: 360-376-3037.

Orcas Island Ferry Landing: Access at the ferry landing is not possible, although local paddlers have reported that an option is to use the nearby private oil company dock through advance arrangement. Another possibility is getting permission to launch from the Orcas Outdoors dock to the west of the ferry. For additional information: www.orcasoutdoors.com.

Friday Harbor: The launch is the dinghy dock at the public wharf north of the ferry landing. There is a launch fee, which is paid at the marina, and there are two kayak launch slots there. The marina has public restrooms and coin-operated showers. Parking in Friday Harbor is extremely scarce during the summer. Boating traffic in Friday Harbor in the summer can be very busy. Keep clear of ferry traffic on these routes.

Shaw Island: There is no launching at the ferry terminal. The closest access point is at Shaw Island County Park on the south side of the island. Plan on driving if you use this option as access to the waters of the San Juan Islands. It is too far to wheel a kayak unless you are extremely determined. The distance is 2 miles. Take Blind Bay Road from the ferry south. Take a left on Squaw Bay Road and look for signs for Shaw Island County Park. There is camping at the park.

Routes

Deer Harbor to Jones Island: *Moderate.* The paddling distance is 2.9 miles. Follow the western shore of Deer Harbor toward Steep Point, passing rocky shores covered with madronas, cliffs, and occasional homes. All of the shoreline along this route is private, so plan to stay in your boat until you reach Jones Island. This route would qualify for a *Protected* rating if not for the Spring Passage crossing. Here currents can reach almost 2 knots. You may need to ferry upstream at a large angle to hold your position during the crossing. Seas in the passage can get quite rough when the wind opposes the current. Tide

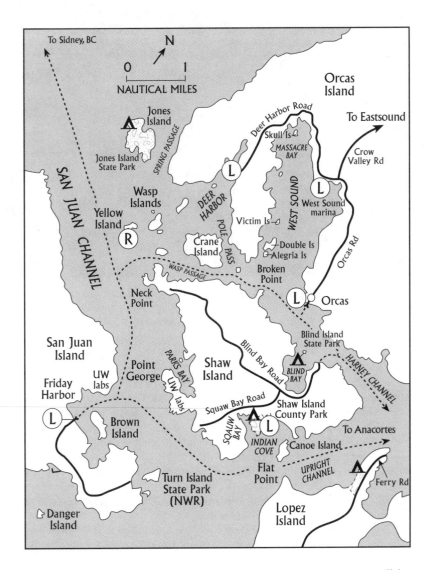

rips are also possible. To be safest, time this crossing when currents will be flowing in the same direction as the probable wind direction.

Jones Island State Park is a very popular destination for kayakers and other boaters. Approach from the south and take-out in the cove for a short walk to the Cascadia Marine Trail campsite. There are two sites, a picnic table, a compositing toilet, and fire pit. Water is only available in summer. Fees for the Cascadia Marine Trail site are $12 a night for up to eight people. Other campsites are first-come, first-served and difficult to find on summer weekends.

A kayak tour paddles through the craggy rocks and madrona lined shorelines of the Wasp Islands.

Only group reservations can be made by calling Washington State Parks: 360-902-8844.

Generally, most powerboaters prefer the more protected northern cove where there is a dock. There are other sites scattered around the island, connected by the 2 miles of island trails. Protect your gear and food from the island's posse of commando raccoons, which will do anything to gain access to your food.

Friday Harbor to Jones Island: *Moderate.* The paddling distance is 6.2 miles. This is a route often used by kayakers riding the ferries as foot-passengers. Aside from Yellow Island (described below) there are no public shorelines along the route, but with favorable current and wind, this trip should take less than two hours. Currents in this part of San Juan Channel can attain about 1 knot. Planning to use them is worthwhile. Watch for ferry and recreational boating traffic when crossing to Jones.

The shoreline of Shaw Island is probably the more interesting side to follow (see the circumnavigation route in the Shaw Island chapter for details) and under the appropriate conditions, you can cross to the San Juan Island side at Point George. Point George and Parks Bay behind it are part of a University of Washington biological preserve; landings are not allowed.

At Friday Harbor the public dinghy dock north of the ferry landing provides the closest place to the ferry to launch and land. Check in with the marina office for information on launching and parking fees.

West Sound on Orcas Island to Jones Island via Pole Pass: *Moderate.* The paddling distance is 5.5 miles from the public launch west of the West Sound Marina. Take a short side trip to the north to Massacre Bay to view the migratory waterfowl that fill the bay. Victim and Skull islands were named after the bloody Indian war of 1858, when the Haidas from British Columbia ventured south to catch slaves. One hundred local Lummi people were killed. Human remains from this period were found at Haida Point in 1900. Head south to paddle on west shore by the inside of Victim Island, Double Island, and Alegria Island. Enjoy views of 1500-foot-high Turtleback Mountain to the east. Round Caldwell Point and enter Pole Pass on the inside of Crane Island.

Pole Pass is a little tide race that can run at more than 2 knots for a short distance. It is rarely dangerous, but boat wakes in the riffles on the downstream side can make it quite rough. It is possible to go through against the current because it is quite weak in the approaches. There are eddies to use on the Orcas Island side with a hard push required for the short distance in the narrows against the flow. Be especially wary of boat traffic in Pole Pass, as it is difficult to see what is coming the other way as you approach. Currents in the passages between Shaw and Orcas islands generally flow westward during the flood tide and eastward during the ebb.

Currents in this area are rarely fast enough to be hazardous, but can substantially affect paddling effort. With the exception of Blind Island State Park (see the Shaw Island chapter for details) and the public tidelands at Broken Point, there is no public access ashore along this route. However, it can be covered in less than two hours with favorable currents.

Orcas, Shaw, and San Juan Islands to Jones Island via the Wasp Islands: *Moderate.* Use chart 18434. While paddling to Jones, take a side trip to the Wasp Islands, a series of rocky islets with a colorful history and great wildlife viewing. Located north of Wasp Passage on the west side of Crane Island, the name Wasp came from a warship in the War of 1812. Wasp Passage is known as the "rockpile" by locals.

South of Jones Island, scattered with rocks and islets, the Wasp Islands make for interesting and scenic paddling. Most of the Wasp Islands are privately owned and a few smaller ones are part of the San Juan National Wildlife Refuge in which landings are prohibited. Coon's pocket beaches and 2000 feet of the southern portion of McDonnell Island are public tidelands. The public areas are only below the mean high water level.

Currents in this area are moderate. Wasp Passage runs swiftly enough to produce rips in the area of Crane Island. The major hazard here is the ferry that takes this route between Friday Harbor and Orcas Island. It can come around the corner quite suddenly from either direction. Do not dawdle in midchannel at Wasp Passage and keep your group tightly together for all channel crossings. Also watch out for ferry wakes colliding with an opposing current (when the ferry is traveling against the current), as these can become steep and nasty breakers. The wake will smooth out after entering eddies along the sides of the passage.

The Shaw Island shore of Wasp Passage is a fine place to practice using shore eddies to travel against the current, especially if you need to do so! Note that the currents in this area run counter to what might be expected; they flow west into San Juan Channel on the flood tide.

In 1946, Lee and Tib Dodd purchased Yellow Island. The cabin was built from driftwood from the island's beaches. A guest house and sauna on the west shore are now gone. In 1960, Lee died on the island and his ashes were buried on his favorite spot on Hummingbird Hill. Tib lived on the island for six months a year until 1978. Owned by The Nature Conservancy, Yellow Island is managed to perpetuate the island's floral communities. The main attraction is the spring flowers that begin to bloom in late March and are at their best from mid-April through early summer. Resident caretakers live in the cabin on the southwest shore.

Kayakers should be aware that Yellow Island has limited access, and there are no camping, restrooms, or other facilities. Collecting plants or intertidal life, smoking, pets, picnicking, and fires are prohibited. The island is open 10:00 AM to 4:00 PM year round. Only land on the southeast beach below the Dodd cabin. The east spit is open to landings only in the spring and fall. Do not beach watercraft on the west spit. For more information, contact The Nature Conservancy in Seattle: 206-343-4345.

52 South and West San Juan Island

Kayakers come here for two distinct reasons. The first is whales: Haro Strait is the best place to see orcas during the summer months. Lime Kiln State Park was developed primarily for public observation of the whales that pass offshore regularly. The second is the barren beauty: the largely tree-less southwestern coast of San Juan Island is unique for the Northwest. The exposure to southerly and westerly winds and big seas along its beaches make it all the wilder. But to the north, western San Juan Island has a gentler face with inter-island channels and the accessible historical attractions of English Camp.

Duration: Part day to multiple nights.

Rating: *Moderate* or *Exposed*. *Exposed* routes involve strong currents with probable tide rips, characteristically strong winds with fully developed seas, and resulting surf on the beaches. See the description of wind patterns under the South Beach to Griffin Bay route.

Navigation Aids: SeaTrails WA 002, 003; NOAA charts 18423 SC or 18421 (both 1:80,000), or 18433 and 18434 (both 1:25,000); San Juan Channel current table.

Planning Considerations: Avoid mid- to late afternoon for paddling west of Cattle Point, when westerlies from the Strait of Juan de Fuca are strongest. Plan your trips accordingly with the currents, which can be strong in certain areas on the island. Heavy fog in August can make visibility difficult along the west and south sides of the island.

An orca sighting off Lime Kiln State Park, San Juan Island

Getting There and Launching

There are several options for launching on the island whether you're doing a day trip, shuttle, overnight, or a 30-mile circumnavigation. San Juan Taxi can also help you transport your paddling craft from the ferry to a put-in, or between launches. For additional information: www.sjtaxi.com.

Friday Harbor: The launch is the dinghy dock at the public wharf north of the ferry landing. There is a launch fee, which is paid at the marina, and there are two kayak launch slots there. The marina has public restrooms and coin-operated showers. Parking in Friday Harbor is extremely scarce during the summer. Boating traffic in Friday Harbor in the summer can be very busy. Keep clear of ferry traffic on these routes. Contact the marina office for additional information: 360-378-2688.

Roche Harbor: Starting from the north, Roche Harbor Resort is a popular launch spot for a number of routes (see the Stuart Island chapter for directions and details on launching here). You can launch on the south side of the main dock by the parking lot. Kayak and SUP rentals are available on the water in front of the resort through San Juan Outfitters: 866-810-1483. To contact the Roche Harbor Resort, call 800-586-3590.

English Camp: This launch is about 8.2 miles from Friday Harbor. From the ferry landing follow Spring Street to Second Street on the right. Follow this street, bearing left where it becomes Guard Street. This eventually becomes Beaverton Valley Road and then West Valley Road. Turn off to the left for the entrance to English Camp and go down the hill to the lot. Boats will have to be carried several hundred yards along a gravel walkway and lawn, smooth enough for carts, to the sand and cobble beach. Park rangers prefer that you launch at the north end of the beach. The park provides restrooms and interpretive facilities that are open during the summer months.

San Juan County Park: Directions for the park start the same as for English Camp, except that you turn left onto Mitchell Bay Road about 9.3 miles from town. Then turn left where it becomes the Westside Road and follow it to the park at Smallpox Bay. There is a small parking lot with easy access to the gravel beach. Check with the park office for the best place to park your vehicle. Campsites, restrooms, and water are available. Overnight parking for boaters and paddlers of smaller watercraft is $20 a night. Note: You are required to watch a video at the park office about paddling etiquette around whales. Heavy paddling traffic in recent years has put public water access on the west side of the island in jeopardy. Please respect paddling etiquette here so access stays open for others in the future. Call the San Juan County Park's line for additional information: 360-378-8420.

Eagle Cove: This launch point is located just north of the American Camp portion of San Juan Island National Historical Park. To reach the area from the Friday Harbor ferry landing, follow Spring Street three blocks to a Y intersection and go left on Argyle Street. This becomes Cattle Point Road and reaches the park after about 5 miles. Just before the park entrance, turn right onto Eagle Cove Road and go 0.5 mile to the parking lot. Boats must be carried 100 yards downhill on a sometimes-slippery path to the gravel beach. This launch point will have more protection from surf than the beaches at Salmon Banks Lane farther south.

Fourth of July Beach: Traveling south in the park, the next launch spot is Fourth of July Beach. It provides access to the southeast shore of the island in Griffin Bay. Turn left off Cattle Point Road 1 mile south of the park entrance and drive to the small picnic area lot. The beach is about 100 yards on a gravel path beyond the lot and busy on warm weekends.

South Beach: With a huge parking area giving easy access to continuous gravel beaches facing southwest, this launch is reached by turning right off Cattle Point Road onto Pickett's Lane a short distance south of the Fourth of July Beach intersection. Launches could be rough here in even a moderate wind.

Cattle Point Picnic Area: This day-use launch gives access to the southern tip of the island and the tidal rapids at Shark Reef. Continue 0.75 mile past the point where you leave the eastern edge of the national park to the small lot on the right. Boats must be carried 50 yards down a steep embankment to a sandy beach. Cattle Point itself offers some protection against surf at the west end of the beach.

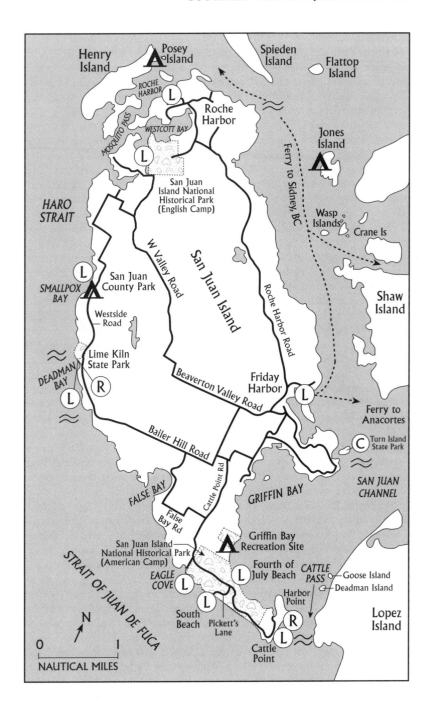

Routes
South Beach to Griffin Bay via Cattle Point: *Exposed.* The paddling distance is 5 miles. Logistically this is the easiest route, as the 1.5-mile walk between the launch and take-out points can eliminate the need for a car shuttle. A lunch stop could be taken at Cattle Point Picnic Area. Plan for plenty of time in Griffin Bay to explore its three lagoons.

The *Exposed* rating is based on both currents and wind. Currents at San Juan Channel's south entrance can reach 5 knots when heavy tide rips are likely, especially around Goose Island and Deadman Island on the Lopez Island side. Staying close inshore on the San Juan Island side may prove best. The current usually flows east off Cattle Point because a large eddy forms there during the ebb cycle. This, combined with the typical daily fair-weather wind pattern, suggests paddling from west to east. A flood current is most favorable.

The Haro Strait side of southern San Juan Island is exposed to bad-weather winds from the south and is a very windy area in fair weather as well. When high pressure builds, strong offshore in-flowing winds in the Strait of Juan de Fuca often produce westerlies of up to 25 knots in the afternoon. They are strongest from about 2:00 AM to 6:00 PM. A little farther north in the strait they become southwesterlies. At the north end of San Juan Island the effects of the strait are less where northwesterlies blow. Pacific swells can penetrate through the Strait of Juan de Fuca and, amplified by local wind, develop considerable surf on southwestern San Juan Island beaches, such as South Beach. Surf is likely to be smallest in the morning on sunny days. Locals have been known to find good surfing here, saving a longer trip to the strait or coast for waves.

If wind makes travel west around Cattle Point imprudent, consider beginning at Cattle Point Picnic Area, which cuts the paddling distance to 3 miles. There is plenty to explore in Griffin Bay. There are three high-tide lagoons and a maze of old roads meandering through the woods above and between them. If the currents are close to slack you can add 2 miles to the route by paddling across the channel narrows to Lopez Island. Here you can visit undeveloped Shark Reef Recreation Site just south of Kings Point. If you enjoy playing in tidal rapids, Shark Reef on a strong tide exchange can provide some fun.

Smallpox Bay (San Juan County Park) to Lime Kiln Point: *Exposed.* The round-trip paddling distance is 4 miles often in fast-moving current with a few tide rips. This route can be paddled one way with a 3-mile car shuttle to Deadman Bay just south of Lime Kiln State Park. Please respect private property above the beach. To go ashore at the park, continue around the point and land on the north end of the beach at Deadman Bay. Deadman is part of the San Juan Preservation Trust. Shores along the way to Lime Kiln Point are consistently rocky with residences here and there. In a bight just north of the point are the old lime kilns, which are easily identified by the white piles of material on the hillside.

This is the best coastline for whales. The population of orcas called the "Southern Residents" are listed as endangered by Endangered Species Act. These whales frequent Puget Sound and the San Juan Islands in the summer and fall months each year. They include at least three separate extended Orca families, called J, K, and L pods. Strict regulations for paddlers and boaters have been imposed to protect the whales. A voluntary motor boat exclusion zone stretches from Mitchell Bay to the north end of Eagle Point. This requires motor boats to stay a quarter of a mile offshore in most areas and a half mile offshore by Lime Kiln Point. Read about the Kayak Education and Leadership Program (KELP) before entering these waters. For additional information: www.bewhalewise.org. The basics of conduct include not paddling within 200 yards of the whales and not positioning yourself in their path of travel or behind them. You should also paddle at minimum speed within 400 yards of the animals.

Facilities and interpretive displays at Lime Kiln State Park are geared toward whale watching. On a busy summer day, hundreds of people may line the viewing areas in the park. Whale watching boats will be seen offshore as well as kayaking tours. Minke and pilot whales, Dall's and harbor porpoise, and even occasional gray whales are sighted here, along with daily sightings of the pods of orcas.

Roche Harbor to English Camp via Mosquito Pass: *Moderate.* The round-trip paddling distance is 5 miles or half that for one-way paddling with a 4-mile car shuttle. This entire route is very well protected from winds and an excellent route for most weather conditions. However, currents in Mosquito Pass can be strong and erratic. There are no predictions for them in the current guides. Paddlers not experienced with currents should stay close to the eastern side of the channel near Mosquito Pass. This is probably the easiest route for going through against the current. South of the pass, turn left to enter even more protected waters in Garrison Bay. Land on the north end of the beach. There is a visitor center in the white barracks building just inshore from the blockhouse. Restrooms are nearby.

Great San Juan Island Tour: *Exposed.* The circumnavigation distance is about 30 miles. Shorter partial circuits include Cattle Point to Roche Harbor (17 miles) and Smallpox Bay to Friday Harbor (20 miles). Campsites around San Juan Island are sparse and irregularly spaced with a 14-mile gap at the southwest portion. Choices include: Turn Island State Park just south of Friday Harbor (see the Shaw Island chapter for details) and three Cascadia Marine Trail sites—Griffin Bay Recreation Site, San Juan County Park at Smallpox Bay, and Posey Island north of Roche Harbor (see the Stuart Island chapter for details). There is no paddling launch at Snug Harbor on the northwest side of the island.

The Griffin Bay campsite, a Cascadia Marine Trail site, is located just south of Low Point in a meadow area directly inshore from Halftide Rock. Vault toilets, picnic tables, and three campsites are 400 yards inland at the trees. There is no water. The grassy path is smooth enough for boat carts if you feel the need to keep your boat nearby. There is no formal access to this recreation site from the road, and private property borders it.

The site on Posey Island is one mile northwest of Roche Harbor Resort. It has two sites with a maximum of sixteen people allowed. There are picnic tables, a fire ring, a vault toilet, and no water. Check the WWTA Website as fees vary throughout the year. Reservations are recommended in summer.

San Juan County Park in Smallpox Bay is a very popular campground with eighteen common sites and one Cascadia Marine Trail site, often full during the summer months. Fortunately, they have a reservation system and a group area for those who arrive under their own power. For additional information: 360-378-8420 or www.sanjuanco.com/Parks/sanjuan.aspx.

53 Stuart Island

Paddling to Stuart Island is among the "wildest" of the San Juan Island trips for two reasons: this destination is in a rarely experienced natural state, and the tidal forces are some of the strongest. This is no place for novices. You are likely to generate some excitement just paddling to and from Stuart Island, but its shorelines, two park areas, and Cascadia Marine Trail tent sites are sure to make the visit a pleasure.

Duration: Overnight or longer; two nights recommended.

Rating: *Protected* or *Exposed.* Strong currents and tide rips are likely throughout this area.

Navigation Aids: SeaTrails WA 003; NOAA charts 18423 SC, 18421 (both 1:80,000), or 18432 (1:25,000); San Juan Channel current tables with corrections for Limestone Point, Admiralty Inlet current tables with corrections for Turn Point, or the Canadian *Current Atlas.*

Planning Considerations: Currents in this area are very strong, and powerful tide rips form in all weather conditions. Coordinating travel with currents is essential for both efficiency and safety, particularly when there are larger-than-average tides.

Getting There and Launching

Launch from San Juan Island at either Roche Harbor or Friday Harbor.

Roche Harbor: Drive on Spring Street from the Friday Harbor ferry landing two blocks through town to Second Street and turn right. After three blocks Second Street bears left, becoming Guard Street. After one block, turn right onto Tucker Avenue. At the fork bear left onto Roche Harbor Road. The total distance is about 10 miles.

Launching at the Roche Harbor Resort is allowed from the boat launch ramp at the far end of the parking area west of the main resort facilities. Restrooms, a shower, water, and provisions are available. Kayaks and SUPs also can be rented at the resort through San Juan Outfitters: 866-810-1483. Contact the resort for additional information: 800-451-8910.

Friday Harbor: Use the public dinghy dock north of the ferry landing. There is a fee to pay at the marina office: 360-378-2688. Overnight parking is very limited and almost unobtainable in Friday Harbor during the summer. An alternative launch point is Deer Harbor on Orcas Island (see the Jones Island chapter).

Routes

Roche Harbor to Stuart Island: *Exposed.* The round-trip paddling distance is 10 miles. This is the shortest, least hazardous, and most popular approach to Stuart Island. Add 10 miles to the round-trip distance if launching from Friday Harbor.

Paddling between San Juan Island and Stuart Island probably requires more careful timing with the currents than anywhere else in the San Juan Islands. Though the crossings are generally 1 mile or less, the strong currents that run through these channels and the associated tide rips earn this trip its *Exposed* rating. However, since tidal cycles are predictable, careful planning and timing can make this a safer trip than those trips with the same rating due to longer crossings and associated bad-weather exposure.

The primary hazards occur in Spieden Channel. At the eastern end between Green Point on Spieden Island and Limestone Point on San Juan Island is some of the fastest water in the San Juan Islands; it runs over 5 knots on the year's biggest tides. Most significant are two powerful and extensive tide rips that form off both points on both the flood and ebb sets of the tide. The rip off Limestone Point forms 100 yards or more offshore, but the Green Point rip extends in quite close to Spieden Island's shoreline. There are less severe rips at the western end of the channel in the vicinity of Danger Shoal, Center Reef, and Sentinel Island.

The channels north of Spieden Island on either side of the Cactus Islands also run very swiftly, though you will find no local reference stations for them in the current tables. Currents here and in the northern San Juan Channel are somewhat fickle, particularly after the tide changes when patterns of flow around each side of San Juan Island are not yet established. One kayaker bound for Jones Island from Flattop Island reported being carried to Spieden Island on the flood current when it should have been flowing in the opposite direction.

Since the total distance from San Juan Island to Stuart Island is too far to paddle in a single slack current period, give most low current priority to Spieden Channel. Then you may round Spieden Island in whichever direction is the most convenient, keeping in mind the possible rips close to Green Point. Don't land on Spieden Island as it's private property. In 1970, the Jonas Brothers, taxidermists from Seattle, purchased the island and renamed it "Safari Island." They imported exotic animals such as Sitka deer, Spanish goats, Coriscan mouflon, and Indian blackbuck. They spent their free time driving around sipping martinis while hunting their imports. Environmentalists forced them to shut operations down, and the island was sold to another private land-owner. Many of the wildlife still roam the island.

Currents in Spieden Channel are slower between Davison Head and Sentinel Island than farther to the east. At the tail end of a flood tide is a good place to start, next riding the ebb current west along Spieden Island, and finally taking advantage of that same ebb current to reach Reid Harbor by compensating to the northeast against its flow.

Most of the small islands and rocks north of Spieden Island are within the San Juan Islands National Wildlife Refuge; do not approach them. If you

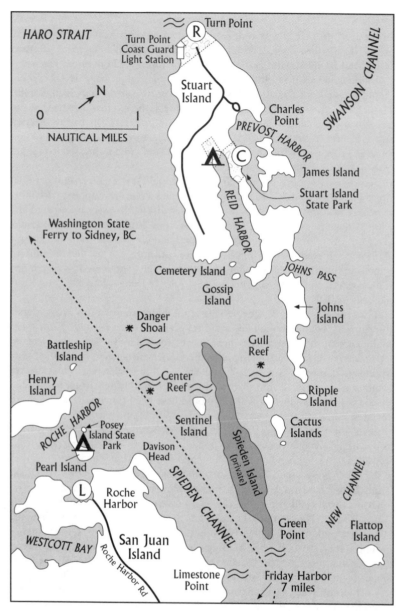

make a late start from Roche Harbor or run late on the return, the Cascadia Marine Trail group site on tiny Posey Island State Park outside the harbor's two approaches makes a suitable overnight spot. A composting vault toilet and a couple of picnic tables are provided; water is not available. The tent sites are located on the south, east, and west sides, with wind protection from the trees and brush at the center depending on wind direction. The maximum number of campers allowed at one time is sixteen, and it is strictly enforced on this fragile island. Since Posey Island is close to Roche Harbor's many summer homes, you can expect company in the summer months from young party-makers bringing their music with them.

For camping at Stuart Island, both Reid and Prevost harbors are suitable for kayakers. Both locations are within Stuart Island State Park, one of the few marine parks in the San Juan Islands where you can count on finding fresh water; the well rarely runs dry, yet state parks only provides assurances in the summer boating season.

The Cascadia Marine Trail tent sites at Reid Harbor are on either side of the marsh at the head of the bay. Number 15 through 18 are marine trail sites only. The rest of the sites are located on Prevost Harbor or on the ridge that separates Prevost and Reid harbors. Composting toilets are near the dock at Reid Harbor and to the right of the Prevost Harbor dock. Pit toilets are available at the head of Reid Harbor.

The beach here dries for a fair distance—great for clam diggers, but not so good for gear-laden kayakers on minus tides. The four tent sites have water only in summer.

Allowing a day layover at Stuart Island for some exploration by foot or boat is strongly recommended. Hiking the island's ample trails and little-used, unpaved country roads is a pleasure. There are also fine opportunities for day-long paddling loops, each skirting the island from one harbor to the other via Johns Pass to the east or Turn Point to the west.

If you circumnavigate Stuart Island, note that the currents flow around both ends of the island on their way to or from the Strait of Georgia. With the right timing both trips can be made with favorable currents for almost the entire distance. Consult the Canadian *Current Atlas* for specifics.

Reid Harbor to Prevost Harbor via Johns Pass One-day Loop: *Protected.* The total paddling distance is 4.5 miles. The Johns Pass loop is easier and shorter than the Turn Point loop (below). Most of this shoreline is residential. Except for Johns Pass, currents along the shore are usually benign, hence the *Protected* rating. Tiny state-owned Gossip Island and Cemetery Island at Reid Harbor's entrance are the only opportunities for shore exploration along this route.

Turn Point Loop: *Exposed.* The paddling distance is 7 miles. The western circuit around Turn Point is exceptionally appealing. The wild, rugged shores and boisterous Haro Strait waters provide a setting in our inland waters. But remember, the steep shores with few safe landings, the strong currents that race around the point, and the open north and south fetches with potential for rough seas require kayakers with good skills and experience.

From Prevost Harbor the pastoral civility of Stuart Island is left behind at Charles Point. From there to Turn Point is a progression of rocky kelp beds, sea crags, and overhanging vegetation. Extensive eddies occupy most of these beds all the way to the point, and progress is fairly easy even against the current. These waters are prime fishing grounds for both bottom fish and salmon.

The largest marina in the islands, the historic Roche Harbor Resort is the launch for Stuart Island.

Turn Point is a 10-acre coast guard light station reservation surrounded by a 53-acre park managed by the Bureau of Land Management. The light facility is now automated and diverse tenants such as Stuart Island teachers and whale researchers occasionally occupy the former residences. The parkland is undeveloped with no recreational facilities. Camping is not allowed. However, it does provide excellent day hiking and is a popular 5-mile round-trip hike from the Reid and Prevost harbors via an unpaved road.

Turn Point provides few easy landing sites for visiting the light station. Though the rocks have eroded into fairly flat shelves, you will have to be adept at landing on rocks in the waves that are usually present. Also beware of the powerful wakes of ships that pass quite close offshore.

A much more practical landing with a rough trail access to the point is found at a small gravel beach about 0.25 mile to the south, just beyond some spectacular sea cliffs and still within Turn Point Park. Secure your boat well above the drift logs and passing freighters' wakes. Plan to be gone for at least one hour if you intend to visit the point.

The rough, little-used trail switchbacks steeply up from the beach. Follow the gully above the beach uphill for about 100 yards to a well-defined trail that climbs across the hillside to the left through open fir and madrona woods. It then trends upward for another 300 yards, passing open, grassy meadows above and below, a perfect spot for secluded sunbathing. Finally it reaches a high, bald hilltop with sweeping views over Haro Strait, Boundary Pass, and the Canadian Gulf Islands beyond. Walking down to the cliff edge you can see Turn Point light station below. A few yards behind this bald hilltop is the old road linking the light station to Reid and Prevost harbors. Follow it to the left and downhill to the point.

GULF ISLANDS & VANCOUVER ISLAND (BRITISH COLUMBIA)

54 Sooke Harbor

Eighteen miles west of Victoria is a very protected body of water called Sooke Basin. Sooke was named for the first inhabitants of the area, the *T'Sou-ke* people. Locals say "Sook." The inside of the harbor is calm and lined with beach homes and docks. The exterior of the basin, which parallels the Strait of Juan de Fuca, has a different personality with rugged shores pounded by the wind and ocean swell, which are common on the strait. The town of Sooke is the main center for supplies, and numerous B&Bs can be found along its shores. The bay is protected by a narrow sandy stretch of beach called Whiffin Spit, popular with locals for an afternoon walk. On the outside of the harbor going toward to Victoria is East Sooke Regional Park. The park is an advanced coastal paddler's paradise with pocket beaches, caves, fast current, and a sense of wildness within a short drive to the city.

Duration: Part day to overnight.

Rating: *Protected* or *Exposed.*

Navigation Aids: Canadian Hydrographic Service chart 3410 (1:20,000), 3411(1:12,000), 3440 (1:40,000); NOAA 18400 (1:200,000).

Planning Considerations: Sooke is great for novice paddlers or those seeking calm waters. Note that Sooke Basin is the inner part, and Sooke Harbor is by the town of Sooke. Watch for boaters in summer. East Sooke requires experience with outer coastal paddling and currents.

Getting There and Launching

(Check the Victoria Harbor, British Columbia, chapter for transportation options from the United States.)

From Victoria, British Columbia, take Highway 14 west to Sooke, approximately 18 miles. Driving can be slow going in the first half as you begin to shed the city behind you.

Flowline Launch: Sixteen miles west of Victoria on Highway 14, you'll drop down a big hill and begin to see Sooke Harbor on your left. The Flowline launch is in Sooke Basin just before Ludlow Road on your left. Look for Sooke Adventures Tourism and Stickleback West Coast Eatery, 5449 Sooke Road, Sooke, British Columbia. This launch has restrooms, a boat ramp, a beach launch, and parking. The cove is protected and also a nice paddle in itself.

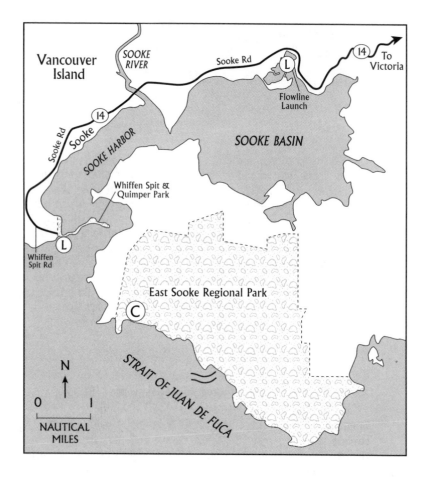

Whiffin Spit Launch: Take Highway 14 west of Victoria for 18 miles. Pass the town of Sooke and take a left on Whiffin Spit Road. Follow through a residential area for about a mile into Quimper Park just past the Sooke Harbor House. Parking is tight on sunny days. Launch on either side of the sandy spit over small rocks and driftwood. Most of the beach below the walking area is sandy. Whiffin Spit is on the south side of Sooke Harbor.

Routes

Sooke Basin is the inner bay and Sooke Harbor is the outer bay near Whiffin Spit and the Strait of Juan de Fuca.

Sooke Basin: *Protected.* Explore the curvy and jagged shoreline of the south and east sides of the basin. A few small inlets and mini islands are fun to visit as well. The cove near the launch at Flowline is very protected and a great place for beginners or those seeking an idyllic wind-free paddle. Paddling west

Driftwood stumps on Whiffen Spit, with East Sooke Regional Park in the background

toward the harbor, a point sticks out nearly splitting the two bodies of water in half. This is the beginning of Sooke Harbor. Behind the point is Sooke River, a melancholy Class I (no rapids) river. Paddle up the river on a flood tide and enjoy the river's slow current and winding curves. Take the ebb down the river for a free ride back to the harbor. On the other side across the river are beach homes and docks along the shoreline adding an interesting paddle farther into the harbor.

Sooke Harbor: *Protected.* In the town of Sooke, you'll pass a marina and a few homes with docks. Whiffin Spit can be seen to the south, extending from the west shore nearly across the harbor entry to the east. The spit is popular with afternoon walkers, bicyclists, and paddlers seeking a rest stop. The Strait of Juan de Fuca is beyond the spit, and views of the Olympic Mountains in Washington State can be seen as well. Paddle around the outside of the spit following the shoreline west along the strait. If the wind and ocean swell are active, stay in the harbor unless you have outer coast paddling skills. Much like anywhere along this stretch, it could be glassy calm or full on storm conditions.

East Sooke Regional Park: *Exposed.* East Sooke Regional Park, which begins on the eastern entry to the harbor resembles the wild coastline from the west side of Vancouver Island. The rocky, windswept wilderness has pocket beaches, caves, petroglyphs, sheltered coves, and solitude only a short distance from the urban center of Victoria. When the current and wind are strong and there's ocean swell penetrating the shore, the park can have dangerous conditions only an advanced paddler can handle. Check current tables, weather, and swell forecasts (and buoys) before heading out to this section.

55 Victoria Harbor, British Columbia

Captain James Cook is the first European known to have visited what is now Victoria. It wasn't until 1843, when the Hudson Bay Company began to operate out of the harbor that Victoria began to grow as a town. Today, Victoria is a bustling city surrounded by water. Known for its British-like charm, the city's tourism industry keeps the downtown corridor buzzing. Victoria's paddling opportunities are equally as exciting with a variety of water in or within a short distance of town.

Duration: Part day to full day.

Rating: *Protected.*

Navigation Aids: NOAA chart 18400 (1:200,000); Canadian Hydrographic Service chart 3412 Victoria Harbor (1:5,000), 3440 (1:40,000), 3424 (1:10,000). Victoria Harbor tide table.

Planning Considerations: Stay clear of the considerable boating and seaplane traffic in Victoria Harbor, especially in summer. Bring along a Victoria Harbor Traffic Scheme map when paddling here, and make sure to paddle along the shore for the entire trip. Plan around the tides when paddling in the lower reaches of the Gorge Waterway. Currents creating a tidal rapid up to 11 knots can rip under the Tillicum Bridge.

Getting There and Launching

To get to Victoria from the United States, you have a few options. The *Victoria Clipper*, a hydrofoil, runs daily from Seattle. The *Clipper* doesn't accept kayaks or SUPs, but Ocean River Sports in Victoria has kayak and SUP rentals as well as paddling tours. Kenmore Air, a seaplane service, has daily flights from several Northwest towns to Victoria. Another option is to take the Tsawwassen ferry near Vancouver to Schwartz Bay on the Saanich Peninsula, north of Victoria. There is a ferry from Anacortes through the San Juan Islands to Sidney, British Columbia, also north of Victoria. If you're coming from the Olympic Peninsula, a good option is to take the Black Ball Ferry from Port Angeles to Victoria. For additional information: www.kenmoreair.com, www.cohoferry.com/main, www.clippervacations.com/ferry, www.bcferries.com. Canadian Customs is north of the Empress Hotel on the waterfront below Wharf Street.

Victoria–James Bay Angler's Association: From the downtown waterfront area take Belleville Street west two blocks and turn left onto Oswego Street in front of the Black Ball Ferry terminal. Go eight blocks to the water. Turn right on Dallas Road and go about five blocks. On your left, look for the James Bay Angler's Association boat ramp. Use of the ramp is $5 a day per car or $20 a year. The parking lot is small and there are no facilities. The ramp puts you just inside the Ogden Point breakwater. A seaplane airport is next to the ramp—be

Always busy, Victoria's inner harbor provides picturesque views.

cautious of seaplane activity as you launch. This is great access for Inner Harbor paddling or going outside the breakwater.

Victoria–Ocean River Sports: A few blocks north of downtown Victoria, this paddling shop has a public launch on the Gorge Waterway. From the waterfront in Victoria, take Wharf Street north to Store Street. Ocean River Sports is three more blocks on your left. They also rent canoes, kayaks, and SUPs. For additional information: 800-909-4233, www.oceanriver.com.

Government Wharf–Inner Harbor: You can launch from the two public wharfs below and to the north of the Empress Hotel in the Inner Harbor. Both are accessed from Wharf Street. Expect heavy traffic and limited parking in summer months. The Canadian Customs office is by both wharfs.

Victoria–Gorge Waterway Park: To access the upper Gorge Waterway, this long strip park has several options for launching. From downtown Victoria, take Government Street north. Veer left on Gorge Road East, which becomes Gorge Road West. At 1.9 miles you'll see the park on your left extending several blocks. Take a peek at the current flowing under the Tillicum Bridge just south of the Victoria Canoe and Kayak Club.

Route

Look at the Victoria Harbor Traffic Scheme map before paddling here. The harbor is busy with boating traffic from ferries, mini tourist boats, seaplanes, shipping traffic, and other small craft like yours. Paddle close to the shore while in the harbor and never assume you have right-of-way over boats and seaplanes. Also check the Victoria tide tables if you decide to paddle up the Gorge

Waterway or near the mouth of Victoria Harbor—current can affect progress in these places. But inside the main harbor the water is generally calm and protected. A good place for paddlers of all skill levels, the harbor presents you with views of the Empress Hotel, the Royal BC Museum, and the dome of the capitol building. North of the Empress Hotel are several marinas and waterfront restaurants. As you paddle away from downtown, the harbor narrows and then opens again as you go past colorful houseboats. Small islands can be explored in the harbor's northern reaches by Lime Bay Park and Barnard Park.

As you reach the harbor entry to the Strait of Juan de Fuca, the shore becomes rocky and less developed on the north side at Macaulay Point Park and north to Saxe Point Park. Pay attention to the current here. Refracted waves can bounce off the exterior of the Ogden Point breakwater in windy conditions or from boating traffic. Called clapotis, these conditions can be tough going if you're unfamiliar with rough-water paddling. For experienced paddlers, this could be a fun play spot.

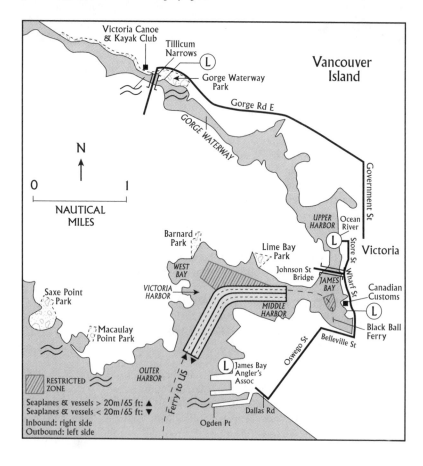

The bucolic waters of the Gorge Waterway are a great place for paddlers of all levels.

56 Victoria: The Gorge Waterway

Located in the heart of Victoria is the Gorge Waterway, a 6-mile-long natural saltwater canal that winds and bends through residential neighborhoods and empties into Victoria Harbor. The gorge was used for thousands of years by the Songhees First Nations people as a source to catch Coho salmon and herring. Under the south end of the Tillicum Bridge, a 4100-year-old midden of shells, charcoal, and scorched rock can be found. The Canal of Camosack as it was known in the 1800s is now called Tillicum Narrows. Here the shore narrows to a 45-foot-wide bottleneck forcing the tidal current to flush through at higher speeds. Current has been reported of ripping through there at 11 knots—enough to create a wild white-water rapid below the bridge. The rest of the Gorge is wider and very calm, ideal for novice paddlers or those seeking a casual, easy paddle.

Duration: Part day.

Rating: *Protected* or *Moderate.*

Navigation Aids: NOAA chart 18400 (1:200,000); Canadian Hydrographic Service chart 3412 Victoria Harbor (1:5,000); Victoria Harbor Traffic Scheme map; Victoria Harbor tide table.

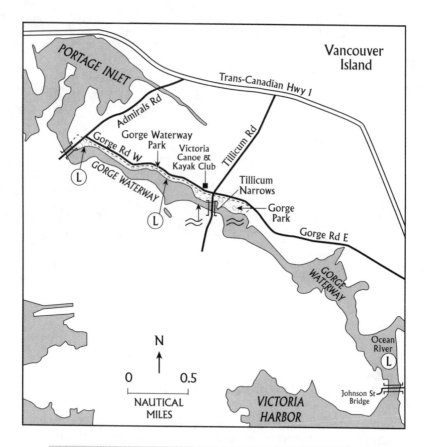

Planning Considerations: Read the Victoria tide table for this trip. If you're paddling through Tillicum Narrows and are uncomfortable with fast moving currents, go at slack. The ebb current here is the strongest and can create turbulent white water during large tidal exchanges.

Getting There and Launching

Victoria–Ocean River Sports: This paddling shop has a public launch near downtown on the Gorge Waterway. They also rent canoes, kayaks, and SUPs. From the waterfront in Victoria, take Wharf Street north to Store Street. Ocean River is three more blocks on your left. For additional information: 800-909-4233, www.oceanriver.com.

Victoria–Gorge Waterway Park: To access the upper Gorge Waterway, this long strip park has several options. From downtown Victoria, take Government Street north. Veer left on Gorge Road East, which becomes Gorge Road West. At 1.9 miles you'll see the park on your left extending several blocks. Take a peek at the current flowing under the Tillicum Bridge just south of the Victoria Canoe and Kayak Club.

Route

Check your tide table before launching. A flood will push you up the gorge, an ebb will take you back to the harbor. Going against a strong tidal exchange can be a lot of work.

From Victoria Harbor the paddle begins north of the stout-looking Johnson Street Bridge. Explore the area's industrial scenery then pass under the Galloping Goose Trail Bridge, a walking and biking trail. The gorge opens here with an interesting inlet on the right and a nice wooded park on the left. The gorge narrows again as you pass waterfront homes and their docks. About 1.3 miles from the start, the Tillicum Road bridge comes into view. This narrow gap speeds up the current. On lighter tidal flows the ride under the bridge can be a fun free ride, in heavier flows dangerous rapids can occur here. Make sure you time your paddle so you either pass through at slack or at a level that is appropriate for your skill level or interest.

Passing upriver through the Narrows, the Victoria Canoe and Kayak Club appears on the right. On your right is the Gorge Waterway Park, a long walkway with several possible launches. The rest of the way is residential through bucolic lake-like sections both narrow and some wider. Five miles from your launch, the gorge opens up into Portage Inlet, a large lake-like body of water surrounded by homes. Portage Inlet is an important bird area known for its shallow water and low salinity. The inlet has extensive eelgrass beds and mudflats providing rich foraging areas for shorebirds. Canada geese breed in Portage Inlet, and double-crested cormorants can often be seen feeding on herring that spawn there.

57 Victoria: Outer Harbor to Cadboro Bay & Trial, Oak Bay, and Discovery Islands

A short drive or paddle from downtown Victoria to the Outer Harbor opens the door to a variety of trips with spectacular scenery for paddlers of all skill levels. The Outer Harbor has several convenient put-ins, a curvy shoreline, and protected bays with sandy beaches. The islands offshore are ideal for the experienced paddler seeking a long day trip, challenging conditions with turbulent water, or an overnight through swift currents to Discovery Island.

Duration: Part day, full day, or overnight.

Rating: *Protected, Moderate,* or *Exposed.*

Navigation Aids: NOAA chart 18400 (1:200,000); Canadian Hydrographic Service chart 3412 Victoria Harbor (1:5,000), 3440 (1:40,000), 3424 (1:10,000); CHS: Oak Bay Station #7130; Victoria Harbor tide tables. Add 22 minutes for Plumper Passage.

Planning Considerations: Check tide and current tables, and wind and ocean swell forecasts prior to launching. Exposure to the Strait of Juan de Fuca can bring unexpected weather.

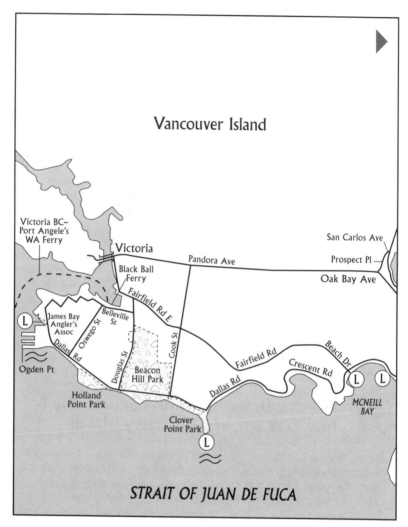

Getting There and Launching

Victoria (Inner Harbor)–James Bay Angler's Association: From the downtown waterfront area, take Belleville Street two blocks. In front of the Black Ball Ferry terminal, take a left on Oswego Street, and go eight blocks to the water. Take a right on Dallas Road and go about five blocks north. On your left, look for the James Bay Angler's Association boat ramp. Use of the ramp is $5 a day per car or $20 a year. The parking lot is small and there are no facilities. The ramp puts you just inside the harbor breakwater. A seaplane airport is next to the ramp—be cautious of seaplane activity as you launch. This is great access for Inner Harbor paddling or going outside the breakwater.

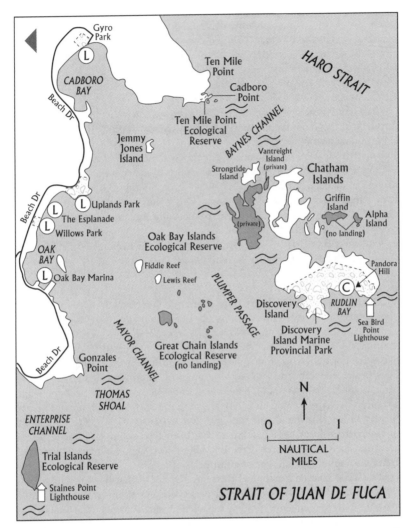

When leaving the harbor for the Strait of Juan de Fuca, watch for rips and rough water from the strait side of Odgen Point. Current leaving the harbor can collide with wind and boat wakes creating turbulent conditions.

Clover Point Park: From the waterfront in Victoria, go east on Fairfield Road, then take a right on Cook Street and drive to the water. At Dallas Road, turn left and follow to Clover Point Park. Clover Point extends into the strait and is easy to find. Drive to the point and park. There's a steep, paved boat ramp at the end. Watch for wind at this launch.

McNeill Bay Launch: From the waterfront in downtown Victoria, take Fairfield Road east. This road will take you all the way to McNeill Bay albeit a long and windy 3.8-mile drive through the city. Fairfield will soon become Beach Drive. Once you see the water, Beach Drive will veer left along the waterfront at McNeill Bay. Look for the cobble beach and park and launch. You can also access McNeill Bay from Dallas Road from the west. (Note: There are several roadside launches east of here, including Gonzales Bay.)

Oak Bay Launch: From the waterfront in downtown Victoria, take Pandora Avenue east. Pandora Avenue soon becomes Oak Bay Avenue. At 2.7 miles, veer left onto Prospect Place, which will curve right, become San Carlos Avenue, then connect with Beach Drive. Take a left at Beach Drive and follow for 0.3 mile to Willows Park on the right. To access the launch in the park, go down the steps to get below the seawall. Beyond Willows Park, another 0.6 mile, is Uplands Park, which has two concrete boat ramps. Other launches from Oak Bay include Oak Bay Marina on south side of the bay and the Esplanade, which is halfway between Uplands and Willow parks.

Cadboro Bay Road: From the University of Victoria take Sinclair Road south. Take a left on Cadboro Bay and enter Cadboro-Gyro Park.

Routes

Victoria Harbor to Cadboro Bay: *Protected, Moderate,* or *Exposed.* Choose your route and launch. This region is a beautiful winding route to paddle with easy access, urban views, undeveloped offshore islands, and picturesque white sand bays. On a hot summer day the lovely crescent-shaped sandy coves look like Southern California. Enjoy views to the south across the Strait of Juan de Fuca of the snowcapped Olympic Mountains in Washington State. Something for all, novice paddlers can enjoy turquoise-colored protected bays while advanced paddlers seeking an adrenaline rush can surf large winter wind waves or play in the tidal rapids off the Trial and Chatham islands. Paddle a short distance or go from Odgen Point to Cadboro Bay, about 10.6 miles. There are three ecological reserves here: Ten Mile Point, Oak Bay Islands, and Trial Islands. Landing is prohibited at all three reserves.

The Trial Islands Ecological Reserve: *Exposed.* Enterprise Channel, which separates the Trial Islands Ecological Reserve from shore, is only a 0.2-mile crossing but has currents ranging between 3 and 6 knots. The islands are known for their rare plant life, which is more common in southern Oregon or California. Watch for Hooker's onion, shooting star, death camas, blue-eyed Mary, chocolate lily, and sea blush. Wildlife include harbor seals, cormorants, eagles, hawks, and herons. The islands' south tip, Staines Point boasts a historic lighthouse built in 1906, which is still in use. Swift tidal rapids occur off the point and can be quite rough, particularly on the flood tide.

Oak Bay Islands Ecological Reserve: *Moderate* or *Exposed.* The Oak Bay Islands Ecological Reserve includes the Chain Islets, Great Chain Island, Alpha Island, Jemmy Jones Island, and an offshore section of Ten Mile Point to the east. The Chain Islets and Great Chain Island have British Columbia's third-largest colony of double-crested cormorants and largest breeding population of

Outer Victoria to Cadboro Bay has both calm, protected bays and exposed islands with swift currents for the more experienced paddler.

glaucous-winged gulls. The cormorants are on the BC Ministry of Sustainable Resource Management's (MSRM) "Red" list, meaning they're endangered or threatened in British Columbia. Other birdlife seen in the islands includes pigeon guillemots, black oystercatchers, and pelagic cormorants. Great Chain Island is located 1.07 miles off Oak Bay Marina. Mayor Channel, which is on the west side of the island, can run up to 3 knots with the flood running north and the ebb running south. If you come from the north watch for the "Goal Posts," which are two reefs, Lewis and Fiddle, both marked by buoys. If coming from the south, keep an eye out for Thomas Shoal located northeast from Gonzales Point.

Discovery Island Marine Provincial Park and Chatham Islands: *Exposed.* Located 2.6 miles from Oak Bay Marina, Discovery and Chatham islands offer a nice day trip or overnight paddling option for experienced paddlers. The islands allow for exploration over shallow reefs, through narrow passageways, by rocky shores, and around small islets. Garry oak and arbutus trees line the shores of the Chatham Islands, which are thankfully undeveloped. Stronger current can work its way through the various islets and passageways making for a fun paddle for those skilled in moving water. The islands also mark where Haro Straight and the Strait of Juan de Fuca connect. The northern part of Discovery Island and all of the Chatham Islands are a First Nations reserve.

Griffin and Alpha islands, both ecological reserves, are tucked between the eastern sides of both Discovery and Chatham islands and landing is prohibited. Strongtide and Vantreight islands, on the north side of the Chathams, are private.

Camping is only allowed on the south side of Discovery Island, in Rudlin Bay, or in a large field southwest of Pandora Hill. Boaters generally don't frequent Rudlin Bay due to several shallow reefs offshore. Facilities included a pit toilet, picnic tables, and information kiosk. No campfires are allowed and fees are $5 per night, per person. Hiking trails lead from the 1885-era lighthouse on Sea Bird Point to the western shore of the park going up to Pandora Hill. Sweeping views of the Olympic Mountains and surrounding area can be enjoyed from the top of Pandora Hill.

Traveling to the islands requires knowledge of open-water crossings, in sometimes-fast-moving current. Separating Great Chain Island from Discovery Island is Plumper Passage. Here the slack tide can be short and the flood can run for three hours and forty-five minutes, leaving about seven hours before slack begins again. Rips and rough water are not uncommon.

Baynes Channel separates the Chatham Islands from Cadboro Point by 0.8 mile, which can be a rough ride especially during large tidal exchanges. Current can run 4 to 6 knots by Strongtide Island, where rips are common, and up to 2 to 3 knots on the southern section of the channel. The flood currents flow northeast while the ebb currents flow southwest. Reefs are numerous off Cadboro Point and may create surface disturbances with stronger tides and wind.

58 Portland Island

Originally a First Nations camp, Hawaiian immigrants called "Kanakas" settled the island in the mid-1800s. The island was given to Princess Margaret in 1958 as a gift when she visited the province. She returned it to British Columbia as a provincial park in 1967. Now a National Park Reserve, it's known for its sandy beaches, little coves, hiking trails through thick forests, orchards, and its easy access to the Saanich Peninsula. The northwest shore of the island below Kanaka Bluff has excellent intertidal life at low tides.

Duration: Full day to overnight.

Rating: *Moderate.* Currents can be strong enough to produce tide rips and rough seas when opposing wind. Boat and ferry traffic is heavy.

Navigation Aids: Canadian Hydrographic Service cruising atlas 3313 (charts in spiral-bound format) or 3441 (both 1:40,000); H&R Nautical Ventures Small-Craft Nautical Maps: Sooke to Victoria and the Gulf Islands (strip charts mostly 1:40,000); Canadian Hydrographic Service current tables (Volume 5) for Race Passage with corrections for Swanson Channel; Canadian *Current Atlas.*

A short paddle from the mainland, scenic Portland Island is an easy getaway.

Planning Considerations: Now included in the Gulf Islands National Park Reserve and the BC Marine Trail system, the island receives heavy use at its three designated fee-based camping areas. Arrive early to secure your site on summer weekends. Travel with current flow; the flood moves north and the ebb south. The fee for wheeling a kayak on the BC ferries varies, so check rates on the routes you plan to use. Make sure to arrive early, line up your boat with the motorcycles on the side, and you'll be directed on to the car deck.

Getting There and Launching

Launch sites at either Sidney or Swartz Bay are respectively adjacent to the Washington State ferry terminal (to and from Anacortes) or the BC ferry terminals. Follow signs to the appropriate one.

Sidney–Tulista Park: Use the beach just south of the launch ramp for the Washington State ferry terminal. When you exit the ferry, take a left on Ocean Avenue, then another immediate left on 5th Street. Look for park signs. There's a busy boat ramp and a gravel beach to the north end of the park.

Swartz Bay: Use the Swartz Bay public wharf to launch. The wharf is just east of the BC ferry terminal. If you've come in from Tsawwassen, go south on Highway 17 and take the first exit off the highway, then turn back onto Highway 17 heading northbound. Take the Dolphin Road exit and follow the ferry terminal fence to Barnacle Road. You'll soon see the wharf with its limited parking. If you've wheeled your kayak off the ferry, walk it directly to the wharf and launch on the gravel beach nearby. When launching here, watch for ferry traffic and don't cross the path of an incoming ferry.

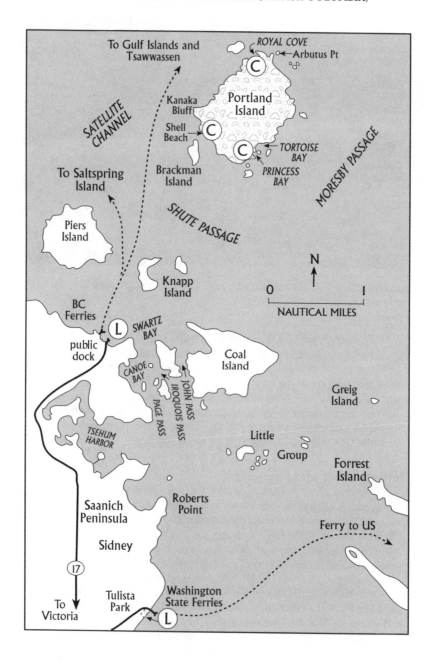

Route

The one-way distance from Swartz Bay to Portland Island is 2 miles; it's 4 miles from Tulista Park in Sidney. Those originating from Sidney can sightsee through John, Iroquois, or Page passes where sumptuous homes and moored yachts line the shores. Paddlers starting from either place should go east of Knapp Island to avoid the busy ferry lanes on the west. Currents in Shute Passage flood northwest at up to 1.5 knots, and in the opposite direction at the same speed on the ebb, requiring a substantial ferry-angle course adjustment to control the amount that you are set by it. The Canadian *Current Atlas* is very helpful for timing with this current.

Portland Island has several First Nations shell middens along its beaches. Do not disturb the middens. Enjoy the extensive trail system; it can take up to three hours to cross the island. The three campsites are at Arbutus Point, Princess Bay, and Shell Beach. Shell Beach is on the south side having protection from Brackman Island. Arbutus Point has tent pads in the forest on the north side of the island. Princess Bay has no views and requires hauling gear up stairs that originate from the dinghy dock. Camping is in a grassy old orchard.

Facilities include pit toilets, picnic tables, but no water. If a fire ban is not in effect, campfires can be built in designated rings, but it's best to rely on your cookstove on this wildfire-prone island.

59 Salt Spring Island–Wallace Island

On the northeast corner of Salt Spring Island is Wallace Island Marine Provincial Park. Located 1.6 miles across Houston Passage from Salt Spring, Wallace is an easy paddle and great for paddlers of all skill levels. The narrow island has several protected coves, an easy portage over the middle, and hiking trails through thick forest. The coves are popular with boaters so expect a crowd on a sunny weekend. As a paddler you can easily find enough privacy in the island's numerous pocket beaches and rocky alcoves to feel much farther way than you are.

Duration: Part day to overnight.

Rating: *Protected* or *Moderate.*

Navigation Aids: Canadian Hydrographic Service chart 3442 (1:40,000); Canadian Hydrographic Service current table for Active Pass.

Planning Considerations: Summer weekends can be crowded on the island. While current is light in Houston Passage, wind opposing current may create rough conditions.

A protected cove at low tide on Wallace Island

Getting There and Launching

From Ganges, take the curvy Robinson Road northeast out of town. Robinson will become Walker's Hook Road and begin to follow the shoreline along Trincomali Channel. In 3.4 miles you'll be in Fernwood, a tiny community of a store and a café. On your right is a government dock. There are two launches in Fernwood. Drive past the dock and on your right look for a small pull-out alongside the road. A shaky wooden stairway will lead to the gravel and sandy beach. Farther north about a quarter of a mile is a boat ramp with limited parking. The beach gets muddy at low tides. The south end of Wallace is directly across from Fernwood.

You can also easily access Wallace from Galiano and Thetis islands, each with short crossings.

Route

Launching from Fernwood, cross Houston Passage, a 1 mile distance to the south end of the island at Panther Point. Light current runs through there with little affect on paddling. Panther Point is made up of rocks above and just below the waterline that sunk the coal ship "Panther" in 1847. The protected cove inside Panther Point empties out in low tides but is a beautiful rest stop with easy walking access to Conover Cove. Paddle around the east side of the island, passing several small offshore rocks, some covered in harbor seals, starfish, and anemones. You'll soon come to a little cove with a small gravel landing area. Above the beach in a grassy area is a campsite. You can also portage from here over to Conover Cove. The picnic shelter above the cove is covered in driftwood art, well worth a peek. Restrooms are on the hill above.

Continuing down the east side, the rocky shore becomes a wall with twisting madrona trees perched on the edge. Near the northeast end of the island is Cabin Bay, another campsite tucked into a sheltered rocky cove. The campsite is on the flat area for two or three tents. There is no outhouse. The north end of the island is Chivers Point surrounded by long rocky reefs. A path leads up to six campsites on gravel pads. The Secretary Islands to the north, unfortunately are private, landing is prohibited. Round Chivers Point and head south down Houston Passage. You'll pass several slender rock shelves and one in particular that parallels the island for some distance. At higher tides paddle through the slot, staying close to shore to enjoy the sea life and geology. Enter Princess Cove, a popular gunkhole for boaters extending nearly 1800 feet. Walk the gravel passageway connecting Conover Cove to the south. Two offshore reefs provide a chance for more exploration, especially at low tides when more sea life will be visible.

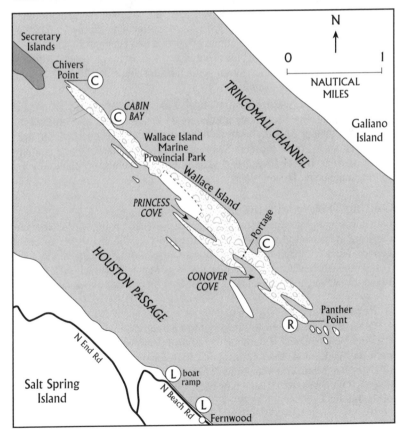

60 Pender, Saturna, and Mayne Islands

This part of the southern Gulf Islands offers the most opportunities for small-channel paddling but with swift currents in some passages that are inappropriate for the inexperienced. There are many route variations, especially for those who carry kayaks aboard the BC ferry and can use different island stops to begin and end their paddling trip.

Duration: Part day to overnight.

Rating: *Moderate* or *Moderate +*. Currents in parts of this area are strong, with at least two local tide races. The most challenging one is avoidable.

Navigation Aids: Canadian Hydrographic Service cruising atlas 3313 (charts in spiral-bound format) or 3442 (1:40,000) and 3477 (1:15,000); H&R Nautical Ventures Small-Craft Nautical Maps: Sooke to Victoria and the Gulf Islands (strip charts mostly 1:40,000); Canadian Hydrographic Service current table (Volume 5) for Active Pass with corrections for Georgeson and Boat passages, current tables for Race Passage with corrections for Swanson Channel, or the Canadian *Current Atlas.*

Planning Considerations: Travel with current flows as much as possible. The flood goes northward in Pender Canal and northwest in Plumper Sound. These have no current predictions but can be estimated from those in Swanson Channel. BC ferries have limited daily service to Mayne and Saturna islands. There is no public kayak camping on Mayne Island.

Getting There and Launching

Unless you integrate this trip with the Portland Island route to the west (see the Portland Island chapter), you will have to take the BC ferries to either Pender, Mayne, or Saturna islands. If you are coming from the mainland at Tsawwassen, you will have to transfer ferries at Mayne Island to reach Saturna Island, or at Swartz Bay depending on which ferry schedule works best.

Pender Island

Otter Bay Launch: From the ferry terminal the closest launch is 0.3 mile at the Otter Bay Marina. Drive to the top of the hill above the terminal and take a right on MacKinnon Road. Immediately look for the small, poorly placed sign to Otter Bay Marina on your right. The road drops sharply down a hill to the marina. There is no fee to launch or park. Check with the marina office per use of the marina facilities: 250-629-3579. There is overnight parking.

Pender Canal Bridge can be a busy bottleneck for boaters. Its sometimes-swift tidal currents give the paddler a push under the bridge.

Launch at Port Browning: To get to this launch from the ferry landing, take Otter Bay Road east to Bedwell Harbor Road, take a right. Follow the road for about 2 miles. Bedwell Harbor Road soon passes the town center, a good place to get groceries, coffee, and other supplies. Take a left, from Bedwell Harbor Road to Hamilton Road. Follow the road to Port Browning, which will be on your left at the bottom of the hill. Facilities include a marina, library, kayak shop, and café. Camping in the large field is available by checking in with the marina office. Launch from the beach below the field and café.

Launch at Mortimer Spit, South Pender: After Port Browning, take Canal Road south. Follow Canal Road for several miles and eventually cross Pender Canal Bridge (one lane). Continue left beyond the bridge to Mortimer Spit Road, which comes up very quickly on your left. This day-use site has no facilities. Launch from any side on the spit, and watch out for boat traffic entering Pender Canal.

Launch at Medicine Creek: From town center, take Canal Road south. Before the bridge, take a right on Wallace Road. Take a left on Schooner Way to the beach. There's ample parking and a beach launch. A small grocery store is located one block north of the launch beach.

Launch at Poets Cove, South Pender: Continue south past Mortimer Spit on Canal Road. In a few scenic miles take a right on Spalding Road, and follow to Poets Cove Resort and Spa. Park anywhere and launch at the beaches below the resort. If you park overnight check with the resort office. There's a kayak rental on the right below the steep cliffs. A full service marina and resort, Poets Cove has lodging, restaurants, and an outdoor pool to relax in. Beaumont Marine Park is a short paddle to the north of the resort. Poets Cove also has a Canadian Customs office. For additional information: www.poetscove.com.

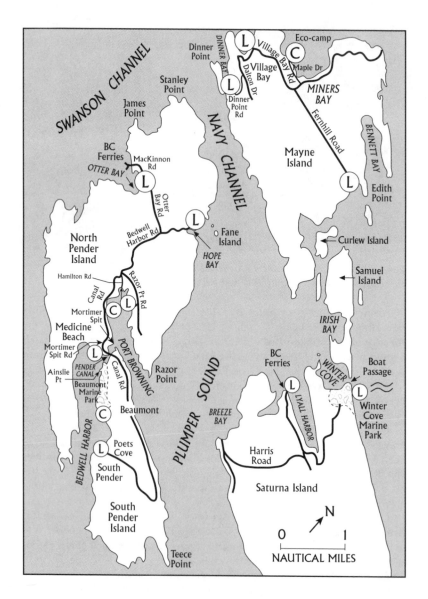

Launch at Hope Bay, North Pender: From Pender town center, take Bedwell Harbor Road north a few miles to Hope Bay. From the ferry, go up the hill and take a right on MacKinnon Road then another right on Otter Bay Road. In about a mile, take a left on Bedwell Harbor Road and follow it to Hope Bay. Park along the road and launch in the bay 50 yards west of the café along the gravel stone beach. Check with the café for overnight parking.

Mayne Island

Village Bay Launch: Foot passengers can wheel their boats on and off at Village Bay on Mayne Island. Turn left immediately after leaving the ferry through a gate leading to a path to the beach. If driving from the ferry terminal, take a right on Mariner's Way and right again on Callaghan. Below is a boat ramp on the south side of Village Bay.

Dinner Bay Launch: From the BC ferry terminal at Village Bay, take a right on Dalton Drive, left on Merryman, and a right back on Dalton Drive again. Take a right on Mariners Way, left on Dinner Point Road, and follow the road 0.3 mile to Dinner Bay Park. The launch is from a sandy beach below the park, providing easy access to Navy Channel or a protected bay for beginners to enjoy.

Miners Bay Launch: Miners Bay has the only water-accessed, nonmotorized watercraft camping on the island at Mayne Island Eco Camping, www.mayneisle .com/camp/. Take a left from the BC ferry terminal in Village Bay onto Village Bay Road and follow this windy route for 1.4 miles to Miners Bay. Take a left on Fernhill Road and a right on Georgina Point Road, which leads you into the main commercial district for Mayne Island.

Bennett Bay Launch: Bennett Bay on the south side of the island is an easy launch from a flat, rock-shelf beach. From the ferry, take Fernhill Road south for several miles. It'll become Bennett Bay Road, which will take you to the beach.

Saturna Island

Ferry Terminal Launch: From the ferry terminal on Lyall Harbor, turn left to the public wharf. This is the easiest launch on the island. Inquire locally about overnight parking options. A store is located just above the ferry dock at Saturna.

Winter Cove Launch: A public day-use area with a boat ramp and gravel beach provide access for the northeast side of Saturna. Boat Passage is just beyond the launch.

Routes

There are three options. You may paddle locally in Port Browning and Bedwell Harbor, make a full day of exploring between Saturna and Mayne islands, or take an extended overnight route that includes both of the above. Enjoy idyllic protected coves or play in tidal rapids such as Boat Passage or run the speedy current of Pender Canal.

Port Browning and Bedwell Harbor: *Moderate.* The round-trip distance is 4 to 6 miles. This could be a day trip or an overnight, with camping at Beaumont Marine Park or Port Browning.

This trip would fall within the *Protected* rating were it not for the current in Pender Canal, which can run at up to 4 knots for a short distance under the bridge. There are no predictions about the current's schedule other than it flows north on the flood. This passage requires some care, but should be no

A lazy summer day on Port Browning

problem for paddlers with average boat-handling skills. Whether going through with or against the current, look carefully for powerboats going through the cut, as they must maintain speed to have maneuverability in the current and have limited deep water in which to avoid you. Bigger boats going through against the current make large breaking wakes on the beaches. You should be able to find eddies in both the north and south approaches to the canal. Avoid paddling through the narrow slots between bridge supports unless you have strong skills with fast moving currents.

The canal area, which was a portage until being dredged at the turn of the century, was a long-used Salish townsite. An archaeological team dug here for a number of years in the 1970s. The bridge was built in 1955. Enjoy examples of modern architecture well blended with the natural surroundings as you paddle south of the canal into Bedwell Harbor.

Beaumont Marine Park is also a Gulf Islands National Park Reserve. The park begins on the northern shore of Bedwell Harbor at Ainslie Point. There are several nice beaches for a break ashore with an extensive trail system that leads toward 800-foot Mount Norman. Panoramic views of the nearby Gulf Islands can be enjoyed from there. The park's shoreline is of little pocket beaches and craggy steep shores with madrona trees overhanging the water.

The Coast Salish have a rich history on the island dating back 5000 years. Shell middens and burial sites can be seen within the park sometimes under picnic areas. In 2011 a burial site was robbed at the park. Make sure to not disturb the middens while visiting this site. Pit toilets and tables are the extent of the facilities. Poets Cove Resort is 1 mile south of the park. The resort has a full-service marina and resort facilities. You can launch and park there overnight for no charge. Check in with the office to let them know you're using the lot. There is a Canadian Customs office should you want to paddle in from the United States.

Alternative launches for this trip include Medicine Beach on the northwest end of Bedwell Harbor and Mortimer Spit on South Pender, just east of the bridge. Both are day use only.

Between Mayne and Saturna: *Moderate.* The distance from the Saturna ferry landing can be as little as 3 miles round trip to Winter Cove or lengthened to about a 7-mile circumnavigation of Samuel Island. A trip to Winter Cove avoids significant currents but allows a close-up look at fast water in little Boat Passage, sometimes reaching up to 8 knots. Those who enjoy playing in tidal rapids could have a lot of fun in the passage. Give right-of-way to boaters who have to maintain a constant speed through the passage to negotiate the current.

The east side of Winter Cove is a marine park that is day use only. A gravel beach just east of Boat Passage gives access to trails for a view of the passage and the Strait of Georgia beyond.

Circumnavigating Samuel Island should be attempted only if you are comfortable with strong currents and sharp eddy lines, or if you plan to traverse its tide races at slack, especially Boat Passage. If your skills are up to it, Boat Passage can be run in midstream with few problems. Going through against the flow is difficult without portaging, as there are no eddies. Currents at the western end of Samuel Island are slower but still provide challenging eddies and possible tide rips between Samuel and Curlew islands.

Village Bay, Winter Cove, and Bedwell Harbor Triangle Loop: *Moderate.* This loop trip involves about 20 miles of paddling. Travel in the Pender Islands and between Mayne and Saturna is as described above. Use Swanson Channel predictions for Plumper Sound and Navy Channel, but note Navy Channel floods east at a maximum of 3 knots from Swanson Channel, meeting the west-flowing flood current from Plumper Sound off Hope Bay. Current speeds in Plumper Sound between Saturna and South Pender Island can reach 3 knots.

Consider alternative launches than listed for this trip to avoid weather issues or for a more preferable current flow. For example, Hope Bay on northeast Pender provides a shorter crossing to Mayne Island. Overnight parking here is only available on residential streets nearby.

resources

Online Resources:

Washington State
Below are a list of links to help you plan your next trip. They include aerial maps of the region, a site that teaches paddlers how to paddle around whales, and ferry schedules for Washington State.

Aerial Shoreline Photos of Washington State:
www.apps.ecy.wa.gov/shorephotos/index.html

Cliff Mass Weather Blog
www.cliffmass.blogspot.com

Department of Natural Resources (DNR)
Many shoreline areas in the state are DNR managed. This link will help you map them. Follow links to Recreation.
www.dnr.wa.gov

Discover Pass
This is required for cars in state parks, public access areas, wildlife areas, and boat launches. www.discoverpass.wa.gov/

Google Maps
Map and satellite with easy tools for measuring distance:
www.google.com/maps

National Weather Service, Seattle
www.weather.gov

NOAA Marine Forecast for Puget Sound, Strait of Juan de Fuca, and Outer Coast
www.weather.gov/sew

San Juan County Parks
www.sanjuanco.com/921/San-Juan-Island

Seattle Chittenden Locks
Website for nonmotorized boats: www.nws.usace.army.mil/Missions/ Civil-Works/Locks-and-Dams/Chittenden-Locks

US Customs and Border Protection
List of offices in the NW waters: www.cbp.gov/contact/ports/wa

Washington State Ferries
www.wsdot.wa.gov/ferries

Washington State Webcams
www.wsdot.com/traffic/Cameras/default.aspx

British Columbia

The following are a variety of online links to assist with travel, weather, and finding the appropriate charts.

BC Ferries
www.bcferries.com/

BC Ministry of Sustainable Resource Management (MSRM)
www2.gov.bc.ca/gov/content/environment/plants-animals-ecosystems

BC Parks
www.env.gov.bc.ca/bcparks/

British Columbia Tourism
www.hellobc.com/

British Columbia Webcams by Big Wave Dave
(includes Strait of Georgia):
www.bigwavedave.ca/webcams.php

Canadian Border Services Agency
www.cbsa.gc.ca/publications/pub/bsf5082-eng.html#s2x4

CANPASS Private Boats
www.cbsa.gc.ca/prog/canpass/canpassprivateboat-eng.html

Environment Canada: BC Weather
www.weatheroffice.gc.ca/marine/region_e.html?mapID=03

Fisheries & Oceans Canada—Nautical Charts
www.charts.gc.ca/index-eng.asp.

Gulf Islands National Park
www.gulfislandsnationalpark.com/

Gulf Islands National Park Reserve
http://pc.gc.ca/en/pn-np/bc/gulf

Paddling with Whales—Regulations and Etiquette

Be Whale Wise
www.bewhalewise.org/

KELP—Kayak Education and Leadership Program
https://whalemuseum.org/products/kelp

The Orca Network
www.orcanetwork.org/

Tides and Currents

Below are online resources to help you find the tide levels and current directions for both British Columbia and Washington State.

British Columbia Tides and Currents:
www.tides.gc.ca/eng

Current Atlas for Puget Sound (shows graphic current directions):
www.deepzoom.com

National Oceanic and Atmospheric Administration:
Tidal Current Tables: www.tidesandcurrents.noaa.gov/tide_predictions.shtml

Tide tables for iPhones: www.tides.mobilegeographics.com/

West Coast tide tables: www.saltwatertides.com

NOAA and Saltwater Tides have tidal and current data that can be downloaded to store on your computer and phone, making them accessible even without internet access.

Saltwater Tides: www.saltwatertides.com/dynamic.dir/mobileapp.html

Surf and Wave Forecasts

If you're planning on surfing or paddling the Strait of Juan de Fuca, it's important to know what the ocean swell is doing. The following sites can help you determine the swell size, direction, period, wind speed and direction, and other important info. There's several other sites out there, find what works best for you.

www.ndbc.noaa.gov/data/Forecasts/FZUS56.KSEW.html
www.magicseaweed.com/
www.surfwa.org/
www.stormsurf.com/

Surfing Etiquette

All paddlers traveling in a surf zone should know how to surf and should practice surf etiquette. These sites are a start to introduce you to being a safer surfer.

www.surfinghandbook.com/knowledge/surfing-etiquette/
www.youtube.com/watch?v=SXhGp07uAMs (Video)
www.hobuck-hoedown.com/the-competition/surf-etiquette

Water Trails

Water trails allow camping and public launching access for nonmotorized watercraft in a region where public access is diminishing rapidly.

BC Marine Trails
www.bcmarinetrails.org

North Kitsap Water Trail
www.northkitsaptrails.org/maps/water-trail

Washington Water Trails Association
www.wwta.org

Useful Publications

These are a number of excellent how-to books, manuals, guidebooks, and references available for improving your paddling skills and for travel in Pacific Northwest waters.

General Paddling

Alderson, Doug. *Sea Kayaker's Savvy Paddler: More than 500 Tips for Better Kayaking.* Camden, ME: Ragged Mountain Press, 2001.

Broze, Matt, and George Gronseth. *Sea Kayaker's Deep Trouble: True Stories and Their Lessons from* Sea Kayaker *Magazine.* New York: McGraw-Hill, 1997.

Burch, David. *Fundamentals of Kayak Navigation,* 4th ed. Boston: Globe Pequot Press, 2008.

Casey, Rob. *Stand Up Paddling: Flat Water to Rivers and Surf.* Seattle: The Mountaineers Books, 2011.

Dowd, John. *Sea Kayaking: A Manual for Long Distance Touring,* 5th ed. Seattle: Greystone Books, 2004 (revised).

Henderson, Dan. *Sea Kayaking: Basic Skills to Advanced Paddling Techniques.* Seattle: The Mountaineers Books, 2012.

Lull, John. *Sea Kayaking Safety and Rescue.* Berkeley, CA: Wilderness Press, 2001.

Mattos, Bill. *Kayak Surfing.* Guilford, CT: Falcon, 2009.

Washburne, Randel. *The Coastal Kayaker's Manual: A Complete Guide to Skills, Gear, and Sea Sense.* 3rd ed. Old Saybrook, CT: Globe Pequot Press, 1998.

Paddling in Washington State

Cummings, Al, and Jo Bailey-Cummings. *Gunkholing in the San Juans.* Edmonds, WA: Nor'westing (out of print).

Hahn, Jennifer. *Pacific Feast: A Cook's Guide to West Coast Foraging and Cuisine.* Seattle: The Mountaineers Books, 2010.

Korb, Gary. *A Paddler's Guide To the Olympic Peninsula.* Self-published, 1997.

McGee, Peter, ed. *Kayak Routes of the Pacific Northwest Coast.* Vancouver, BC: Greystone Books, 2004.

Mueller, Marge, and Ted Mueller. *Middle Puget Sound and Hood Canal Afoot and Afloat,* 2nd ed. Seattle: The Mountaineers Books, 2006. www.mountaineersbooks.org/

———. *North Puget Sound Afoot and Afloat,* 3rd ed. Seattle: The Mountaineers Books, 1995.

———. *The San Juan Islands Afoot and Afloat,* 4th ed. Seattle: The Mountaineers Books, 2003.

———. *Seattle's Lakes, Bays & Waterways: Including the Eastside.* Seattle: The Mountaineers Books, 1999.

———. *South Puget Sound Afoot and Afloat,* 4th ed. Seattle: The Mountaineers Books, 1996.

Nyberg, Carl, and Jo Bailey. *Gunkholing in South Puget Sound: A Comprehensive Cruising Guide from Kingston/Edmonds South to Olympia.* Seattle: San Juan Enterprises, Inc., 1997.

Rogers, Joel, *Watertrail: The Hidden Path through Puget Sound*. Seattle: Sasquatch Books, 1998.

Sept, J. Duane. *The Beachcomber's Guide to Seashore Life in the Pacific Northwest*. Madeira Park, BC: Harbour Publishing, 2009.

Thrush, Cole, *Native Seattle: Histories From the Crossing Over Place*. Seattle: University of Washington Press, 2008.

Washington Water Trails Association. *Washington Water Marine Trail Guidebook*. wwta.org, 2007.

Yates, Steve. *Marine Wildlife—From Puget Sound through the Inside Passage*. Seattle: Sasquatch Books, 1998.

Paddling in British Columbia

Chettleburgh, Peter. *An Explorer's Guide: Marine Parks of British Columbia*. Vancouver, BC: Special Interest Publications, 1985 (out of print).

Cummings, Al, and Jo Bailey-Cummings. *Gunkholing in the Gulf Islands*. Edmonds, WA: Nor'westing, 1989.

Ince, John, and Hedi Kottner. *Sea Kayaking Canada's West Coast*. Seattle: The Mountaineers Books, 1992 (revised).

Kimantas, John. *The Wild Coast 3, A Kayaking Hiking and Recreation Guide for BC's South Coast and East Vancouver Island, Vol. 3*. North Vancouver, BC: Whitecap Books, 2010.

Mueller, Marge, and Ted Mueller. *British Columbia's Gulf Islands: Afoot and Afloat*. Seattle: The Mountaineers Books, 2000.

Obee, Bruce. *The Gulf Islands Explorer*. North Vancouver, B.C.: Whitecap Books, 1997 (revised).

Vassilopoulos, Peter, *The Gulf Islands Cruising Guide*. Nanaimo, BC: Pacific Marine Publishing, 2006.

Snowden, Mary A. *Sea Kayak the Gulf Islands*. 3d ed. Surrey, BC: Rocky Mountains Books, 2010.

Tides and Currents

Burch, David, *Tidal Currents of Puget Sound, Graphic Current Charts and Flow Patterns*. Seattle: Starpath Publication, 2009.

Canadian Hydrographic Service. *Current Atlas: Juan de Fuca Strait to Strait of Georgia*. Ottawa: Canadian Hydrographic Service Department of Fisheries and Oceans, 1983. This atlas provides the most accurate and detailed information on tidal currents in this complex region. For a given hour and tidal range, the user is directed to a chart showing currents at that time. Calculations required to arrive at the correct chart make this resource a bit difficult to use. (See *Washburne's Tables* for a simplified method of finding the proper current chart.)
www.charts.gc.ca/charts-cartes/index-eng.asp
www.epiphyte.ca/proj/currents.

Department of Natural Resources, State of Washington. Public tideland. *Tidelog: Puget Sound Edition.* Tiburon, CA: Pacific Publishers, published annually. http://tidelog.com. This is a useful combination of tide and current information for the year. It provides daily tidal curves that show slacks and associated current strengths and lunar and solar phases as they affect tides. It also includes current charts for Puget Sound and current schedules for Deception Pass and the Narrows at Tacoma.

Washburne's Tables. Bellevue, Washington: Weatherly Press, published annually. www.waggonerguide.com/. Use these tables in conjunction with the helpful Canadian Hydrographic Service's *Current Atlas: Juan de Fuca Strait to Strait of Georgia.* These tables provide direct access to the proper current chart at any hour of any day without need for calculations or adjustment for daylight saving time. www.charts.gc.ca/twl-mne/index-eng.asp.

Marine Weather

Burch, David. *Modern Marine Weather.* Seattle: Starpath School of Navigation, 2008.

Lilly, Kenneth E., Jr. *Marine Weather of Western Washington.* Seattle: Starpath School of Navigation, 1983. www.starpath.com/

Mass, Cliff. *The Weather of the Pacific Northwest.* Seattle: University of Washington Press, 2008.

Renner, Jeff. *Northwest Marine Weather: From the Columbia River to Cape Scott.* Seattle: The Mountaineers Books, 1994.

Maps

SeaTrails Maps

Waterproof maps designed for paddlers and other small boaters, these blend the features of nautical charts and topographic maps, with updated information about parks and other attractions ashore. Available for Washington waters in regional sets or individual sheets. wwww.seatrails.com/

Maptech Nautical Charts

These are "flip-fold" waterproof navigational charts small enough to carry on a kayak, canoe, or SUP. www.maptech.com/

The Green-Duwamish River Map

Duwamish River Cleanup Coalition, 2010. www.duwamishcleanup.org/

index

THE MOUNTAINEERS, founded in 1906, is a nonprofit outdoor activity and conservation organization, whose mission is "to explore, study, preserve, and enjoy the natural beauty of the outdoors...." The Mountaineers sponsors many classes and year-round outdoor activities in the Pacific Northwest, and supports environmental causes through educational activities, sponsoring legislation and presenting educational programs. The Mountaineers Books supports the organization's mission by publishing travel and natural history guides, instructional texts, and works on conservation and history.

Visit www.mountaineersbooks.org to view our complete list of more than 700 outdoor titles:

 The Mountaineers Books
1001 SW Klickitat Way, Suite 201
Seattle, WA 98134
800-553-4453
mbooks@mountaineersbooks.org

 Leave No Trace strives to educate visitors about the nature of their recreational impacts and offers techniques to prevent and minimize such impacts. Leave No Trace is best understood as an educational and ethical program, not as a set of rules and regulations.
For more information, visit www.lnt.org, or call 800-332-4100.

about the author

Rob Casey has honed his kayaking and stand up padding knowledge over a decade of paddling year-round in all water conditions—from flatwater to rivers and surf. Rob is the founder and director of PSUPA, the Professional Stand Up Paddle Association, and is a consultant for recreational business.

Rob is the author of the first book on stand up paddle instruction, *Stand Up Paddling: Flatwater to Surf and Rivers.* A photographer for many years, Rob is a regular contributor to *SUP Magazine,* and *Standup Journal.* You can read his blog, https://suptips.blogspot.com or visit his website, www.salmonbaypaddle .com. Look for book updates and new trips on another of his blogs, https://60tripskayakpugetsound.blogspot.com.